Building Guide for

Basic Hot Rods

By LeRoi Tex Smith

First printed in 2004 by Hot Rod Library, Inc., P.O. Box 748., Driggs, ID 83422.

Hot Rod Library, Inc. Books are also available at discounts in bulk quantity for industrial or sales promotional use. For details, contact the marketing director at Hot Rod Library, Inc., 12 N. Main St. C-3, Veyo UT 84782. (435) 574-2174

ISBN 1-878772-20-1

Printed and bound in the United States of America

Author . . . . LeRoi Tex Smith
Publisher . . . . . . LeRoi Tex Smith
Editor . . . . Jim Clark
Associate Editor . Freda Clark
Art Director . . . . Jim Clark
Covers . . . . Jim Clark

Building Guide for *Basic* Hot Rods

Contents

A real hot rod or custom car is not necessarily a basic hot rod or custom! A real hot rod or custom is a personalized automobile created to have increased performance and/or modified styling. Despite modern definition that strays considerably from what we originally meant, such a "Real" car is not limited in scope as to performance or styling, nor in the attendant building costs. Which means there may be no upper limit on effort or expense. It can be anything from a stripped down Model T Ford to an automaker's lat-

This, then, is what Basic Hot Rods is all about…the grin and giggles that only a sweet running hot rod can produce.

est concept show car. On the other hand, a basic hot rod or custom car normally will be much more modest. In out-of-pocket expenditures as well as expectations.

Essentially, a basic hot rod is a no frills approach to a classic problem. Often, it can cost very little. It will be a pure pleasure to build, own, and use if some time-proven tenets are followed.

In the world of design, it is said that form follows function. The shape and construction of an object is directly related to what the object is supposed to do. Enough is enough, just a tiny bit more is too much. Just as long as it is enough to get the job done for which it is intended, it becomes a basic object.

In hot rodding, that is what this book is about.

This is not a how-to hot rod manual as such, although we do include a few interesting building scenarios. Our extensive Hot Rod Library of hot rod and custom car technical books more than cover the how-to needs of most builders, amateur or pro. Instead, this is a guide, intended solely to give you ideas for your own basic hot rod. We present a gamut of not-so-typical street driven hot rods (at least in the new twenty-first century of designer rides,) the kinds of hot rods that were dominant in my earlier years with the hobby/sport.

Largely forgotten and only recently rediscovered by rodders intent on regaining the roots of the hobby, these cars are known variously as retro-rods, rat rods, nostalgia rods, etc. The description that has come to the fore within the ranks of experienced rodders is to call these cars "Scrappers". As in cars that are made up of scrap parts. Whether such cars are patina covered barn finds (which used to be the dream of people into stock vehicle restorations) or contemporary builds made to look old, the final truth is that a basic hot rod is just that—just enough, usually minimal, always absolute fun.

While the rat rods are really more about a lifestyle, the Scrapper rods are more about the cars. As such, they are beginning to surface at all major and minor rod events as well as general automotive races. Interestingly, many of the photos we show here, courtesy of LeGrand Lee and Larry O'Toole, are from the annual Bonneville salt Flats SCTA/BNI Speedweek. This is the event where real hot rods still exist, and as such it is a magnet and focal point for the street oriented Basic Hot Rod crowd. These cars have been coming to Bonneville for decades, but in 1999 they really started to appear in numbers until by 2004, there were almost 70 of these examples plying the race course pits/spectator areas and the nearby

A basic hot rod does not need to be pre1948, or pre-anything for that matter. Author Tex Smith bought this great 1960 Chrysler hardtop in 1982 from an enthusiast in Tacoma, Washington: price $500. Objective was to build a budget beater that could run at least 135mph at the Bonneville salt flats.

No, the Chrysler wasn't in prime shape, but rust was limited to very small repairable areas, the glass was all good, and the 413 wedge V8 was still strong enough to handle another 10 years. All the body repairs and paint was handled by well known custom painter Carl Brunson, who now has a shop at the Las Vegas Motor Speedway.

Left—In keeping with the hot rod theme, the Chrysler was dechromed a bunch, all badges removed so that many think the fin car is a Cadillac, then Porsche brilliant red was sprayed on. Result is a machine many mistake for a 300 series hardtop; latest engine is a hot 440 wedge.

This old photo of the Tom Hynes T tub, powered by a four-banger engine and running hydraulic brake backing plates on early Ford spindles, is an absolutely perfect example of a basic hot rod. And, it was built when similar cars were common. The same no-frills formula works as well in the twenty-first century.

Nothing captures the true essence of real and basic hot rodding like an open wheel rolling along the highway. Just be sure and wear goggles.

Wendover casino evening hours. What has been lost at the major street rod events is still very much a part of the Scrapper hot rod movement.

However, don't automatically classify a basic rod or custom as a Rat Rod, or a Prime Croozer, or a Nostalgia Ride. It isn't even automatically a Scrapper. It will usually be more than such spare definitions, and such a vehicle must, really, satisfy only one requirement: It must be what the builder/owner/driver wants it to be! And, it should be safe!!

Basic rodding is for the owner, not for the spectator. If the latter becomes predominant, then the vehicle becomes a show car. Rough and tumble show car, perhaps, but still it exists more for someone else than for the owner. Which is ok, if the car is built specifically as a show car. Just as in racing, it is extremely rare for a basic hot rod or custom to be truly dual purpose, first class competitive in either arena.

Fifty and more years ago, those of us into hot rods understood that the basic vehicle of our choice was little more than a used car. A Model T Ford or twenties era Chevy were not usually our choice, because we could get a much better used car for about the same price of $25. Something like a '32 or so Ford, maybe even a thrashed '40 Ford or Chevy. Most of those cars still had good paint and upholstery, so all we had to concentrate on was the powertrain, brakes, and rubber. With

MOON
Equipped

FOR SALE

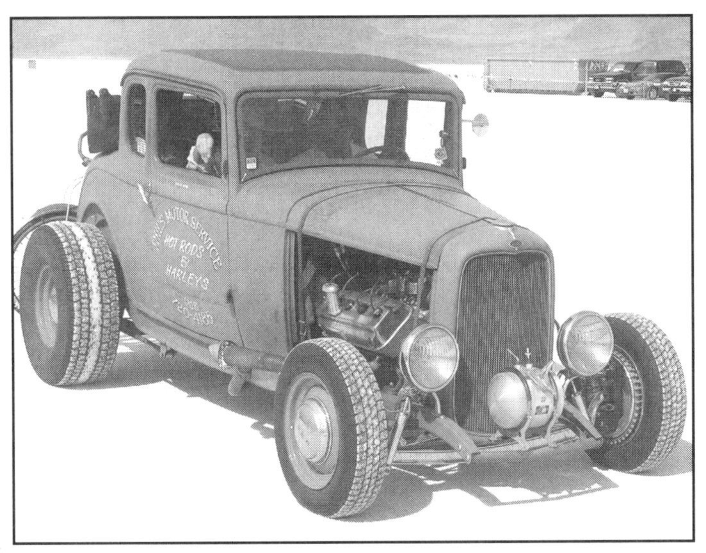

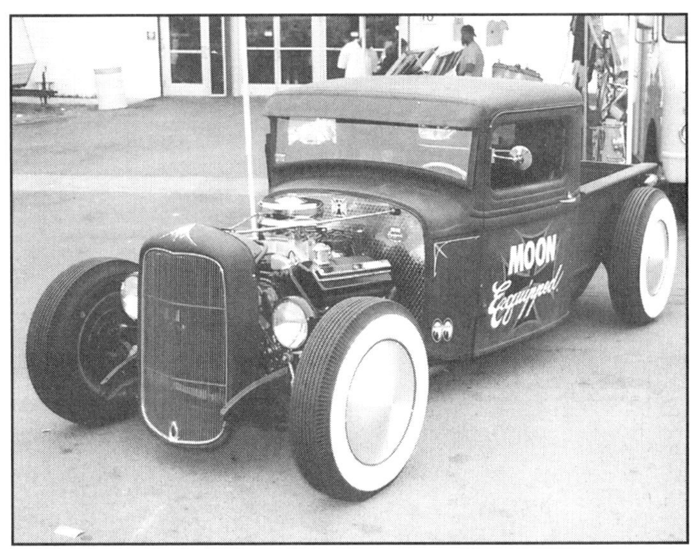

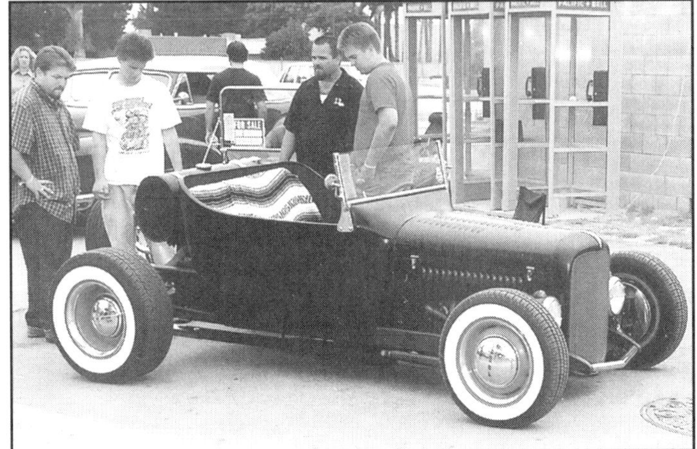

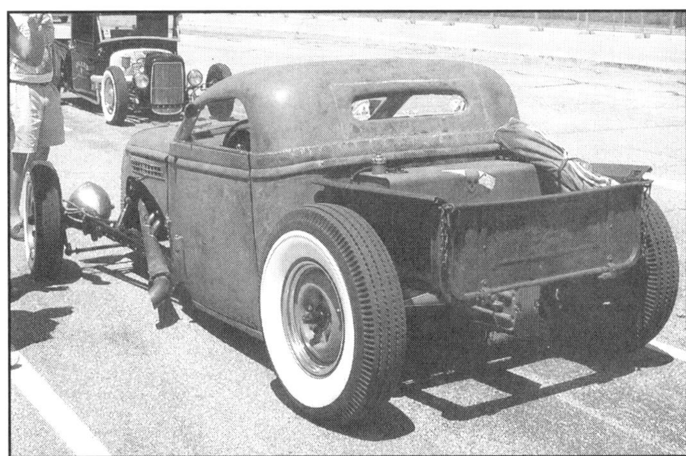

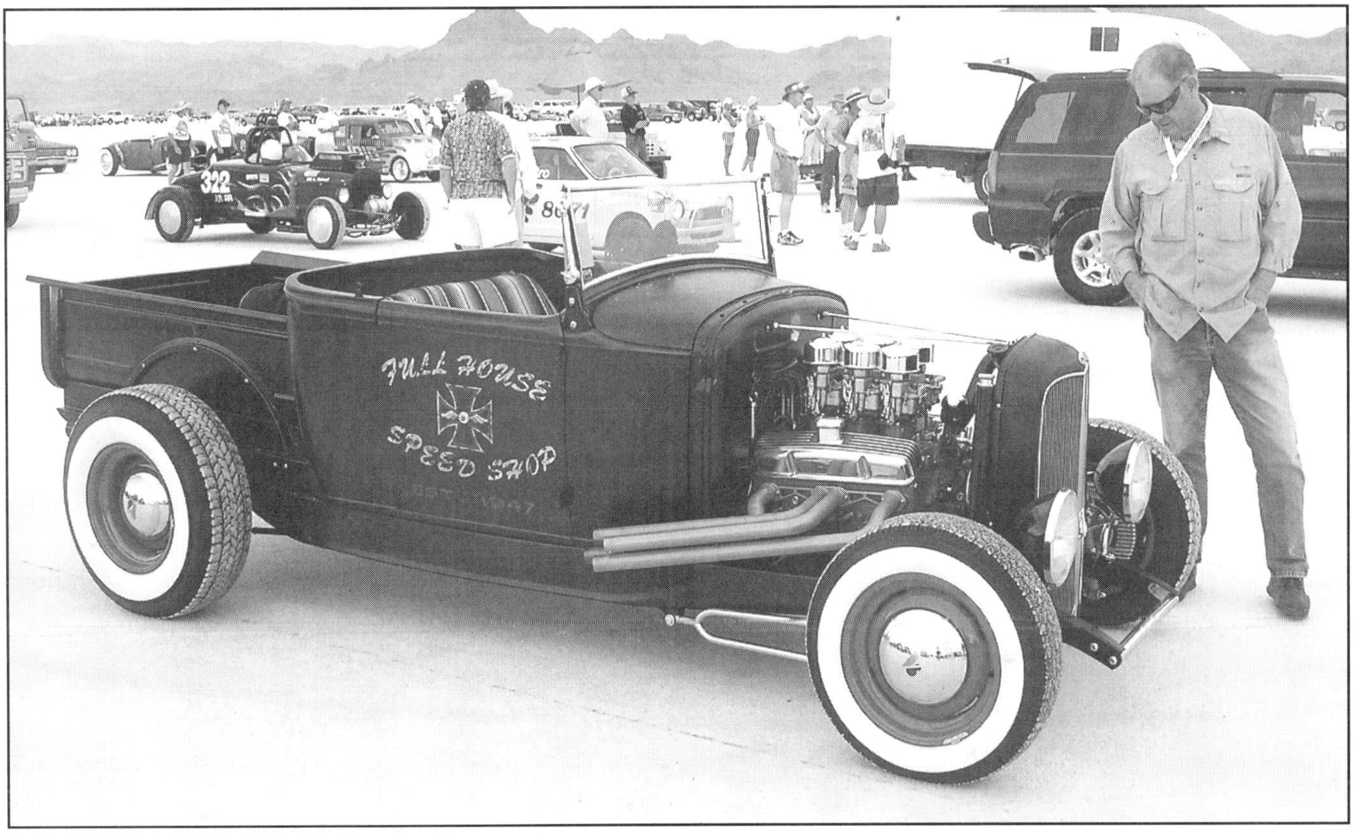
FULL HOUSE
SPEED SHOP
322

little money and much ingenuity, we had our basic hot rod or custom.

Yet one of the side delights to owning a basic hot rod is to step aside and listen as other hot rodders talk about how neat it is to see the old-timey hot rods coming back into favor. At the same time, it is nice to own the hot rod, not to be owned by the hot rod. With a basic hot rod, there need be no long hours of lost sleep or concern about theft or fire or damage. The car is what it really is, a mobile platform of metal or fiberglass. A simple wash job is enough preparation for a car show, minor tuning is enough for a drag race, an oil change is enough for a cross-country trip.

I've been accumulating the material for this book for some time, so some of the features are dated by the calendar, but fresh as today by the truth that a really good hot rod is always new.

I love all of the contemporary high profile hot rods, whether they are meant as personal drivers or as concept ego trips. But, neat as they may be as idea platforms, I'll guarantee you one thing for certain, you will never have as much enjoyment from any specialized automobile as you will from one that is nothing more than a Basic Hot Rod!

LeRoi Tex Smith

Photos by Larry O'Toole, LeGrand Lee

Something old intended

Russ Young has been a serious hot rodder all his life, and his newest basic rod ride is proof that you don't need to be a rocket engineer to build one in the backyard. Of course, being a whiz-bang electrical engineer doesn't hurt. Which is where the paradox about this little T roadster pickup comes in.

Russ first told us about this venture some half a dozen years before we got our first test ride on the salt flats. He said he wanted to build a "new" old style rod, using a mixture of old Ford and new Ford aftermarket parts, with the real emphasis on achieving a vehicle that would intrigue some, confuse some, but amuse all. Most importantly, Russ wanted to have a rod that would be fun.

Look the photos over carefully. You'll note that the Ford Model T roadster pickup body is redundant in rust hues. No fake patina here. But the Model A frame rails are plenty fresh. You can even see where he extended the rails up front for more wheelbase, and added a suicide spring perch for the Posies cross spring. In fact, inspection reveals that much of that basic Ford engineered front end is aftermarket. So are a lot of the parts under the car. Not so the transmission, or the rearend. Note that the headlight bar is of Russ' design, and how the windshield glass utilizes the same top curve (which is a kind of mid-Twenties strip-down flavor).

This car is a classic Scrapper, a pure Basic Hot Rod, and a heap of fun to bang around in. It steers good, it stops good, it goes really good, and the gears grind just the right amount. Russ Young done his northern California truck just right.

Oh, and when someone asks him when he will finish it, guess what his reply is…?

WHERE TO START

Building plan, what to use, where to find stuff, buying an unfinished or older car...

Where to start? Seems a simple enough question, yet it is the very point where so many projects first bog down. As with everything the human does, it works best if you have a plan. It can be highly detailed, or just a vague outline, but the plan should be made. You can put it on paper, or just have it noodle around in your head. It may be a compilation of ideas you have seen in magazines and at rod runs, or maybe it is fragments of a long held dream. The point is, if you have an idea of where you want to go, piecing out the road map is the very best way to avoid costly delays and wasted money.

Most of the successful builders I know, whether pro or first time builders break the plan down into three or four components: Chassis, powertrain, and body. Once they have the initial elements decided on, they then take each unit and decide exactly what they want it to become. As they progress with each element, they try and forecast any problems or difficulties that may arise. Easy enough for the experienced builder, but the newcomer probably doesn't even know what those problems may be, what questions to ask/answer,

much less how to solve them. This is where the neophyte needs to take the plan, at this point, to someone with experience for insight. Usually, it need be no more than a local acquaintance with experience in cars. This will be most successful if

the rodder who you call on for help is experienced in home-built rods and customs. A professional builder may actually be more of a professional assembler. That is, he or she buys nearly everything mail-order. Good information, but not exactly what the basic rod will utilize.

MENTORS

A really good way to locate such a mentor is through an area hot rod or custom car club. Every group will have someone who can help with answers, and is willing to help screen out potential pitfalls. There are also dozens of hot rod how-to books available through such people as Neal East at Colorado Car Books, Motorbooks International, and certainly our own Tex Smith Hot Rod Library. All the available magazines are a must read to gather ideas.

At this time, the budding plan is becoming something of a Build Sheet, with what needs to be done (along with parts needed) listed in some kind of order. This author (Tex Smith) has built many cars through the years; most of them through to completion and some discarded along the way. Perhaps my personal method of planning may be of help in the building of your project.

BUILDING PLAN
Tex Smith's Hot Rod Build Sheet

ONE—Think about the project. What is the purpose? I start by letting my imagination roam freely, any-where and everywhere. Ideas come from our surroundings, and I try to be as liberal with input as possible. Example: I see a really neat track roadster and file the nose/hood treat-ment to casual memory. Somewhere else I notice a rad-ically chopped '29 Dodge sedan. Four door. Hmmm. Suppose the MoPar body was mounted on a four-spring Dodge pickup frame, the frame kicked just behind the front spring aft mounts and just ahead of the rear spring mounts. That would make a really low down puppy but retain some decent interior room. Then modify the race car nose on the lower portions to cover the frame horns, (exactly as race car builders of the 1930s did). Very interesting ride bucko. The most difficult part of the build would be shaping the nose, and with fiberglass or contemporary metal fabrication skills, even that would be a no-brainer.

TWO—Allow several build ideas to perco-late at the same time. So I'm building the Dodge sedan, but I think how neat a roadster pickup on the same or similar chassis would be. Maybe even use the front doors and cowl from a sedan, top cut off and rear body panel moved up behind the doors. Pickup bed from a 70s-80s import truck, cut down.

Just let the mind noodle, dream along. Good for the blood pressure.

THREE—Make some sketches. I'm no artist, so my attempts are really amateur, but all that doesn't matter, because what I am trying to do is capture the ideas of the moment, to be suitably filed away for future reference.

FOUR—Consider the powertrain. Since I like to try things just for the sake of experiments, it is in the planning stage where I do my homework on engine/trans/rearend combos. Keeping in mind that a good Donor Vehicle will keep costs way-way down, I consider carefully what engine I want/need. While the transmission should be orig-

inal with the engine, or at least compatible, the rearend can be most anything.

FIVE—The suspension and brakes largely depend on what front axle/spindle combination I use, and what rearend.

SIX—I normally decide on the interior and gauges as I build, but I'm thinking of them as I survey what is available, either aftermarket, wreck-ing yard, or swap meet.

This is the sum total of my build sheet, but it works remarkably well. While I will most certain-ly stray from my original ideas and intent as I build the car, I have learned that it is best to be true as possible to my original concept. It is best not to change horses or horsepower in mid stream. After all, there are dozens of other projects just waiting to get my attention (and garage space).

Sometimes, you still find 'Barn Fresh" rod material, this was an abandoned restoration project.

HOMEBUILT A-BONE

Building Plan for a Basket Case. *By Brian Quinn*

Four years before I got into this basic hot rod I got wind of a half-restored basket case Model A coupe that had been left sitting across town in a single car garage. A backyard body shop that had gone under ten years before. The car had been forgotten by all concerned. After a long and intense battle with stubbornness I eventually found the true owner, and a transfer of ownership to me.

With help from my buddy Brad, we dragged the frozen-wheeled chassis out of a foot of accumulated leaves that had blown into the small garage over the years. We hunted around, gathering parts and finding half-done bodywork, rusty seat springs, miscellaneous nuts and bolts…what fun.

We hauled the coupe home and it sat for a year while the design process began. Having never built a rod before and being a carpenter by trade, I was sure of one thing. I needed a game plan laid out as completely as possible prior to getting started.

After many changes in plans, and consultations with experienced rod builders and fellow Strokers club members, the concept appeared to take the shape of an early '50s hot rod. Wanting to see the projected started, Brad (who is a true artist and professional rod and custom builder and who would never have spent so much time planning) made what I am sure was a frustrated suggestion. We then spent a snowy, cold Saturday in the woodstove heated shop at my home in Rowley, Massachusetts. We chopped the rusty top. Starting at 8 in the morning and finishing at 6 at night, we took 5-inches out of the uprights and welded everything back together. That was the kickoff, which Brad knew all along it would be.

Fellow Stroker club member Barron supplied me with a lot of how-to's and a hot little '53 Ford flathead, an old hammered dropped EIE beam axle, a '39 gearbox, and fellow-Stroker Mike's '40 Ford rearend. Russ set me up with a set of fifty-buck Model A frame rails. Three months passed while frame construction proceeded in the shops heated area, the body rested on its original chassis outside. Many trips back and forth referencing one frame to the other.

I boxed the rails with l/4-inch plate and crossed the frame with 4-inch channel left over from a construction site. I extended the frame in

Very first order of business was to chop the top 5-inches, Model A Fords have vertical posts so lowering the lid is not a major undertaking.

Above—Having an extra Model A frame made this project a little easier. The front axle is one of the old stretched and hammered versions, brakes are from a '40 Ford. Headlight mounts are outer stubs of Model A light bar cut and reshaped then bolted to side of frame for an ultra low appearance. Shock mounts are '49 Ford pickup items, steering gearbox is '40 Ford.

Below—1932 Ford grille is classic identification of a Model A hot rod, the tires are 6.00-16 front and 7.50-16 rear with wide whites on red rims.

Above—Model A frame was modified at the rear with some home-made kickup extensions welded to Model A rear crossmember. The A spring connects to '40 rearend. Sections of I-beam became an X-member to considerably strengthen the torsional quality of the frame.

Although this is a hi-boy, the severe top chop makes it seem much lower. The '53 Ford engine uses Edelbrock heads, Thickstun high rise dual intake with Stromberg carbs, a Beehive oil cooler and homemade headers. Stock 6-volt starter doesn't seem to mind short bursts of 12-volts for starting. Taillights are '48 Chevy.

back to accommodate the spring on the '40 Ford rearend. With an old Model A cowl section bolted to the frame I could layout the '40 Ford brake/clutch pedal unit, where the engine should fit and a fan mounted on the generator confirmed where the radiator should be. The hood length would be stock.

The '40 Ford torque tube and driveshaft had to be cut down, the tube cuts nicely with a rental service 4-inch pipe-cutter. The driveshaft was cut off at the tail end and turned down to fit inside the splined coupling, then welded, and the shorter unit is then installed to the pinion shaft with a l/4-inch bolt peened over.

When the body was put in place there was just enough room at my added frame kickup so that a snug rumble seat could be fashioned. I wired the car with all new braided wire and the use of a l953 Ford wiring diagram. The generator is a 6-volt armature with 12-volt field windings, and it works fine.

Finally, out the door for a ride around the yard. Sure was an exciting moment. The first year my wife and I put on over 4000 miles of great riding. The most important things I learned was to have a complete building plan before starting, knowing what end result is wanted, mock up of parts, and a loose assembly during construction.

Just when you think you got the lowest coupe in town, up drives a knee scraper.

THE EVOLUTION OF A BASIC HOT ROD

By Harvey Tarnasky

This tale began in 1965 when a young Canadian hot rodder named Ernie Welta spotted a 1928 Ford roadster body. Ernie had to have it. After some haggling with the former owner, a deal was struck and for the grand sum of five ($5) hard earned Canadian bucks, the roadster body complete with 43 bullet holes was hauled home. Thus began the saga of a real hot rod.

By the summer of '66, Ernie was ready to storm the streets of Regina, Saskatchewan in a channeled roadster, sans windshield and deck lid. It was in primer, had cheater slicks, two Carter AFB's and dual exhausts. Within a few years the topless A sported a bright yellow paint job, a deck lid, and a windshield. And a single carb.

In 1969, a new frame was fabricated from 2x4-inch tubing, the body was unchanneled and a pair of bobbed rear fenders found home. By the early '70s the car was in constant use, and somewhere along the way it turned bright orange. Added were a '32 grille shell, an aluminum hood, and a new brown interior.

But this is one basic rod that doesn't languish in front of rod run lawn chairs. Ernie's done it all with the little A, from drag racing, some street encounters, a few hillclimbs and a sporty car slalom course. It is sometimes towed, it has done

Next up, Ernie whittled the body down over the A frame, installed a thru-cowl steering, and hit the road. Who needs a decklid anyway?

the towing, and it is always driven. The car has been built, then rebuilt. Cussed and discussed. Shown, and almost sold. But it has remained as a family affair. Maw Welta has sewn the interiors while Ernie and the two sons have handled the several reshapes.

In l983, the car was disassembled for the umpteenth time. This time, a much-modified Deuce frame was used, with a Super Bell I-beam axle, Horton slider spring, '56 Ford pickup front brakes on '48 Ford spindles, and a Vega steering box. In the rear a coil spring mounted Nova differential handles power transfer from the 262 ci small-block Chevy

No billet stuff, thank you, just basic hi-temp flat black paint. Even the transmission is a GM 3-speed of unknown origin. An ancient Hurst shifter sorts the gears, topped with a glass doorknob.

Above—Oh, the shades of progress. Now Welta could enjoy a windshield but he still could have used some kneeguards due to the severe channel. Headers were often uncorked for town driving.

Left—Yes, that is genuine Saskatchewan snow bucko, with cycle fenders up front for all year touring. The new top and side curtains were in deference to Ernie's advancing years, the shortened Deuce grille shell replaced the Model T unit, pointed at things to come.

Below—A short time off the street allowed the body to be raised so the lowboy could become a highboy, and rear fenders added to keep some of that winter mud at bay. A decklid had come home, as well.

Left—Chrome wheels and blackwalls replaced the painted wheels and wide whites, the lakes headers were now gone in favor of more traditional Chevy ram's horn exhaust.

Above—Like something from a 1948 Southern California weekend, the Welta A often saw duty as a tow car.

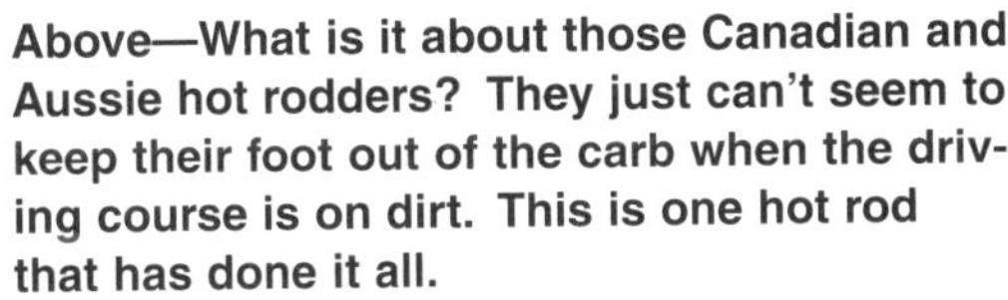

Above—What is it about those Canadian and Aussie hot rodders? They just can't seem to keep their foot out of the carb when the driving course is on dirt. This is one hot rod that has done it all.

Above—The drag strip is well known to this family daily hauler, with some respectable times in the process of evolution.

Left—As most rodders know, sometimes stuff happens. Deciding on a career in off-roading, Ernie started by having the rear radius rod on the left side detach from its mooring. Not much hassle to jack the car up, push the rearend back into place, build better locator brackets, and straighten the fender.

Building Guide For Basic Hot Rods 19

That $5 body had all the seams welded, the windshield was whacked some 2 1/2-inches and the posts leaned back. Welta fabricated a new hood, formed over a propane bottle, with lots of side panel louvers. The radiator shell is a highly modified l936 Ford pickup item with a machined insert. Again, orange paint was applied. Maw made up still another interior, this time in grey vinyl. After this rebuild, Ernie figured the next one would have to be in the hands of the boys. Sure, Welta. We believe you one hunnert percent.

AUSSIE TRIPLE PLAY

Basic hot rodding has been the very foundation of American rodding since the 1920s, but too many enthusiasts think it didn't start until the 1950s. Practically no Yanks know that basic rods have been happening around the world, especially in Australia for almost the same amount of time. Fewer still realize that basic hot rods, sometimes now called Nostalgia Rods, caught on again in the Land Of Oz well before the current American craze to return to the roots. Here are several examples that illustrate the point.

Courtesy Australian Street Rodder magazine,69 Forest St., Castlemaine, Victoria, 3450 Australia. E-mail them at Grafitti@netcon.net.au. A great magazine very much worth a subscription.

COGGIN' ALONG

By Larry O'Toole

When Maurice Cogger first started building his T speedster he wanted something that would appeal to rodders and restorers alike. This he has achieved, judging by the amount of interest it has created. The T also had to be safe and reliable on a long run, hence good mechanicals with safety aspects built in from the start of the project. Maurice has had lots of help and advice from friends along the way, also meeting many people throughout Victoria in the pursuit of parts to complete the speedster, all of whom he would like to thank. The speedster was built 100% at home over a period of several years and on a very small budget.

The chassis is 1924 T Model Ford, obtained from the Holden Museum in Echuca, Victoria. It has been fully boxed with 5mm plate but retains all of the original crossmembers. A lazy L rear step up has been incorporated for that typical speedster style.

The body is full steel 1924 T Ford with the cowl narrowed seven inches to sit on top of the chassis main rails. It features a reversed firewall with Dodge center pressing, full steel floor, fiberglass bonnet with air duct, shortened windscreen posts and hand-made Pegasus bonnet mascot.

Residing under the bonnet is a 1928 A Model Ford engine that has been fully rebuilt using five thou oversize pistons fitted with Hastings rings. The carby is XD Ford downdraft while the extractors are homemades. Starter motor is sidevalve V8, the engine has a modified water pump of foreign manufacture (one that doesn't leak) and the radiator is FB Holden fitted with a thermo fan. Distributor is from a Ford Prefect. The engine sits back in the chassis to distribute weight better and give better handling. Gearbox is A Model Ford three-speed manual with single plate clutch and no synchros and the flywheel has been lightened. The Shortened tailshaft and diff is '39 Ford.

Front suspension consists of an A model Ford front axle fitted with 1/4-elliptic springs, A Model steering arms connected to a VW Kombi steering box and Lucas front shockers are fitted. The rear suspension utilizes a T Model Ford rear spring with coilover helpers on the shock absorbers.

Electrical functions are controlled by a 12-volt system that is very basic with only low and high beam lights, indicators, brake lights etc. The loom was made at home and incorporates a push-button start and one-wire 50-amp alternator. Wheels and tires are '35 Ford wires fitted with Olympic air ride tires. Paint is black acrylic with fine gold metalflake while the interior has basic tan upholstery completed at home. Inside there is a wooden steering wheel and a gauge pod with warning lights; there is no dash as such. A floor mount starting assembly is used and a custom-

made fuel tank is mounted under the floor. It holds 24 litres and uses a Fiat sender unit.

Front brakes are A Model Ford adapted to hydraulic operation by adding a wheel cylinder and a portion of backing plate to the A Model Ford backing plate but retaining the stock A Model Ford internals. Rear brakes are '40 Ford and the master cylinder is a HQ Holden drum unit mounted underneath the floor.

No matter what your particular taste is in street rods, you can't help admire what Maurice has achieved in this simple little car. No doubt it is a bundle of fun to drive. What's more there is almost nothing about this car that couldn't be duplicated by anyone with just the basic tools found in the average hot rodders garage.

$UM FUN

By Doug Hamilton and Larry O'Toole

The reason for the title name on this feature is two-fold. $um Fun is the name of a salt racing roadster that often pushes the limits at Bonneville and has even traveled to South Australia's Lake Gairdner to shake the salt. This is where John De Vries and his little lakester comes in with his hopes of hitting 100mph in the South Aussie outback. John has been into modified rides for about 25 years and has had a nice assortment of rods over the years, but he has always liked lakesters for their no extras, no frills, all fun and all thrills attitude.

The original plan was to use early Ford parts but John decided the cost was too steep for pieces too rusty. Then he hit upon the idea of using Prefect components from Ford's poorer cousin over in jolly old England during a boring lunch break.

Eleven months later the little Prefect prowler had its rego plates screwed on just in time to head

for Castlemaine for the Graffiti 25th anniversary celebrations. Smelling of fresh paint and burning engine oil, the little lakester took John and his mate Nigel to the run, even testing the speed limit at times (the streamlined hair cuts helped).

The guys not only had a ball all weekend but also scored one of the best momentos ever to take home, a commemorative plate engraved to declare it as Tex Smith's pick of all the sweet rods on show. That's not a bad effort for a cash outlay of about $1200.00. (Aussie dollars) $um fun indeed.

John's nine-to-five job as a custom Harley fabricator came in handy as he scratch-built the 1927-ish Ford-ish body complete with suicide doors and a narrowed dash from a circa 1935 English CX Ford. Built entirely from scrounged, cast-off and hand-built parts this mosquito-weight ride is pure fun. Even the way John filled out the tech-sheet for this feature reflects this side of the project. Many handmade parts are featured throughout the car including the V style wind-screen, the headlight bar and the detachable lug-gage rack. Lighting the way at night is a pair of Anglia headlights and following along behind are trailer taillights in handmade housings with turn signals from K-Mart.

A cast-off 100E Ford Prefect provided the basic mechanical parts, including the transverse leaf springs that were cut in half and mounted

quarter elliptic style. An early Suzuki steering box is set up in push-pull fashion and John reports that the handling and steering is so good that he can actually go down rough roads with his hands off the steering wheel. Brakes are also 100E including the non-boosted master cylinder and swing pedal system. Anglia shock absorbers are used at the rear and Morris items at the front.

To watch the suspension working as the rod was driven down a bumpy farm track was quite intriguing. Again the fun element came out when John wasn't phased at all about mud on even fresh green cows stuff, although he did let his wife drive the car home, letting her cop all the stuff flung from the Peugeot 14x4 and 14x5 wheels.

The body was mostly made of folded sections to provide strength and light weight and it could be built to whatever dimensions required. Most of the things such as the windscreen posts, headlight bar, fuel tank, steering column and wheel etc. were hand/homemade to help keep the cost down. The doors have bears claw door latches and the dash has minimal gauges – amps and speedo from a 100E Prefect. The steering column and wheel is handmade with a snakeskin leather wheel trim. John's wife Janina is a professional trimmer and gets the credit for stitching the tan tuck and roll

vinyl after John carried the body shell into the spare room so she could fit everything. Brown cut-pile carpet is used on the floor.

The engine is from a 100E Prefect, described by John as "low compression". It's fed by a Datsun 120Y carby on a homemade inlet manifold and the engine is painted orange – that's all there is to know about it. Oh it does have a handmade lakester style exhaust and it retains the 100E radiator and three-speed gearbox. A Datsun 120Y distributor is the most high-tech item on the whole car and came about because the original dizzy was dead and a Datsun unit was collecting dust on the shelf. As it turned out the Dato Dizzy was almost a drop in fit.

Using a four pot Flathead sandwiched between a laid back '35 Ford CX grille and K-mart supplied taillights may not be everyone's choice of hot rod hardware, but the De Vries' don't care, they're just having $um Fun without breaking the bank, now the next step is to break 100mph. Watch out "Team Piggy Bank" are looking to shake the salt.

John would like to thank his lovely wife Janina for her support and his mate Nigel for his help so they could finish the car in time for the Castlemaine run.

ROLL-OUT A ROADSTER

By: Chris Henry

The car is based on a 1924 Chev chassis and firewall. On the chassis was added partial stepped boxing and three box tube crossmembers. The rear crossmember is from a 1922 T-truck. A 1937 Plymouth front tube axle is hung by a pair of quarter-elliptic springs, which hook via Plymouth U-bolts to the chassis rail ends. Late '40s Morris lever shockers live under the springs.

A Suzuki FV 50 steering box sends directions to the stock Plymouth spindles and steering arms via slingshot steering. All this is sent to the driver via a Mitsubishi Colt steering column and a SAAS leather steering wheel. Brakes consist of standard 1975 XB Falcon panel van drums on the front and Mitsubishi L300 brakes with Falcon finned drums on the rear, both being fed by a stock unboosted HQ Holden master cylinder. A pair of '37 Ford wishbones on Nylathane bushes keep the axle where it should be. Another pair of '37 Ford wishbones, having been

shortened considerably, hold the L300 Mitsubishi van differential in place. The differential is a stock item running 4.36.1 gears. A re-arched T-Ford spring connects the chassis to the diff. Mini Minor shockers keep all the rear under control.

Engine is a Starfire four-cylinder Holden motor. Internally it is basically stock, with the exception of a bit of headwork and a lumpy performance street grind cam. A two-litre Cortina Weber carburetor feeds it and spent gases are exited via a set of tuned tube extractors. The beast is cooled by a re-cored EK Holden radiator, Toyota Corona viscous clutch and plastic fan; all keep within a modified fan shroud made up of steel Toyota Corolla and Subaru pieces. A Daihatsu Charade 35 amp alternator keeps the charge up to a stock electrical system.

Hours and hours of work went into the engine dress-up, fabrication, paint work and detail. A brand new Holden-six alloy rocker cover was cut down to fit the Holden four-cylinder then rubbed and filed up to perfection. An early British truck gave up its sump, which was cut down to make the finned alloy side cover plate. All fabricated brackets, sump, manifold, alternator, starter motor, fan shroud, rocker cover and side cover are painted in PPG Silver two-pack enamel. A selection of small chrome parts provide highlights. A Victa lawn mower petrol tank is now home as a windscreen washer tank.

Hooked to the engine is a stock Borg-Warner Toyota Corona four-speed manual gearbox. It transfers motion to a shortened Mitsubishi L300 tail-shaft, which is bolted via stock flanges to the L300 diff. EK Holden pedals keep some driver control, with a Suzuki Carry Van accelerator in place for forward action. A Toyota AE85 Corolla handbrake helps if things get out of control in a hurry. Keeping in control is aided by a Smiths speedo, a Triumph multi-warning light gauge and a full compliment of Pricol aftermarket gauges, consisting of fuel, water temp, oil pressure, volts, amps and tacho. These all sit in a hand formed steel dash panel. Switch gear consists of Holden, Valiant and Toyota switches, for lights, wipers and heater controls. All are fitted with Valiant knobs. Driver and passenger sit on a modified Toyota seat back and base, which is covered in Tandoori Orange leather look-a-like vinyl, with black piping. Simple door and quarter panel covers are fab-

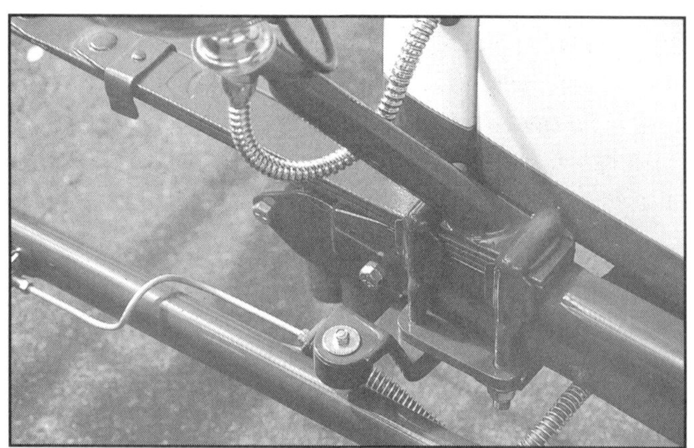

ricated from 2mm sheet-aluminium then covered in the same Tandoori vinyl. Floor covering is a combination of hardwearing black closed grain vinyl and black carpet. An orange spider gear knob tops it all off.

The body starts at the front with a modified '26 Whippet grille shell. It surrounds a black steel weld mesh grille insert. Above it sits a '27 Chev grille badge. Bonnet and side panels are hand-formed. Bonnet is latched by a Suzuki bonnet latch and cable and swung by Toyota Corolla bonnet hinges. Bonnet sides are held by Commodore threaded rubber absorbers. The firewall and topside of the body cowl are stock '24 Chev touring car. To this mounts '26 Oakland windscreen frame and posts that have been chopped four inches. A detachable top frame mounts a Mighty wiper and dual windscreen wipers, with dual small-diameter rear-view mirrors both sides. From the cowl back all the body is scratch built. A steel box tube frame holds everything together. To this the hand fabricated 1mm steel floor is attached. The cowl sides, door skins, quarter panels and tu b section is all hand-formed then welded to the steel box tube frame. Hand-built scaled down EK Holden style door hinges do the opening while Centurion bus latches do the closing. New aftermarket seat belts are fitted. Behind the driver a '24 T-Model truck fuel tank is held in place by stainless steel straps. An Echelin electric fuel pump keeps motor drinking substance up to the engine. Under the fuel tank sits a Heyman Reese tow receiver which doubles as the number plate mount and third taillight holder. Other lighting is done by King Bee repro headlights and Harley Davidson front blinkers on shortened '37 Ford wishbones, used to make the

headlight stanchions. Modified Model A taillights also sit on hand-made tube mounts. A 1928 Hudson gave up its third stop light to go just a little faster. All this is kept on the road by stock 16-inch Plymouth wires on the front, running MS 90-16 Cheng Shin tyres and widened 16-inch Plymouth wires on the rear mounted up to LT 245/75R16 Nankang tyres. These are painted PPG Arancio. These compliment the PPG Vert D'Lamozone and Juane Rialto on the body. Interior paint detail is done in PPG Black Suede, with PPG Starsixer applied to the drivetrain silver items.

So there we are. Now all that remains is to drive it and shake down some of the minor bugs. Obviously time to build went grossly overtime, mostly due to me getting fussier than I originally intended to be. My first plans were for it to be done in two-tone primer. The standard of paint and detail put months extra on the project.

Budget wise we're a long way over. The initial figure was around $8,000. The finished total is $13,045. (Aussie dollars) However everything is either new or reconditioned with the exception of engine transmission or differential. Although all these have been opened up and checked prior to using.

New radiator, exhaust, tyres, electrics, gauges, brakes, bearings and body hardware all adds up. There is $1,900 in paint materials. The trim and carpet was $1,000. Rego, personal plates, roadworthy and engineer's report add up to just on $1,700. There is $4,600 in those three areas alone. With labour included at a reasonable hourly rate, retail wise all up this would be about a $50,000 car done in a good workshop. Obviously not counting labour an average handy guy would do it for somewhere between $10,000 and $20,000. Still good Value!

There are many people to thank. Firstly, I thank Larry and Mary O'Toole for giving me a chance to do something for hot rodding and express my knowledge and views to the world at large. They have given me a chance to do something most people don't get to. As importantly, thank you to my lovely lady, Rita. She has put up with the house not being painted for eighteen months now, and has supported me solely and whole heartedly over the time it has taken to do the car and write the articles.

Thank you to the very best of friends I've had help me over the duration of this project. Steve Callahan, Peter Taylor, Graeme Johnson and James Bowden have all contributed to make this car happen in many and varied ways. A special thanks goes to Brian Pendlebury, who continues to think up ways of doing something. His input has made this car the quality that it is.

Last and not least, thanks to all the readers and people who have followed the project for the last 18 months.

By Ron Lucas

LONG TERM 'A'FFAIR

Sometimes the hot rod of your life has been there all along.

One of the most interesting things about basic hot rodding is that it can be a casual fling, a kind of weekend thing easily forgotten, or it can last a lifetime. Take the case of Russel Daly of Newport, Rhode Island.

The story begins in about 1953 when young Russ and his dad saw a white roadster in a Northern California parking lot. Dad lifted Russ so he could look inside to the green and white tuck and roll upholstery. The white roadster was owned by a guy in the Slicks Car Club of Crescent City, California. Let's

stop right here and point out that if this rings a bell with any reader, please contact Tex Smith at this publication. Anyway, in l959, Russ moved to Eureka, still in Northern Cal. While riding his bike and now in junior high school, he discovered

Top down, the A model is the personification of post-war California rodding, what with the California roll on the seat back, the wide whites on wire wheels, hairpin front radius rods and a black body on red frame paint scheme.

a roadster that looked a lot like that white gem of years before.

After graduation from high school, Russ found out the roadster he had been eyeing was for sale, but the asking price of $800 was exactly twice what his bank account could deliver. Enter good friend Dave Koskeln who was good for the extra $400 loan. At last, the roadster of first love was his.

One day, while scraping the paint off for a restart, Russ found it was white underneath. The very same car he had seen so many years before. By 1963 the hiboy had a Z'd frame, Model A rear crossmember, Model A front crossmember, '49 Olds engine, Cadillac transmission, chopped windshield, Carson style top, and a '32 Ford three window coupe dash. Half-century rodding epitomized.

The roadster became daily transportation, driven to work, to college, and even to a Joan Baez concert in Sacramento. There was even some off roading, by installing chains out back for extra dirt trail traction and taking on high-minded motorcycle jockeys. In 1964, the little car made the pilgrimage to Bonneville.

The story went into hibernation then. Living near the ocean means that metal and airborne salt do not co-exist. Russ decided to disassemble the roadster, eliminate the rust and do some general cleaning. Which is about the time he was drafted into the Army. The car was stored on the second floor of a fire station for the duration. Then, in 1973 Russ moved to Illinois with the roadster in tow. The car was not on the street again until Russ moved to the East Coast in 1979. This time around, it is what you see here. With just enough modern touches to make it good for another fifty years.

It is basic hot rodding at its best, and you simply can't get any better!

Above—Early style dropped axle mounts 1940 Ford hydraulic brakes, tube shocks, spreader bar between the headlight brackets to reduce headlight shake, filled '32 Ford grille.

Above Left—Yeah, it says so right there on the windshield sticker. Bonneville National Speed Trials, Safety Inspected 1963. So take that, all you wannabe's!

Hood is made of aluminum; the entire inside surface has been engine turned and is very effective. Engine is 1948 Mercury flathead of 255 cubic inches, which would have made it a very serious player in the early Fifties. Triple carbs are now fronted by a modern alternator, headers are Fenton, and the oil filter is coveted beehive type.

Left—Deuce coupe dash is tucked behind the original Model A tank facia, with the old Stewart Warner style dash insert. Original spoon throttle remains, along with early type hand brake lever. Steering wheel is Bell champ-car type complete with chest pad. That long shifter connects to a '37 Cad-LaSalle box.

Right—An art deco styled rear nerf bar surrounds the license plate, and taillights from a l940 Dodge. The modern mega-phone exhaust tips might seem totally today, but they were not unknown in early day rodding. 1940 Ford rearend sports a Halibrand quick change.

Below—Because a basic hot rod usually gets the snot driven out of it, a neat padded top on a roadster is pure period perfect. Headlight buckets are from 'l936 Olds, another trick from the post-war II era.

In a single days drive within 100 miles of the Tex Smith Publishing offices in eastern Idaho, several hundred good basic rod projects were spotted. This four door is not a l932 Ford, but it really does look like one and chances are the body would bolt onto a Deuce frame and perhaps even accept '32 Ford fenders. Proof that you don't have to build a cookie cutter hot rod, and you don't have to spend a small fortune.

FINDING TIN

It's probably just around the corner from your place. *By Tex Smith*

Back in the l960s, close friend Tom Medley inherited the reins of Rod & Custom magazine at Petersen Publishing Company. R&C had started as one of the inexpensive "little books" but had become grown-up. With Medley at the helm, the emphasis was diverted to the growing interest in street rods, and I was assigned to write almost as much freelance material as I could produce.

On one office visit, I was showing Medley some photos of an upcoming article when he spotted some adjacent pictures of old abandoned cars I had found in Montana and North Dakota. His enthusiasm was immediate, and he asked for more and more reports on his newly coined Vintage Tin articles.

Overnight, Vintage Tin became one of R&C's most popular series, but in all the years I did those stories, I used perhaps only one percent of the material I uncovered while travelling the states west of the Mississippi. I didn't use anything from Canada or Mexico, both places rich in rusty car treasures. In recent years I have discovered similar treasure troves in Australia.

The original purpose of the vin-tin stories was to prove to a skeptical readership that there truly

Vintage tin in western states usually come with a light coat of rust that normally is not invasive. When a single usable piece is found, such as the Model T touring front seat, the other pieces are often nearby.

Doesn't look like much, perhaps, but this closed I928/29 Ford cowl and floor plate is an excellent starting point for a basic rod. The windshield posts can be modified for an open roadster or tub, or a woodie body, or????

Above—While this sedan floor can be saved, a new aftermarket piece might be more economical in the long run. Learning how to mix and match old/new pieces is part of becoming a wise basic hot rod builder.

Right–No, it isn't a Ford touring body, but the unknown make remains are good enough that some mixing and matching of parts will produce a Fad Car, a roadster pick-up, a touring, a speedster…the list of possibilities are limited only by the builder's imagination.

Probably a Dodge four door. Because floor and lower body rust is not really common in most of the western U.S. and Canada, such a body as this is a good start. Rather than work at fixing damaged panels and doors, it is often easier to find good replacements. This particular body was within sight from a major north/south freeway in open range.

Left–Not a particularly good starting point, this non-Ford isn't the interest of the photo, in the background is a l935/36 Ford five window coupe body still with good fenders/doors/deck lid. You can hang out at your local swap meet and hope to find such a good project for under five grand, or you can lash on the old car trailer and go searching.

Then you might want a two door trunk back '36 Ford instead.

were basis for hot rod or custom car material still available. One such article I did on a short outing in central Nevada was titled something like "Tex Smith's Lost Vintage Tin Mine." Some two decades later, fellow rodder Burley Burlile of northern Utah decided to retrace that original journey (after deciphering the route clues). To his delight, he found that almost all of the old roddable hulks were exactly where they were from my visits 30 years prior.

To give another illustration of how great hot rodding material can go un-noticed was when I traveled from a home base in south central Montana to the street rod nats in Minnesota. I had wife and four kids loaded in my l948 Chrysler eight-passenger sedan, and stopped in a small Montana burg for gas. A young gas pump jockey was admiring the car and ventured, "Gee, I'd sure like to have a car like this. But you can't find them anymore!" When I went to pay, I invited the young kid to follow me around back of his station. "How about that car? Same as mine." He was stunned. Among the obligatory dozen or so abandoned relics was a '48 Chrysler coupe, great

Above—Then again, maybe a Mopar five window is more to your liking. Neat thing about basic hot rodding is that you can build whatever you want without applying for permission from the magazine gods or the rod run power parking guru's.

Left–Hmmm, looks beyond hope doesn't it. Not really, and this Chevy is a twice door to boot. Major roof damage can be cured with graft from another donor, or it could be removed entirely to create a great two-door sedan convert/phaeton.

Nope, not still out there in the Idaho snows. This '39 Buick convert came home to the author's house for safe keeping, was eventually given to another rodder who welcomed the choice piece for a basic low-cost custom.

There are bullet holes aplenty in this Willys twice door, but bodyman/painter extaordinaire Carl Brunson says no problem to bringing it back to life. Easy for him to say.

Although wet weather rust is not normally a problem in the arid west, alkali in the soil will do bad damage as well. Note the sedan almost completely covered with sandy wash soil in background.

Brunson checks out grille in a '4l Ford coupe found in the cedar breaks, where alkali destruction is not usually found. In this case top sheetmetal has been removed, all the easier to make a convert.

So, rodder Burlie Burlile followed up on a Rod & Custom story from the Sixties, doing a stretch of highway in central Nevada. To his surprise, all the cars I had photoed were still in the same place. So much for hot rodders willing to make a search. The dry Nevada weather means that metal doesn't go the way of right coast America.

shape, and from the looks of it all, had been running until recently parked. For me, it is amazing how myopic most wannabe hot rodders can be.

Until years recent, many rodders were reluctant to think of an old car body design as anything than as produced by a factory. With the advent of the hot rod designers and an ever-expanding list of phantom rods and customs, now we have come full circle and everything is fair game. Especially when making an open car from a closed version. In the beginning, this was all a part of hot rodding, but it began to die back during the Fifties. This diversity took a further hit with the introduction of great fiberglass replica bodies. Now, we are back to some reality, and the ingenious rod builder can create a basic hot rod or custom car from just about anything, even the bed from a Japanese import truck.

Right—In the town of Manhattan, you'll find this, what? Buick has had rear of body replace by wooden pickup bed and once served the volunteer fire department.

Left—Yes, it is a portable air compressor made by mating a Ford V8 engine to drive an inline six converted to be an air pump. With a '32 Ford grille shell on either end!

Right—Don't call us, this is the treasure map tip you need. Remember that Vintage Tin is usually as near as your own town, if you just start hunting.

MANGLED TIN

Reclaiming a 1935 Ford Sedan Convertible.

By Tex Smith

I have always had a very soft spot for phaetons and sedan convertibles. I am first and foremost an open car nut. I've owned many closed cars, but open air running is what turns my crank. Especially open cars that have just a tad extra elegance. This means an open car with two seats! After all, the queen never waves from the front seat of a roadster.

Most American automakers created phaetons and sedan converts up until the end of the l930's. Most all of these bodies were hybrids, usually created by cutting and patching up available roadster and sedan body panels…hardly different from what custom fabricators do today. This is more true of the sedan convertibles than of the phaetons.

Whatever, I have lusted after a 1935-36 Ford or Chevy phaeton since the l950's, passing up a Ford beauty that Don Blair had at his speed shop in Pasadena during l959. The asking price of $150 was more than I could scrape together! Thus it was that I ran an ad in Hot Rod magazine in the Sixties looking for such a car. Only one response from nearly l million readers. Robert Martin in Douglas, Wyoming knew where such a car was. Except it had roll-up windows. Not a phaeton, but a sedan convert, and I took it anyway. Well, actually it was just a badly treated bare body and frame, but the top irons were intact. Bit rough, but the price was a trade for two 1934 Ford bumpers that I had.

As many of my projects, this one languished in the yard and through two interstate moves until I

Left—Rick Eccli, long time Cheyenne, Wyoming rodder hauled the sedan convert body to west Yellowstone rod run for Tex, the pieces tucked into a pickup bed.

Right—The first of several thousand miles on a trailer for the sedan convertible, but here there is a roadster body tucked inside. Tex found this body on one of his countless searches for vintage tin.

Below—The SC languished in side yard of Tex's southern California mountain home for several years.

Once rod building work started, the '35 frame as stripped bare to reveal damages.

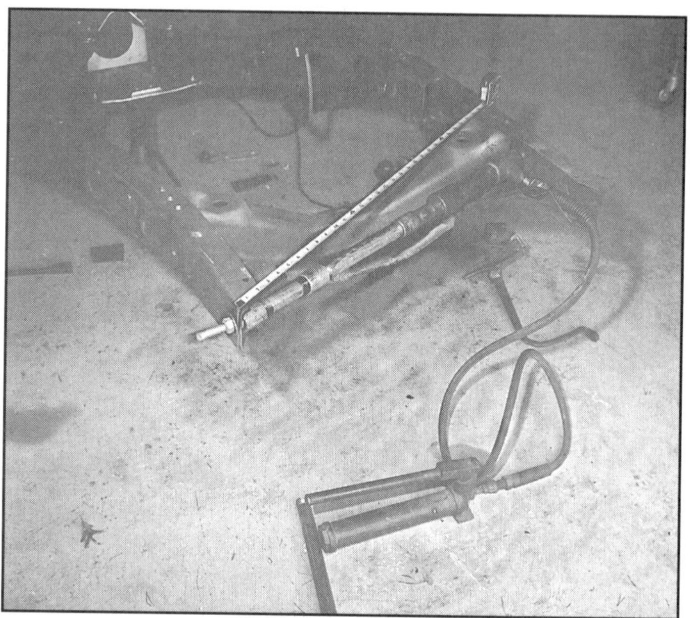

A small Port-a-power hydraulic jack was used to push bent frame members into position.

Crossbraces from frame rail to X-member were straightened with body hammer and dolly; small cracks were welded and ground smooth.

Note a small crack in front crossmember, between the spring U-bolts. Cracks are also common around any rivets in the frame.

started work on it in 1979. Over the span of five years, the car got a typical roadworthy chassis, a Buick V6 engine, and a ton of bodywork. Also typical of such ongoing projects, it went out the door in semi-finished state when another interstate move loomed. Fortunately, the new owner in California finished the car with a ton more work, making it much better than I had anticipated.

In this way, what I was building as a basic hot rod ended upscale, becoming a very nicely finished warrior. So, here is a photo review of how some discarded mangled tin became a show worthy addition to our street rodding world. But I'm ahead of myself.

How to get the frame/body combination from east central Wyoming to southern California? Rick Eccli called to say he was coming to the Yellowstone Rod Run, and he would load the hulk in his pickup, I should bring my car trailer to the run. Since I was going to be in the area anyway, the shuttle worked great, only I had to leave the body at a friend's home in Idaho. The following summer I picked up the treasure just before the Teton Dam broke and did an instant clean-up of my friend's farm. In the nick of time. For several years the project sat in the back yard.

A closer inspection revealed this to be a 1935 Ford, not a '36. Dame fortune smiled at the right

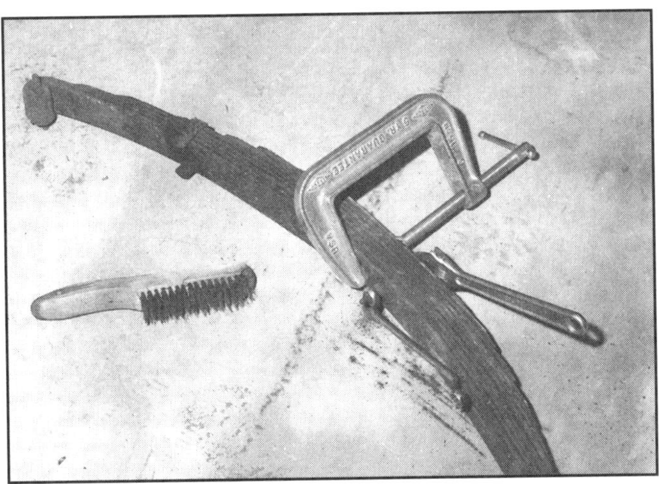

Ford spring was taken apart so that each leaf could be thoroughly cleaned. So the car would sit lower and ride better 4 leaves were removed.

Each leaf was massaged with grinder, and then the square cut ends of each leaf could be tapered so the leaf would not dig into leaf below.

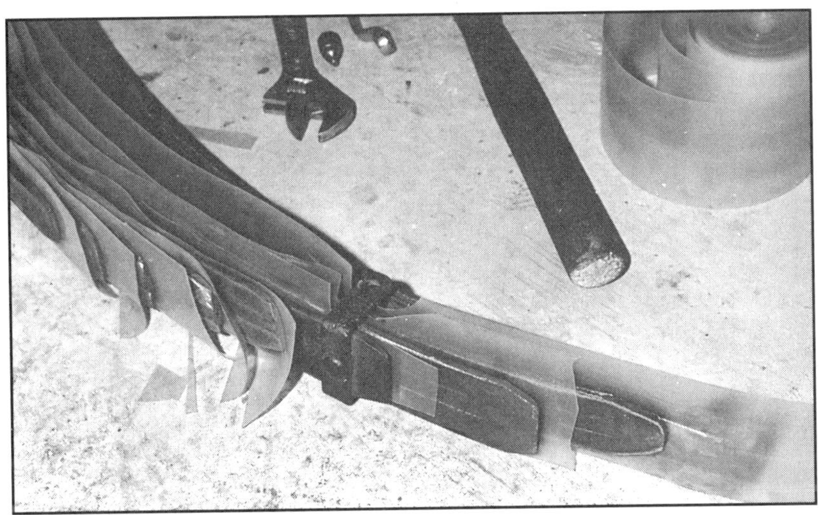

With numbers 3-5-7-9 leaves removed, the spring stack was reassembled with Teflon sheet between each leaf. Result makes a nice limber spring for improved ride.

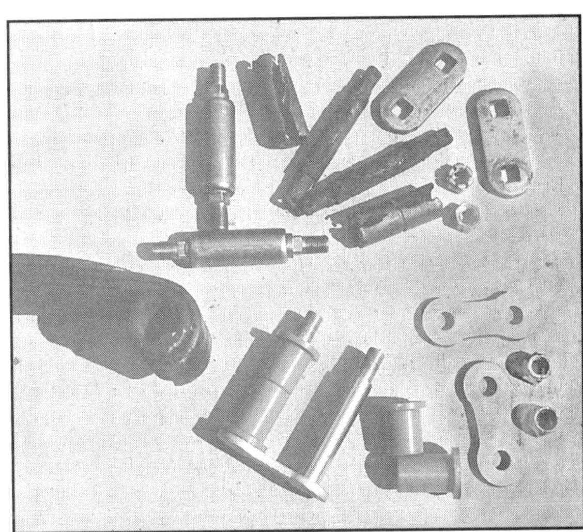

Original Ford style shackle bolts were replaced with new urethane bushings, which also improves spring action.

Stock Ford X-member center saddle is a bulky item, it is removed so that the Chassis Engineering frame kit can be installed.

The rivet holes are opened with a drill so the new center saddle can be bolted in place.

As with most similar kits, the Chassis Engineering cross-member saddle can have the bottom plate unbolted so transmission can be dropped from chassis.

The saddle bottom plate can also serve for the rear mount when Ford wishbone is widened to get more transmission room.

To install the Chassis Engineering parallel spring kit inner lower lip of frame horns aft of rearend centerline must be trimmed slightly.

There really isn't much to mounts for parallel springs on pre-49 Ford frames, but the aftermarket kits are designed to align with existing holes which reduces chances of error in building.

Bracket kits may be bolted in place, or welded.

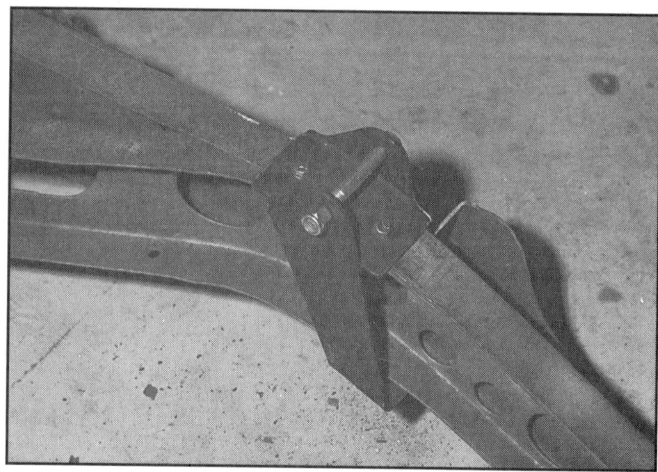

Front end of parallel springs will pivot from single point, if the car is to be lowered an inch or two, this bracket can be recessed into the frame rail.

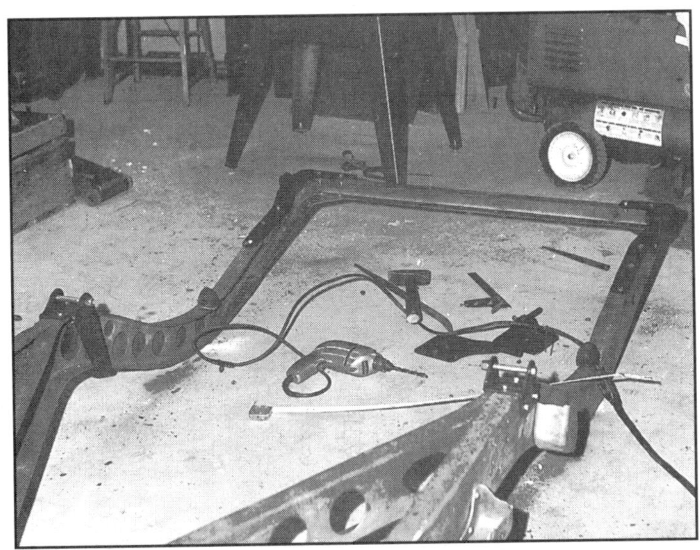

Quick as that, the spring kit was installed.

In this case, a Chevelle rearend was used and everything lines up as intended.

The original Ford style front axle included mechanical brakes and spring mounted ahead of the axle. About all that will be saved in this application are the spring and the wishbone.

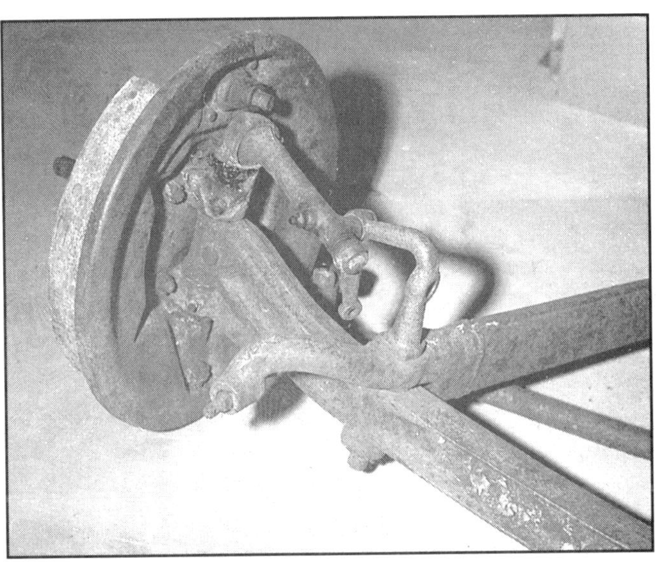

Those Ford mechanical brakes served rodders for years, and they were barely adequate only if kept in absolute adjustment.

time when I located a good set of '35 fenders, hood, and a trio of damaged grilles. Still the car sat until I moved to central Wisconsin. Finally, in the late 1970s I started on the car, chassis first.

Trying to revive an old vehicle frame is a similar process no matter what the nameplate, first the frame must be returned to original dimensions, then modifications can begin. The number one reason to throw away an old frame is rust, number two is crash damage. You can usually fix the latter, not so the former. While you can clean all the grunge from a frame with wire brushes and grinders and chemicals, the best is to either have the frame dipped in chemical stripper or have it sandblasted.

In either of the above cases you only have a short day or two to get the bare metal primed to prevent more rust. Before you put anything on the frame, go over it thoroughly for cracks, which will occur in high stress areas, as where the crossmembers rivet to the side rails. Weld all cracks thoroughly, and replace metal beyond repair.

Straighten those pieces of frame that are damaged. Usually you can use a body hammer and dolly, or even get out the small sledge, but if the frame is double thickness you will need to use a hydraulic jack and, perhaps, some chain. Just know that anyone can straighten most damaged old car frames, sometimes a gas torch is needed for heat. On a double wall frame, visible dings may have to be filled with lead or plastic.

All during work on a frame, constantly meas-

To get the spring hangar bolt out of the wishbone and axle, it is sometimes necessary to resort to the use of a cutting torch.

Severed end of the spring hangar bolt is ground smooth.

Hangar bolt is center punched for a drill bit register, then successively larger holes are drilled until bolts can be collapsed and removed.

The wishbone yoke is cut from each radius rod end, then threaded spuds are inserted into each tube and welded solid. Tie rod ends should screw in about half the length of the shank.

ure the unit to insure is remains parallel and not twisted. Do this by picking like points on each frame rail, front and back, then tape measure on a diagonal. Factories used to have a tolerance of l/8-inch for frame alignment. If the frame is really out of whack, haul it off to your local body shop that has frame repair equipment.

When I had the '35 frame in stock configuration, I started on modifications. I started with a kit from Chassis Engineering that would put the small block Chevy in the '35 frame. Yes I could have made all these brackets, but not worth my time since the kit price is so low, and there are several street rod companies making these kits. I set the frame on stands and made sure it was perfectly level and removed the crossmember centerpiece by cutting the rivets. Then I bolted in the pieces from Chassis Engineering. All this took about an hour to complete.

For the semi-elliptic rear springs the kit includes brackets fore/aft that bolt (or weld) to the frame. While the rearend could be anything, the kit is for a Chevrolet and that is what I used. The springs used were from a late model Dodge pickup front end as they have equal distance from front/rear spring eyes to the spring centerbolt. I

Each tie rod end then mounts through the bottom X-member plate.

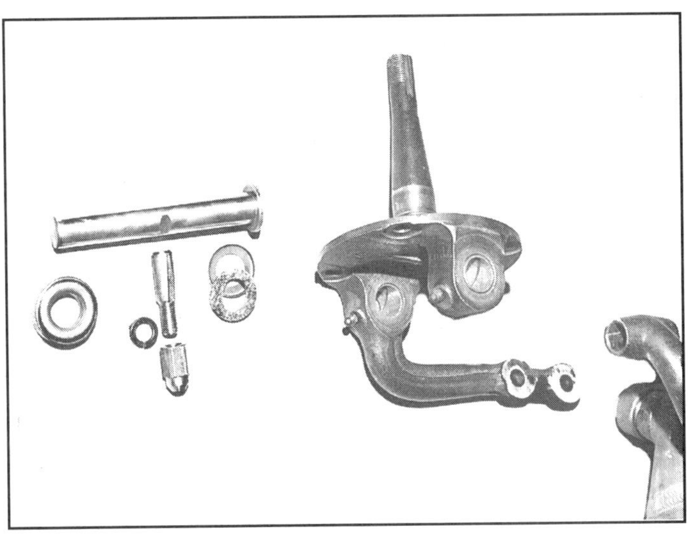

It is vital that the Ford spindles be fit with new bronze bushings with lube holes in bushing aligned with grease zerk hole. New kingpin sets have all the needed renovation pieces.

Here, a dropped round tube Super Bell axle replaces the Ford beam, disc brakes are being adapted to the Ford spindles.

Brake caliper is mounted so caliper bolts in trailing position; there are many different kits available for discs to early Ford axles.

GM Saginaw steering box mounts to the left frame rail via a bracket that can be made at home, but it is cheaper to buy the bracket.

Buick V6 engine mount needed to be moved slightly forward so frame mount would clear the steering box.

Simple flat plate steel was used to create the engine frame mounts. Length of pitman arm can be varied for quickness of steering response.

That's it for modifications to the chassis in order to get an open drive rearend, better front axle and brakes, and a late model engine.

 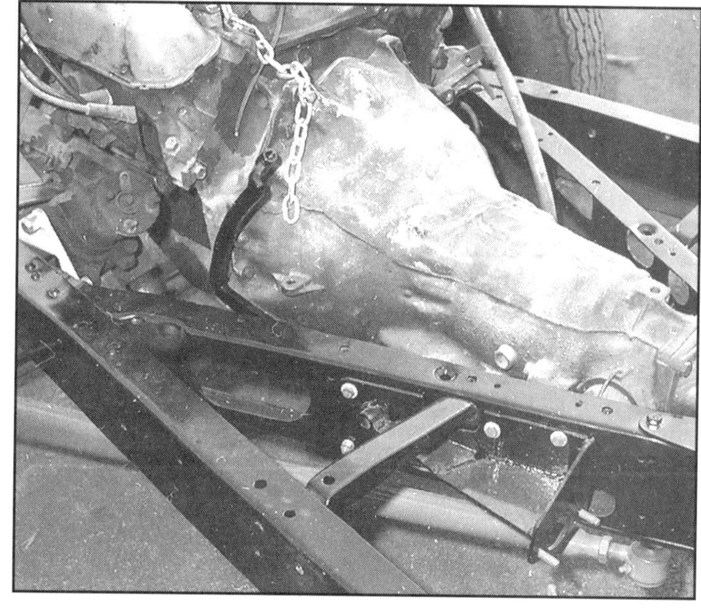

The small X-member oval will require a slight floorboard massage.

Above—With engine and auto transmission in place, attention is turned to making up new brake pedal mount that will bolt in place. This is always a tight area when fitting a bulky automatic transmission to the Ford frame.

Left—The idea is to tuck the rear wheels into the rear fenders without letting the larger diameter tire inner sidewalls rub the body.

took the springs apart and cleaned them up, then reassembled each spring with Teflon between the leaves.

At the front I went with a Super Bell axle of 2 1/2-inch drop, the width determined by telling the company salesman where I wanted the steel wheels to reside in the stock fenders. Simple enough. The Chassis Engineering center crossmember replacement plate had provision for a split wishbone, in this case I used it because the 6-inches separation was all I would need around the transmission pan. Of course, the wishbone ends could have been mounted clear out at the frame rails. With the axle connected to the spring via the shackles and the spring firmly in the front crossmember, I cut the wishbone yoke at the back. Then I heated each rod tube just behind where the axle yoke casting ends (about 5-inches behind the axle, and slowly bent each rod to align with the tie rod end mounting holes in the X-member plate. Each rod was trimmed to allow the rod end stubs to be inserted and tack welded in the rod.

To separate wishbones from the old axles, it usually takes a ton of heat to release the spring

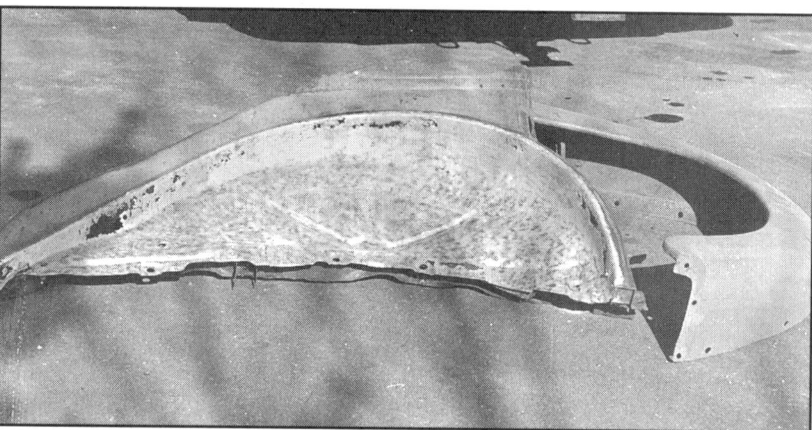

The body was mounted and attention turned to the mangled rear wheelwell area. Some replacement wheelwells were found on an old body, but they had rust in the top curve area. Still, it was a start.

Above—The original gas tank was solid, but needed to be cleaned chemically.

Below—Wheelwell trimmed from a four-door sedan came with some of the rear quarter metal still in place, this had to be carefully matched to the body during trimming.

After trimming, the fenderwells were ready to be matched to the body.

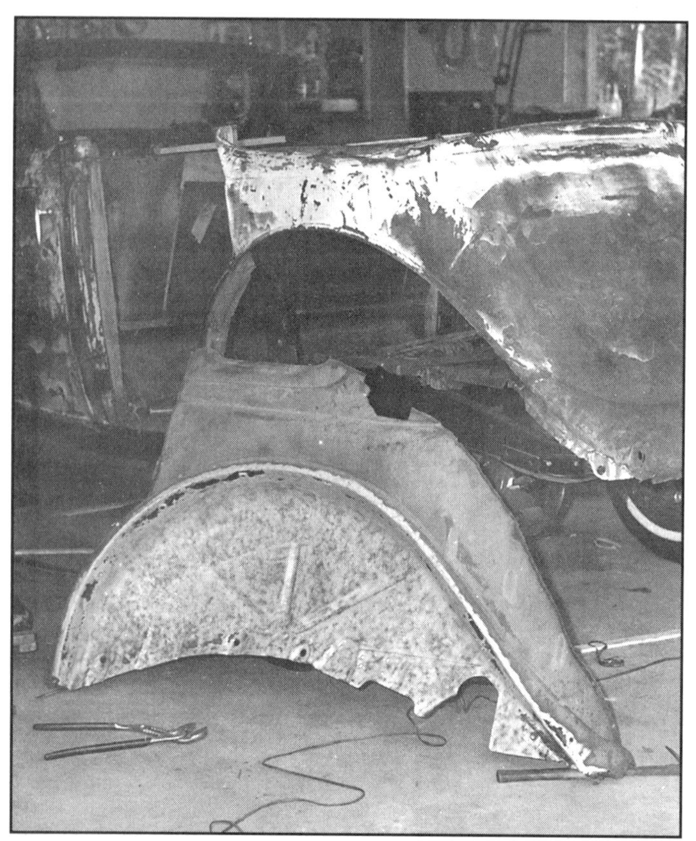

The body fender area was carefully trimmed halfway through the body roll.

Each fenderwell had reinforcing straps attached and held in place at the fender boltholes while the straps were tack-welded in place. Bolts were then removed.

With the replacement fenderwell tacked in place it could be determined where metal would need to be added at lower rear corners.

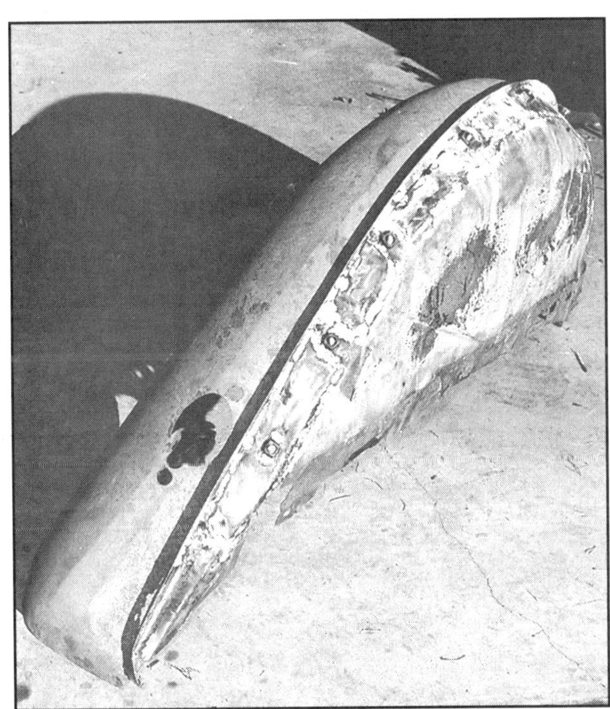

Fenders were bolted to the fenderwells to make sure they would align when the fenderwells were welded to the body.

After being tacked in many places with the fender installed, fender was removed and fenderwells finish welded to the body quarter panels and to the floor.

hangar bolt. And, that usually doesn't work. For expediency, I cut the top of the hangar bolt even with the wishbone, grind it smooth, centerpunch the severed bolt, then start drilling successively larger holes in the bolt. From both top and bottom. The bolt is eventually drilled large enough that it releases the wishbone. In extreme cases, I have had to use the cutting torch to scrag the through

bolts loose. This is not a fun job, and it takes patience. I used a GM steering box.

I chose to go with a good used Buick V6 and Turbo 350 auto rather than the initially considered small block Chevy. The Buick head touched the firewall on one side, so I simply widened the existing stock firewall kickback.

Before going further with the bodywork, I

Left—Now that the body rear section was solid again, attention was turned to the rotten wood that had to be replaced.

Below Left—The years of exposure to western weather had pretty well destroyed all the wood supporting members.

Below—Here, wood has been removed from front end of inner fenderwell; the piece went from bracket on floor at right to the upright.

A good cabinet shop can cut replacement pieces of hardwood if they can have a decent pattern. A body grinder will do the precision shaping.

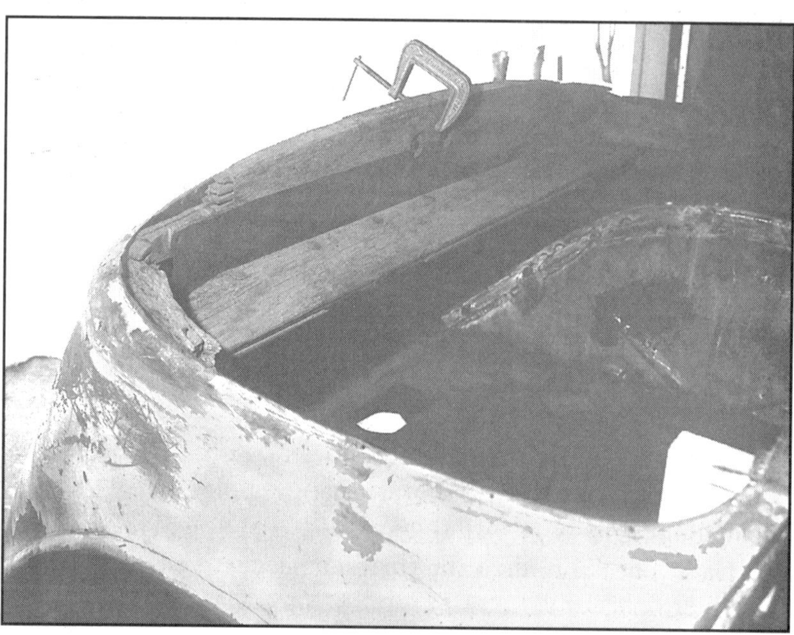

Wood behind the rear seat is where the folding top would rest, rear seat folds forward for a small amount of storage space. All this wood would be replaced later by square tubing.

Sometimes only a portion of original wood remained; in this case the opposite side had enough to show what the piece looked like.

Although some pieces of wood can be done at home with basic wood working tools, it is usually cheaper and faster to have a shop make up the pieces.

The wood will usually come very close to, or actually touch the sheetmetal. Some fitting can be done with a wood rasp.

Dennis Bickford made up all the needed wood replacement for this sedan convertible project.

decided to clean up the front axle spindles and mount an aftermarket disc brake kit, using discs from a 1968 Chevelle. Now I attacked the body.

The body had been hacked up at the rear (it looked like someone had taken the rearend with spring and crossmember, as well as the fenders/fenderwells. Probably for a ranch trailer.) These Ford sedan converts were kind of cobbled together at the factory, using as many stock sedan parts as possible; therefore there is a large amount of lead in the bodies. There is also a bunch of wood. In this instance, I had to replace the rear fenderwells, straighten the body panels, do a lot of metal shrinking, add plenty of lead, and replace every piece of body wood. Hardly anything at all.

For the woodwork I carefully removed each piece of rotten wood, and took the remains to a wooden car restorer. Actually, any good cabinet shop would do the same replication of the bad wood. If the new wood needed to be shaped slightly to fit the body correctly, I did this with the regular body disc grinder. With all the wood and the front stationary seat frame in place I could attach and adjust the doors. Suddenly, the car was

Hardwood is a must for car bodies. Thickness of this piece means it must be cut with a band saw.

Smaller flat pieces may have some curve to them along the flat surface to fit sheetmetal.

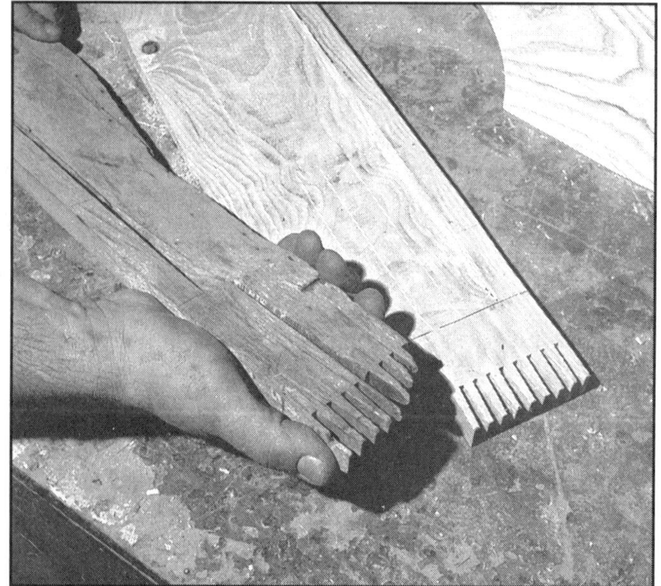

Finger joints were common practice in woodworking earlier on. These pieces can be done with a band saw but it is painstaking, pro shops usually have a special saw for this.

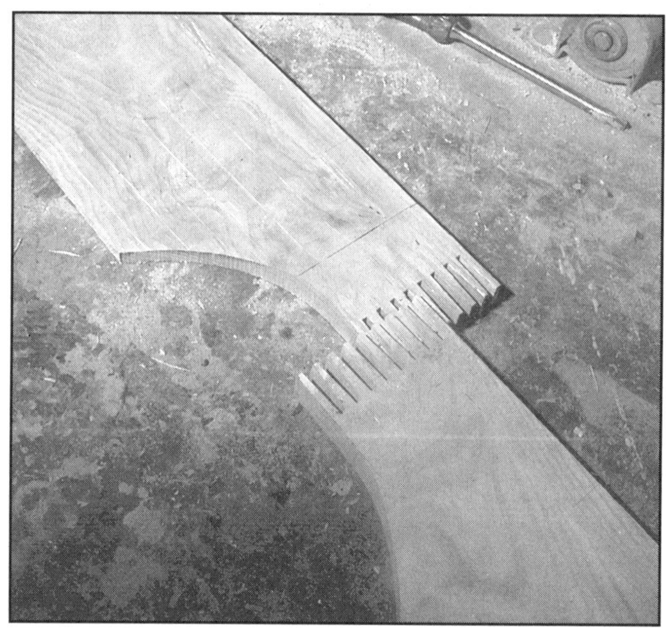

When fingerjoints are glued and joined they are extremely strong.

coming together rapidly.

Which is where it was when I decided to move to Dallas and work for the Great American Race, sponsored by Interstate Battery. It was there that I met Gene Reese who was making up the first of the Mustang/Pinto independent front suspension kits. I made a beeline for my new Texas digs and removed all the great dropped tube axle stuff, and installed one of Gene's kits.

It is not necessary to use such a kit, because you can trim the Mustang assembly and weld it directly to a frame. This is how Kent Fuller did it on Tom Medley's bitchin' l940 Ford coupe. He did it in less than a day, the car rides and handles superbly, and not a single kit piece was purchased. Which is the difference, sometimes, between a basic hot rod and an aftermarket nightmare.

And this is where the story takes yet another turn.

By now I had been in Dallas four years and I just couldn't stand it anymore. My old stomping grounds of Idaho/Montana/Wyoming were calling. So, I retired. Well, that was the first time, anyway. But by now I had been clanging on the '35 so long

Right—With all the inner wood structure in place, the body panels can be straightened.

Below—A really handy tool around any shop is a shape duplicator. Here the fenderwell roll is checked toward the front where it was not butchered; this shape will be reproduced for the full roll.

Right—The body fenderwell opening had been cut severely, so that spacer sheetmetal had to be cut to fill the gaps.

Below—The tools of body leading include a special air mixing tip for the torch, a hardwood leading paddle, some beeswax, lead tinning compound, and lead bars.

Below Right—After metal is tinned, stick lead is carefully melted to the surface. Doing overhead leading is where most amateurs get in trouble, the real secret is in getting the metal surface just warm enough then melting the bar lead slowly.

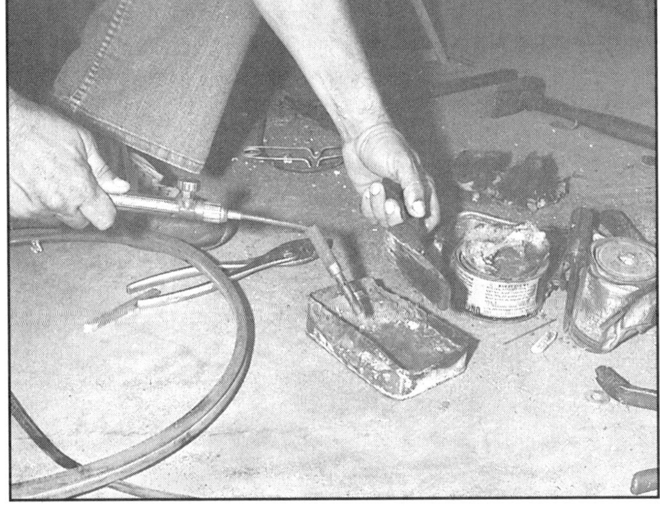

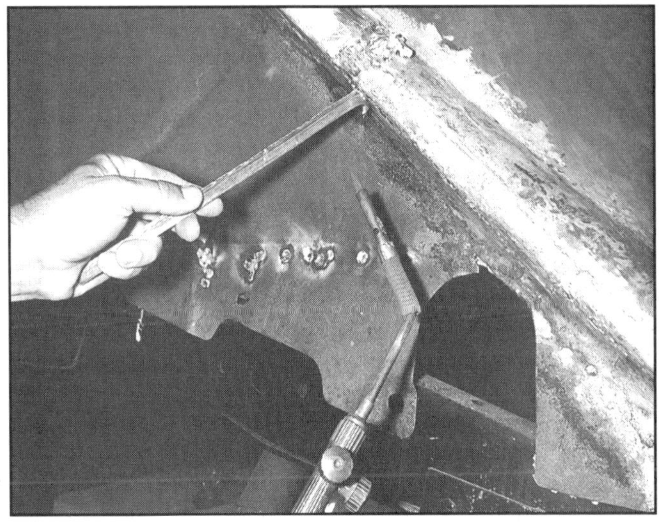

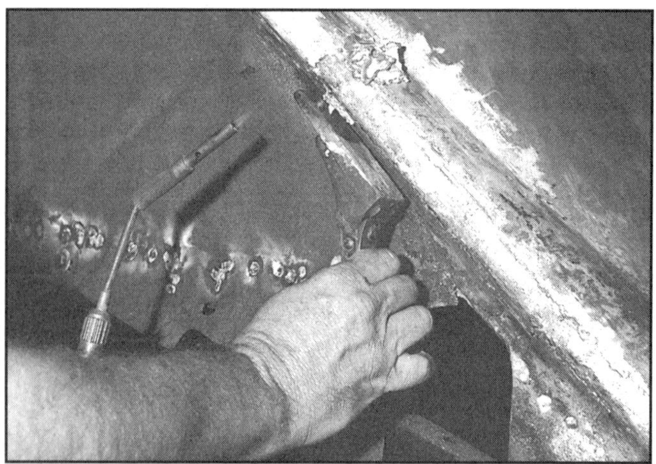

Once lead bar has been applied to the metal, the lead can be heated repeatedly so it can be moved into rough shape with the lead paddle.

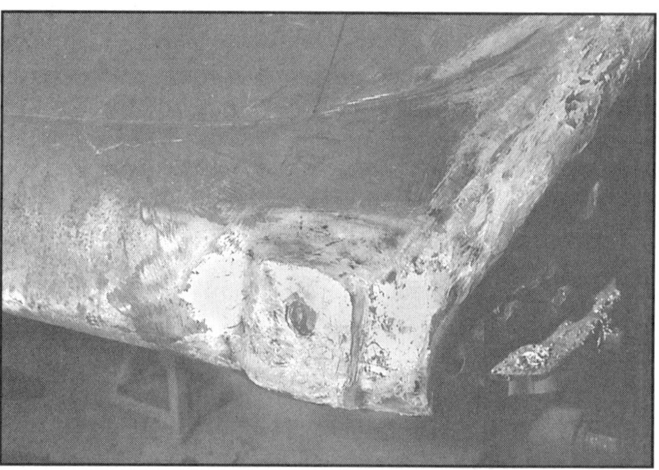

The old way of building up bad body areas included using a lot of lead, that is how the body bumper bracket area was repaired here.

With both rear fenders and fenderwells now attached, the rear sheetmetal panel could be worked into shape. It had been badly mis-shaped through the years of neglect. Start with a couple of vertical lines at either side of back.

At points down the vertical line, make horizontal lines. Here the big problem was in the rounded corners as they flowed into the quarter panels.

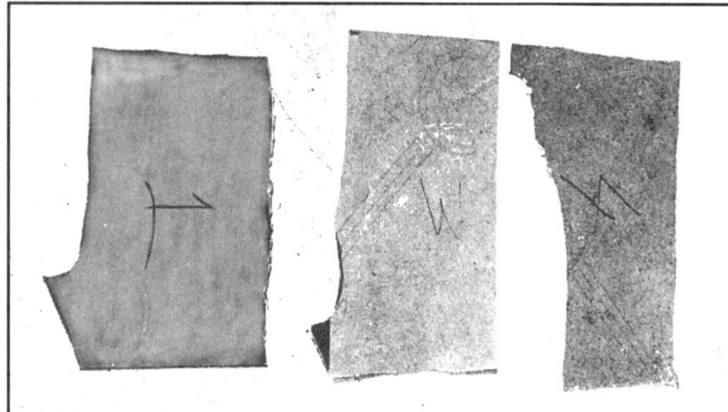

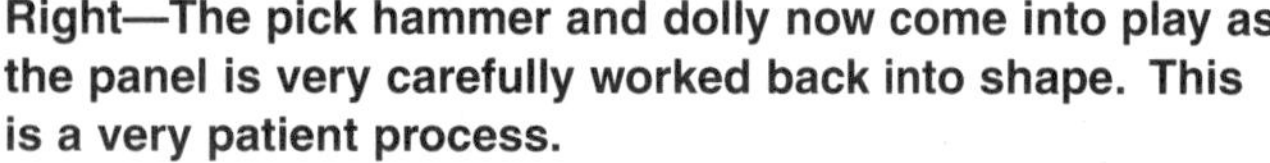

Cardboard patterns were cut to fit one side on each horizontal line; this shape was then created on the other side.

Right—The pick hammer and dolly now come into play as the panel is very carefully worked back into shape. This is a very patient process.

The hand is far better than the eye at locating high and low spots in the metal. If you can feel it, you will see it after paint is applied.

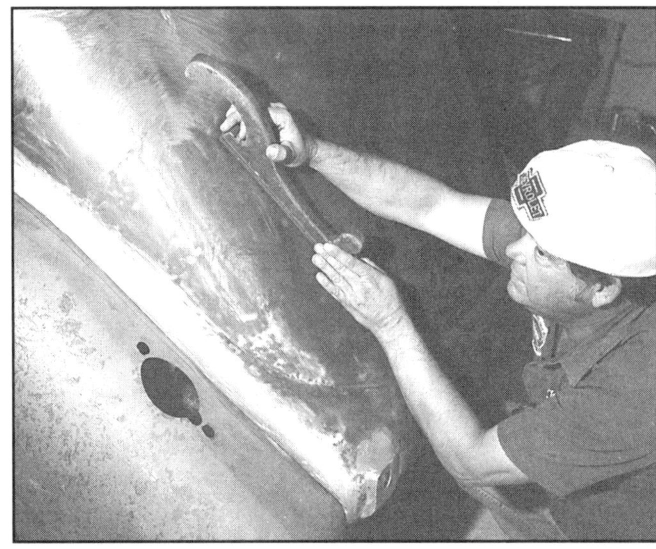

The bodyman's vixen file is best way to spot high and low areas as the panel is being shaped.

The body grinder is not a substitute for the hand file, and it must be used sparingly with minimal force and heat build-up.

Areas of smaller sheetmetal panels are often the best place to learn bodywork; the sedan convertible had a number of small holes to weld shut.

Car body styles such as the Ford mid-thirties convertibles were often made from a mix of production body parts, where body panels mated there was usually a large amount of lead used. If new lead is being added the area must be thoroughly cleaned and tinned first.

I was looking for a new adventure. I put the sedan convertible up for sale, and along came old acquaintance John Rutledge of Wofford Heights, California. Which is right up that winding, twisting river road from Bakersfield, the town where I really got started in hot rodding back before War Two. How we go in circles.

Whatever, John liked the sedan convert idea, so he trailered what I had done back to his Kernville area home, then started all kinds of rebuild to suit his own needs. The result is a very nice, subtle and understated street rod. It is basically the basic hot rod I was building, but with keen changes to make it a trophy winner. Proving something or other. I think.

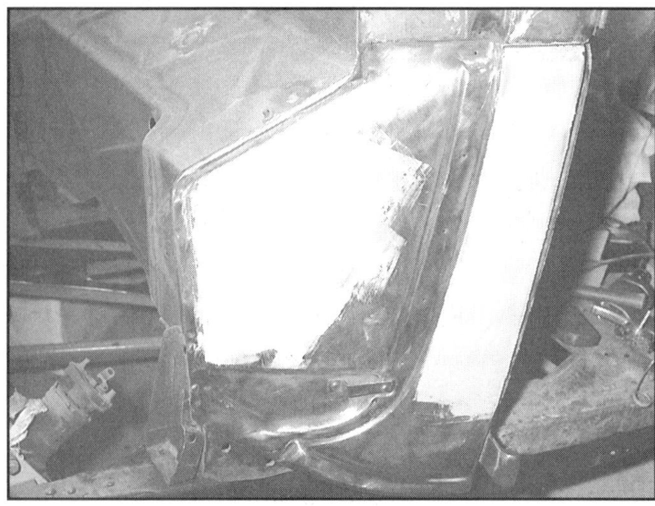

Plastic filler is only used as a very thin coating to get the metal panels absolutely straight.

In this case, the curved sides of the firewall cutout were moved to each side.

Phaetons and sedan convertibles use a rigid front seat framework made up of metal and wood.

A neat way to modify firewall for additional V8 or V6 engine heads is to cut the wall well outside the head lines.

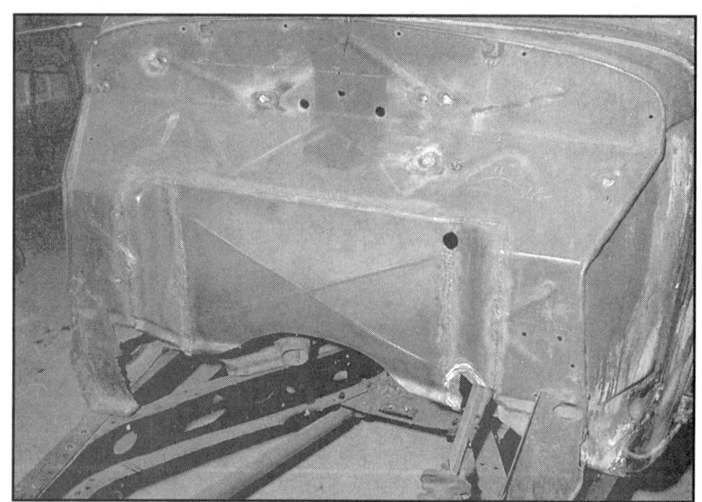

New center panel has beads rolled in to give strength and stop oilcanning.

The rigid seat frame bolts to the body floor and to each door post.

Above Left—Wood should be replaced where needed.

Above—When seat framework is installed to floor and door posts, the body gains considerable strength.

Left—Finally, it was time to spray fenders and doors with primer.

Three different '35 Ford grilles were cut apart in order to build one good unit.

This photo shows the bare top bows on a restored sedan convertible.

Transmission cooler was located under the passenger seat, low enough in the frame to get a good flow of air.

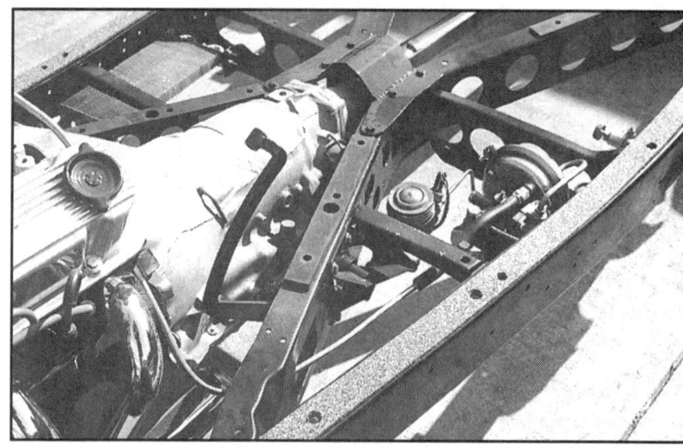

Power brakes include a remote boost.

A rebuild of the frame included adding a Mustang IFS with power rack and pinion steering.

Frame to body padding was available from aftermarket suppliers.

And this is how everything appeared just before the car was sold.

Left—New owner continued the work, but at a much higher level of quality.

Below—The engine was fitted with an aftermarket radiator as well as air conditioning.

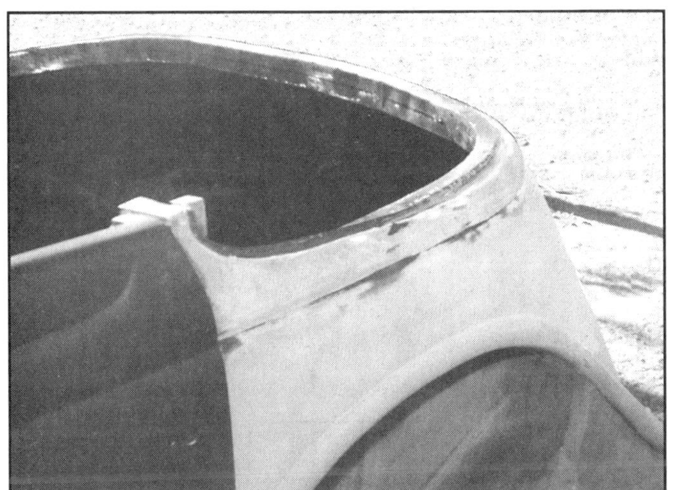

Above—Wood around rear lip of passenger compartment was replaced with much stronger metal square tubing.

John Rutledge hauled the sedan convertible to his southern California home and then proceeded to turn it into a very tasteful blend of modern monochrome and early day rodding.

Left—During the photo shoot along shore of Lake Isabella, John played host to a roadrunner. Is Wiley Coyote nearby?

Below—Grille is painted same off white as body; hood is a three-piece unit.

Above—A dash panel insert in keeping with the update tops an Olds tilt column steering shaft.

The Buick V6 fits the early Ford confines very nicely.

Left—Top is now a lift-off; interior is combination of tweed and ultra leather.

Right—The interior turned out extremely well, with contemporary rod styling in the dash and gauges.

Left—The slope back panel and snap-on Moon wheel covers tabs this as a hot rod rather than a custom.

Right—Now, compare this really nice finished '35 Ford sedan convertible to that mangled hulk hauled from a Wyoming field so many years before. This is proof that a basic hot rod can evolve into a great modern street rod.

BINK'S BASIC BUCKET

B ink is the name, basic rodding is the game. I met Bink Flodberg of the northern California community of Clearlake, at Bonneville in the very early Nineties. He is old like me, a sure enough basic hot rodder who has been doing it for generations. His then current (and still owned) ride was exactly the kind of car this book is about.

Above—So, in Basic Hot Rodding 101, you dance with the one what brung ya. In the case of Bink Flodberg, this bucket is made from just about everything automotive. The frame is from a Model T truck turned around so there is a full taper toward the (now) front. The salt buildup on big and little tires is from afternoon mosey on the Bonneville salt flats. Windshield and posts are 1927 Model T variety, grille shell is also from Henry's finest.

Left—Total construction time for Bink's bucket was just over 6 months, with a cost of $4600. The rearend is from a 1970 Hornet with quarter elliptic springs that were made by combining Gremlin/Hornet springs then cutting them in half. Front half of the body is 1927 Model T open car cowl, the rear of the tub is cut down sedan body of unknown origin.

Left—No fancy footwork here, the interior is spartan but functional. The steering column is a Gremlin, with a shifting arm connected through to a Chevy 3-speed transmission. The seat is a bench type found somewhere that just happens to fit, dash gauges are mixture of aftermarket in a flat panel.

Below—The steering gearbox is l946-7 Ford pickup, mounted flush with firewall to gain engine room. Engine is a stock 307 Chevy with fad-T type headers, since the cars weighs in at well below a ton, performance is crisp.

Above—Upper mounts for rear quarter elliptic springs are extended pieces of diamond plate which double as step pads for entry...the doors are welded shut.

Right—Below the shortened T grille shell is a suicide type mount for a shortened T cross spring that is in turn bolted to an ex-drag car Willys front axle. Front brake combination is an old Curt Hamilton Automotive kit that uses VW calipers on Volvo hubs/rotors. Like the axle, spindles are Willys. Lever shocks are used.

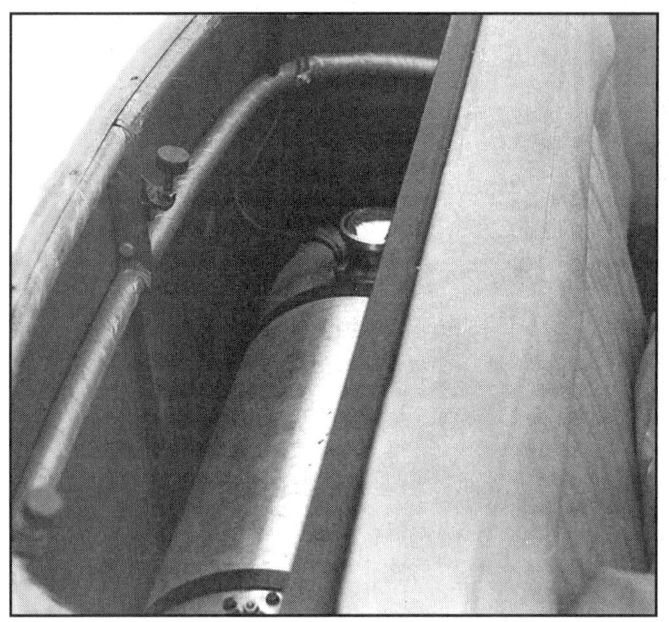

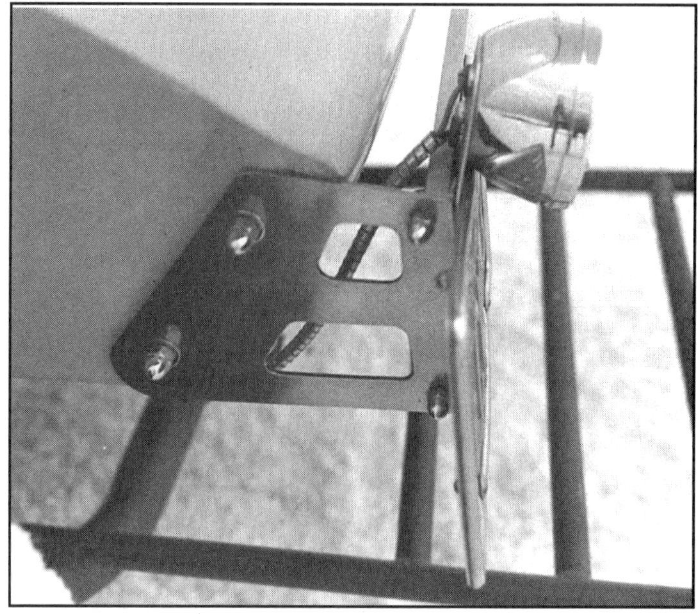

Above Left—Round steel tubing was used to support top of trimmed body, a second piece of tubing is just below for added strength. Round gas tank is of unknown variety, it just works.

Above—When a bracket for the taillights was needed, Flodberg whittled one from plate stock.

Left—Since there isn't room in the car for overnight possibles, a round tubing trunk rack is mounted low and aft of the trailer hitch ball. Dual taillights are all the rage now days.

Right—Moon discs on the rear and slot mags on the front were all the rage in the Sixties, in this case they were what was available in the spare parts pile. Headers lead to muffler tubes that exit just ahead of each rear wheel.

X-MEMBER SUPPORTS AND WIDENED CENTERS FOR 35-48 FORDS. ALLOWS USE OF OVERDRIVE AUTOMATIC TRANSMISSIONS. WELD-IN ONLY.

STILL THE BEST REAR SUSPENSIONS AVAILABLE FOR 35-48 FORDS. WELD-IN OR BOLT-IN KITS AVAILABLE WITH STANDARD OR REVERSED EYE SPRINGS. UNIVERSAL KITS ALSO AVAILABLE

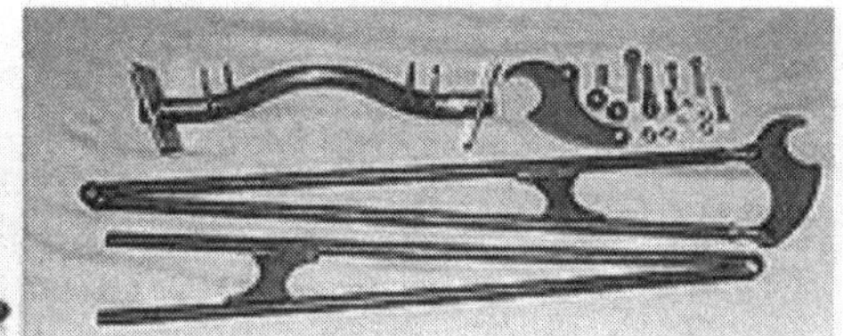

LADDER BAR AND FOUR LINK REAR SUSPENSION KITS AVAILABLE FOR MOST VEHICLES. COIL-OVER OR TRANSVERSE LEAF SPRING MOUNTS ALSO.

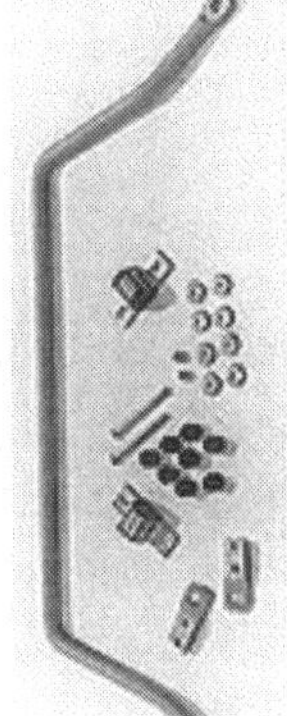

SWAYBARS FOR FRONT AND REAR ENDS. BARS ARE AVAILABLE FOR MUSTANG II OR AXLE FRONTS AND PARALLEL LEAF OR STOCK FORD REARS.

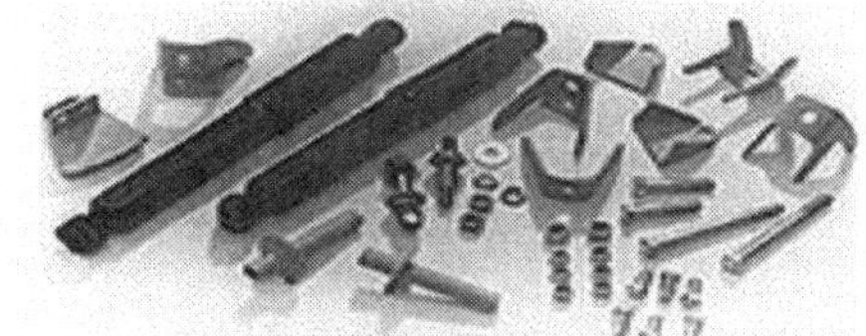

WELD-IN OR BOLT-IN REAR SHOCK KITS FOR 32 TO 48 FORDS AND SOME EARLY CHEVROLET

ENGINE MOUNTS FOR VARIOUS ENGINE/CHASSIS COMBOS

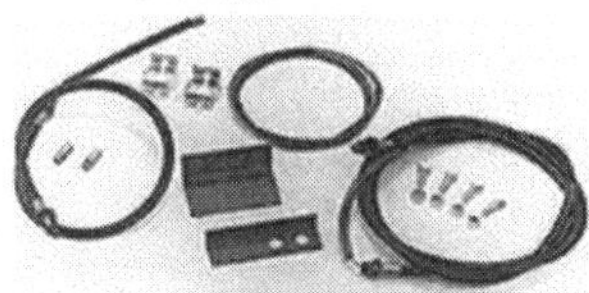

EMERGENCY BRAKE CABLE KITS

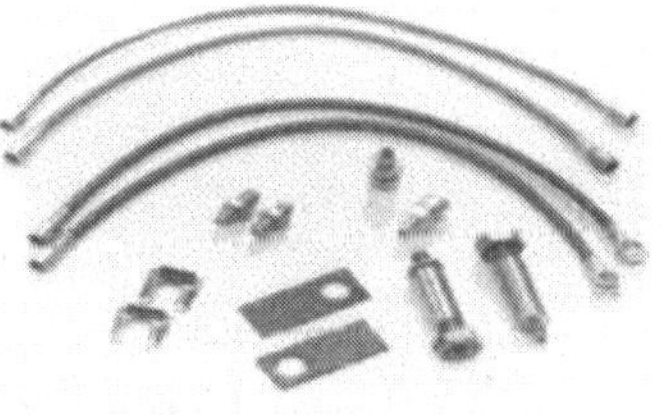

BRAKE AND BRAKE/CLUTCH PEDAL ASSEMBLIES FOR 28 TO 48 FORDS. BOOSTERS AND MASTER CYLINDERS ALSO

STEEL GAS TANKS

BODY AND FRAME PACKAGES ARE AVAILABLE FOR 27 FORD ROADSTER AND TOURING IN FENDERED AND HIBOY STYLE. MODEL "A" FORD COUPE AND ROADSTER IN FENDERED AND HIBOY STYLE. 32 FORD COUPE AND ROASTER IN FENDERED AND HIBOY STYLE. 34 COUPE AND ROADSTER IN FENDERED AND HIBOY STYLE. 39/40 FORD CONVERTIBLE. CALL FOR MORE INFO.

REPRODUCTION FRAMES AND CHASSIS FOR 26 THROUGH 48 FORDS. MANY OPTIONS AND STYLES. SPECIAL "HIBOY" FRAME FOR 26 TO 31 FORDS . USES EXCLUSIVE WEEDETR DESIGNED FRAME RAIL.

BRAKE PLUMBING AND FLEX LINE KITS. RESIDUAL AND PROPORTIONING VALVES.

MUSTANG II FRONT SUSPENSION KITS
CUSTOM IFS
DISC BRAKE KITS
DROPPED AXLES
SPINDLES
STEERING KITS
TRAILER HITCHES
ACCESSORIES

CATALOG $3.00

12649 Paskenta Rd.
Red Bluff, Ca. 96080-9732

Phone: 530-527-2040
FAX: 530-527-3406

weedetr@snowcrest.net
www.weedetrstreetrod.com

BUDGETING COSTS

No matter how many hot rods a person may have built/owned, interest is always for the next one in line. This is why it is vital to keep costs down and to always assume that the current project will be sent packing at sometime in the future.

When deciding to build a basic hot rod, you can look at the bank balance as a guide for all your decisions. Simple as how much you want to spend.

By nature of the hobby, an open roadster is going to cost less to build than a closed car. A T bucket should come in for less cash outlay, and probably skinned knuckles than a '37 four-door. A four-door will cost a bit more than a two-door. And so on, ad nauseam. And the better condition the vehicle is in that you start with, the less the build will cost to complete.

And, the amount of your own time and labor expended will bear directly on the final tab for your ride in the sun. This doesn't mean you can't spend money on a pro for help. But you can shop around for a good price from the pro, while maintaining a modicum of quality. This will play especially important when going for paint or upholstery. Yet, in the long term the more you do yourself, the more fun you will have with the finished project.

HOW TO CHOP TOPS

This is the first and most exhaustive book available on the subject of Chop Tops. It contains over 200 pages, with step-by-step guidelines on hammering the lid on rods and customs, as well as pickups. Also demonstrates glass and window frame cutting technicques. This book covers all categories of tops with instructions applicable to customizing cars from the twenties and thirties, all the way up through today's automobiles.

**Hot Rod Library, Inc
12 North Main St. C-3
Veyo, UT 84782
Toll Free: (800) 513-8133**

Walter P. Chrysler basic hot rod is a most imposing view from the front, some would say akin to a docking aircraft carrier. It hauls 7 people in total comfort and never fails to garner attention from the ladies.

By Oslo Wilhunkie

WALTER P. CHRYSLER

If you've read much Tex Smith stuff through the years, chances are you've run across the reference to a 1948 Chrysler kinda-limo that he built back in the very early 1970s. It all began when Tex got a bit worked up when the new NSRA decided that it should be cast in stone that a street rod had to be a 1948 or earlier vehicle. So he set about making a statement.

He knew where there was a 1948 Chrysler airport limo (no roll up window between front and rear, just fold down jump seats), a very long car. Flathead 6-cylinder power. Cushy ride. This particular car had been used in the VIP fleet for Yellowstone National Park, but it was currently doing duty as a rancher's hay hauler (back seat removed). It was in surprisingly good condition. For $200 Tex got to drive it back to Southern California.

The car got an engine rebuild, and in the process it got an Edmunds finned aluminum head. There, Tex said, It was pre-49 and it had speed equipment, the exact example of what a hot rod had to be. It also got a plush upholstery job and maroon paint to drool over. Off to the

Nationals, and through the years everywhere in between. Then Tex's family grew up, and he moved back to Idaho. Walter P was baggage, so off it went to live with Skip Readio in Massachusetts. Skip has updated the car with dual exhaust and twin carbs, but it remains basically as built nearly forty years before. A basic hot rod, if you follow the traditional definition.

Proof that this pre-49 Mopar is truly a hot rod comes in the form of an aluminum-finned head on the six-cylinder block. Plus, a remote mounted racing oil filter.

Left—Although Walt P has a wheelbase about l0 feet long, it is an elegant looking ride, more so for something called a hot rod. With a 3 speed manual trans with overdrive, the six-cylinder gives surprisingly good mileage.

Below—Pretty nice looking hot rod spoof, wide whites and maroon paint set this lengthy hot rod apart from the norm, but it is still just a basic hot rod.

Above—Although this car had seen thousands of miles hauling VIP folk in Yellowstone, the interior was in excellent condition. Tex had it upholstered in Cadillac cloth, which has lasted very good for almost 40 years during a life of rod running.

Right—Then there is all that back seat room, as demonstrated by Tex Smith on banjo and boots on jump seats.

Now this is a reality learning experience, getting down and getting dirty. Mike picked up a number of skills during construction of the roadster, including a big dose of patience and persistence.

HIGH SCHOOL TRANSPORT

Mike Smith is our kinda guy. No late model rice burning, lowered, five-jigawatt stereo powered mini hunk for him. His choice of machinery for drive-in dazzlement is a roadster straight out of the past. Even his past, because he built this streeter several years ago and as with some of the cars we feature in this book, it was a prominent part of our old Hot Rod Mechanix magazine. Mike's time warp T never fails to draw a crowd of admiring gray beards, most of whom can't believe someone born 20 years after the last flathead was produced did all the work.

While the major part of construction was handled by Mike, LeRoy Smith (no, not the editor of this book) helped his son start off on the right direction by teaching him some automo-

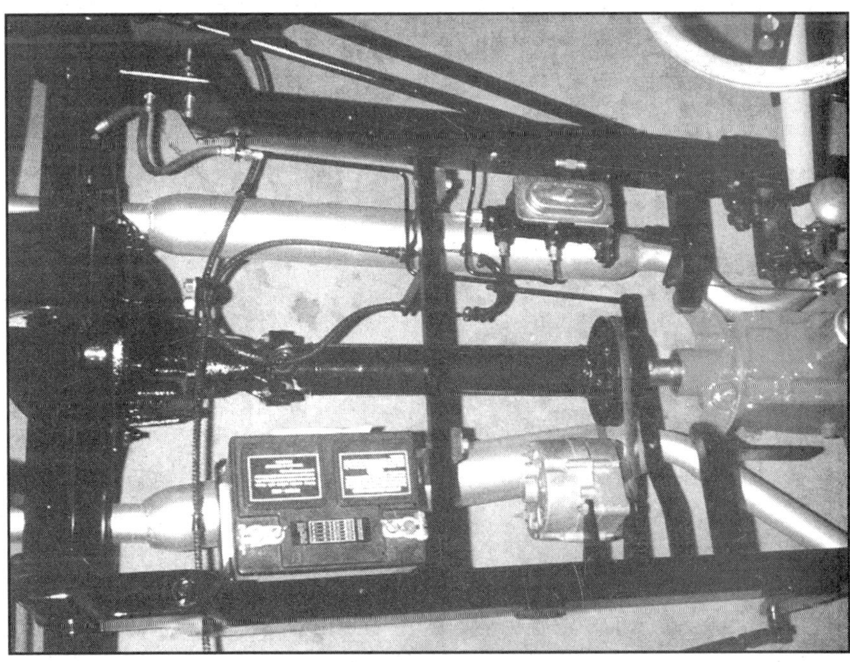

Converted to open drive with original Ford commercial vehicle pieces, the early l939 Ford transmission sends power to a 3:l ratio geared Mustang rearend. The alternator is mounted to the frame and driven off the front driveshaft yoke.

tive fundamentals, and how to weld. Then dad stood back and answered questions. Lots and lots of questions. (Which is exactly how my dad taught me. LeRoi Tex Smith, editor of this book.)

The first homework assignment was to design and build a chassis. The frame was fabricated of 2x3-inch rectangular tube, then fit with a '34 Ford front axle and spring. Spindles and brakes came from a '40 Ford while the shocks are homemade friction units. All this is held in place with a split '32 Ford wishbone and steered by a l970 Ford van gearbox.

When it came time to pick the powerplant, there was only one option for this history project: A Ford flathead V8. It is a '52 block overbored, balanced and holding a Winfield SU-lA cam. (That's a grind I often used, something Winfield said would give me better street performance than a full race profile. LeRoi Tex Smith)

A local swap meet provided an original '25 T body, and after dragging it home Mike decided to get bids to have a pro straighten the metal and apply paint. Finding that the best deal available still exceeded his lunch-money budget, Mike tackled the job himself. With dad's capable guidance, of course.

Construction time for the project was just two years; not bad considering Mike started when he was l4 years old. And, he had done his homework on how such cars were built in the past. By the time Mike was ready to get his driving license at age l6, the T was finished. That first ride was kind of like the ultimate history final.

The car worked just fine on the road test, and as far as we're concerned both car and builder get an "A" in hot rod history.

Left—Mike gave up on stitching the brown and tan interior, but we think he could have done it given an upholstery sewing machine. Steering wheel is an older wood rimmed aftermarket item common in swap meets, the flat dash includes early Chevy pickup instruments. The AM/FM radio doesn't include woofers and tweeters and mega bass, etc.

Right—High school kids once knew the Ford flat motor intimately; at least they did if they wanted to have a set of Ford wheels. By Mike's day this was ancient history so the fact that he created one with .040 bore, used a Winfield cam and Offy heads/triple carb manifold is all the more remarkable. Those are model 94 carburetors to the unknowing.

Left—Kelsey Hayes wire wheels really support the old-timey theme, rears have been widened 2 inches to accentuate the basic hot rod look, wheels, engine block, gas tank are all red while the T body Is bright yellow. Now tell us this didn't wow all the girls in PE class!

LOW BUCK DANDY

By Harrison Miles

Around the central California coast, Gale Brady is well known as the original Rodney Lowbucks. Doesn't bother him in the least, since he believes in low cost, high ingenuity hot rodding. A creation he put together several years back really exemplifies the concept of MFPD (More Fun Per Dollar).

This little rod began when Gale discovered the sad remains of a 1937 Fiat Topolino hiding in a neighbor's backyard. The owner had no idea what it was, and was very pleased to get rid of it for $100. Then, Gale had a friend come up with a high-performance Pontiac overhead cam straight six engine for $300. A good used TH350 GM automatic transmission set Gale back another $100. Brady had a Volvo rearend left from a previous project, and a Pinto disc brake front end appeared, along with the flex shaft Pinto steering gear. A wrecked Honda supplied the master cylinder and power booster along with the brake and gas pedals.

The '34 Ford truck grille sets the pace for purist hot rodders while the high tech nerf bar harks back to much simpler days in hot rodding.

Ever the jet-setting continental croozer, Gale Brady shows that suicide doors were common in Italy well before the current crop of aftermarket hinges. Oxide primer sets the tone, of course.

Pinto independent front suspension doesn't seem out of place on this unusual coupe; the disc brakes compliment similar discs on the coil sprung Volvo rearend.

Right—Pontiac OHC six fits the narrow Fiat style perfectly but put plenty of beef on the road in stock high performance version.

Below—Moon spun aluminum wheel discs seem appropriate for a body style usually associated with early day drag racing.

Instruments and flat panel insert seem kind of truckish, but they don't know what vehicle they are in.

Somehow this begins to sound an awful lot like Tex Smith's famous Junkyard Dawg roadster.

The grille shell came from a '34 Ford truck, Gale made the three piece hood. Taillight origin is unknown, but cost $10 at the Turlock swap meet. Moon discs hide steel wheels, but the glasspack mufflers can't hide the distinctive sound made by a six-banger.

Total cost to build, including license and registration, was just over $1600, which figures at about 85 cents a pound. Good arithmetic when you follow the Gale Brady school of hot rod knocks, "Use what ya' got or can get cheap, and do all your work!"

What we would call sound hot rod economics.

Right—Taillights off something or other are mounted high for traffic congestion, note the factory filled top.

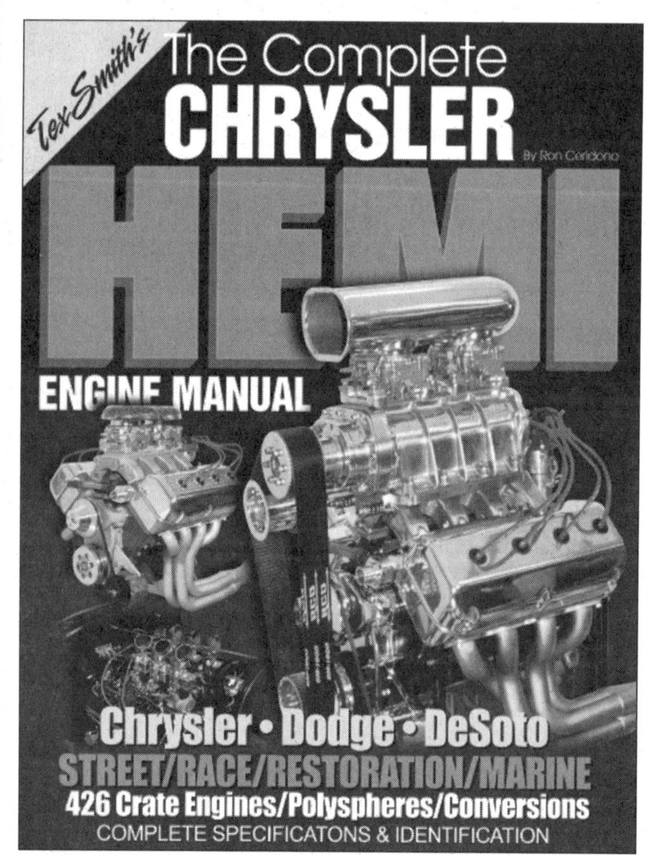

Left—When you drive a basic hot rod like this the same question keeps popping up. Sign in the window tells all the belly-button spectators all they need to know.

BASIC SIXTIES

Left—Wisconsin winters can be brutal, but springtime is great for driveway rod building. Tex bought a dual exhaust set from the local auto parts store and installed it in an afternoon. Good sound is a major first step in basic hot rodding project.

Below Left—By staying with baby moon hubcaps and painted wheels, no unnecessary cost was lavished on the Chevy. The car was a family friend for a full decade.

Above—After some rust repair in the lower panels, light grey primer was laid on in the outdoors, later some white paint finished the job.

Wen you really think about it, just about any brand of automobile, and any year can be a basic hot rod. Take the mid-Sixties Chevys for instance. Dime a dozen, get a good one for lunch money. Actually, same applies to Ford and Mopar. The secret is to not go for the muscle mania. Like this 1966 Chevy Tex Smith bought for $300 back in 1980. Twice door, small-block V8, some body rust. Great runner.

So, home came the car, out went the rusted panels, on went some chrome wheels (bigger rubber in back of course), and then a set of twice-pipes. The factory white paint was good, as was the interior. In about a month of piddling after work, the two-door post was ready for the two high school daughters.

Big factor in keeping late model rod costs down is getting something with good glass all around, engine and trans in good condition.

This coupe in convertible clothing turned out to be one slick custom rod ride, and the change was mostly the result of three bodymen who had patience and persistence. There are lots of stalled projects in hot rod land that need only some attention to hit the streets.

CONVERTEDABLE

Things sure have changed. Consider the convertible for instance. Not so very many years ago, at least to us of the grey and missing hair, convertibles were customs, for picking up girls, and studly guys drove hot rods. Roadsters mostly. In the Sixties, things started to change some more, with customs fading away and girls driving small convertibles, mostly Mustangs and Corvairs. Guys were switching to factory muscle power, but the truly studly dudes were still driving fenderless hot rods.

Fast forward to the twenty-first century and posiers are driving road rockets and studly dudes are driving hot rods and half-a-century-old convertibles. The more things change, the more they change.

And there is no doubt that fat fendered convertibles are no longer considered customs-only. And convertible bodies are in huge demand with the basic hot rod crowd. Cars that once would have been deemed too far gone are now bringing top dollar, and now the race is on to make coupes and sedans into topless runners. That's what happened with this 1941 Buick.

Long years ago I was on a typical summer sabbatical to Montana from Hot Rod Magazine in Los Angeles. Stopping en route to visit with Joe Mayall (now editor of NSRA's StreetScene magazine) in Idaho Falls, Idaho, I noticed a really neat 1941 Buick coupe, somewhat similar to a 1939 coupe that friend Lee Wooley of Pocatello, Idaho had run at the drags and Bonneville in the early Fifties.

Joe Mayall shot a photo feature of the Buick for Rod & Custom magazine, where the Metalflake green paint and Nailhead V8 Buick power set it apart in the emerging street rod world. But then, fame is so fleeting. By the mid-Seventies the coupe had gone from the magazine pages to the back row of a used car lot. That's when Steve

Above—The Idaho Buick was towed to Ohio on a dolly, complete with Model A cabriolet body on top. Convertible top portion of body was grafted on just behind the rear doorpost about 8-inches down from top opening. Convert door tops had the coupe doorskins crimped in place and welded beneath where the beltline chrome strip fit. Rear fenders were molded to the body.

Left—A Sixties era Buick front frame clip was installed to get more modern front suspension and power brakes along with power steering. A 350 Buick engine dropped in place, along with wiring harness from a late GM product. In the rear the original coil springs were discarded in favor of parallel leaf springs and a GM full size l2-bolt rearend.

Below—Freddie made up rolled pans front and rear to replace the rather bulky Buick bumpers; headlights from a Monte Carlo were frenched to fenders.

Lowery entered the picture. Lowery knew the location of some convertible remains, and being a bodyman he figured the transformation would be a no-hassle affair. Steve cut the top off the coupe, then began the installation of the convertible windshield, upper sheetmetal around the quarters, and the doors. He had the body roughed into shape when he was killed in a private airplane crash.

All of this with a minimum cash outlay because Steve just wanted a basic hot rod that had some smattering of custom influence. Can an amateur do this kind of conversion? Absolutely, it happens all the time.

Enter Carl Brunson, a more than capable

metalman and a super ace painter. He bought the Buick. One of the doors needed reskinning, then other commitments set the car aside. Enter Freddie Hurt, then recently of Jackson, Wyoming but removed to Ohio. Also a bodyman, Freddie set about finishing the conversion while adding some custom touches. First was taking the conversion to completion, then making the folding top irons functional again. When the bodywork was done, Freddie applied PPG Deltron black over a pearl base. For power a 350 Buick with a 350 automatic were installed. Then, as things often happen, another project cropped up. Where is the converted convert now? We don't know, hopefully not on the back row of some used car lot.

GAINING SKILLS

By Jim Clark

I always wanted a roadster. A deuce highboy roadster. As a boy growing up in Syracuse, New York in the 50's this was not a practical choice considering the prevailing weather conditions in the region.

Reason had little to do with the choice though. It was influenced by my first encounters with hot rods. Car magazines like Hot Rod that I read featured many classic '32 roadsters and my first model car kit was a deuce highboy. But my

first actual spotting of a real hot rod was a black '32 highboy while I was attending the 1952 Watkins Glen Grand Prix.

My first cars were typical used cars that were affordable by young people entering the workforce at the time. A '37 Ford coupe, then a '53 Merc. At eighteen I join the U.S. Navy landing in Long Beach, California and eventually buying a Chevy-powered deuce Victoria sedan. I bought it from Tom McMullen after failing to buy a '32 Ford

Cabriolet that he was selling for Dick Scritchfield, who along with Tex Smith were the founders of the L.A. Roadster club.

Tom and I became instant best friends, a relationship that continued throughout our lives despite many disrupting incidents. We worked on and raced (street and strip) his roadster and attended many roadster club activities together over the years but I had a sedan so I couldn't join the club.

I drove the Vicky for eight years, moving to New York and back during the period. The move cross country with my new wife Freda and 5-month old daughter Susan, plus all our worldly possessions in the Vicky, made us look like "Grapes of Wrath" era migrators. Mattress on the roof was the final touch. My brother Dave did the heavy lifting on the trip, towing a U-Haul behind his '56 Merc 2-dr hardtop and sharing the front seat with Wife Fay and 6-month old son Davie.

After returning to California I bought two different '32 roadster basketcases that I was unable to do anything with so I ended up selling them. In 1967 I sold the Vicky for $346 to pay for a '48 Harley chopper. Easily one of the stupidest thing I have ever done.

In 1972 we launched Street Rodder Magazine and I was the first Editor so it seemed like the perfect time to build my highboy project.

The one I bought was basically rust-free but being a former race car it had the decklid removed

The Chevy-powered deuce Vicky that I drove for 8-years before stupidly selling it to buy a Harley chopper.

Posing with the roadster in 1973 for the introduction of the project in Street Rodder magazine. Welded rear deck was done when car was used on dirt tracks.

Shot of inside rear deck shows how the driprails had been removed and the quarter panels trimmed.

Panel behind the seat back was torched off and the single piece of sheetmetal welded over the entire opening.

and sheetmetal welded over the entire rear deck area. I was naive enough to think this was easily fixable. Many of us have sold cars for "peanuts" and later regretted it, so when I bought this deuce roadster I vowed to keep it regardless of whatever transpired.

Unfortunately I had neither the talent, tools nor money to restore the rear of the deuce to stock condition. Now we have reproduction pieces that can be used to rebuild complete bodies, like those from Brookville Roadster, but at the time we had to cannibalize other cars to get the replacement parts needed.

While covering the '73 Street Rod Nationals for 1001 Rod Ideas magazine I obtained the rear-

section of a '32 Cabriolet from fellow deuce highboy owner Ronnie Smith of Odessa, Texas.

Ross Magee, one of the premier bodymen at the time, grafted it into the rear of my car but had to work with a flat replacement-top panel available from California Metalshaping. The panel was well made but didn't follow the curvature of the deck lid, preventing me from installing the new decklid. The work he did was excellent; I was the one unable to complete the process.

The chassis and powertrain work progressed over the years but I never could finish the body restoration. A solution to the problem finally came a couple of years ago when I met and became friends with Carl Brunson, one of the few premium

Salvaged driprails from '32 Cabriolet were trimmed and joined to quarter panels at flattest point on panel to minimize metalwork.

Ross Magee performed the surgery using reproduction upper and lower deck panels and lead to reconstruct area.

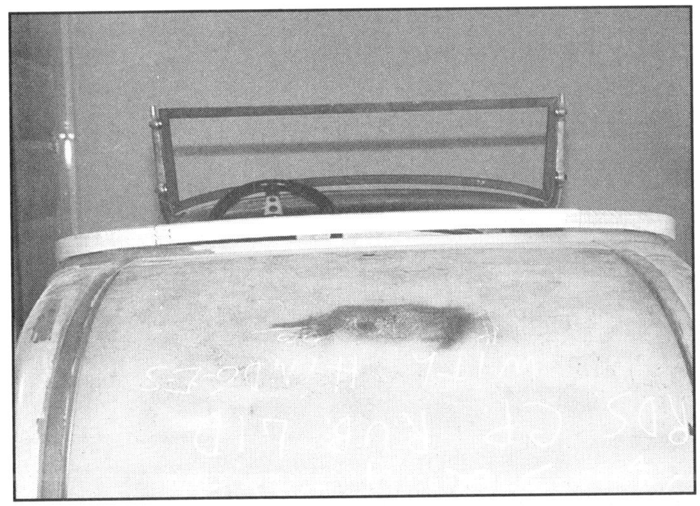

First upper panel from California Metalshaping was flatter leaving gap between trim roll wood and decklid curve.

New Brookville panel matches the contours of the decklid restoring the original fit.

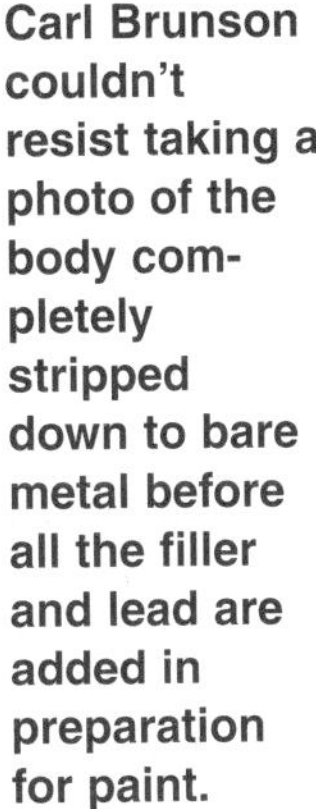

Carl Brunson couldn't resist taking a photo of the body completely stripped down to bare metal before all the filler and lead are added in preparation for paint.

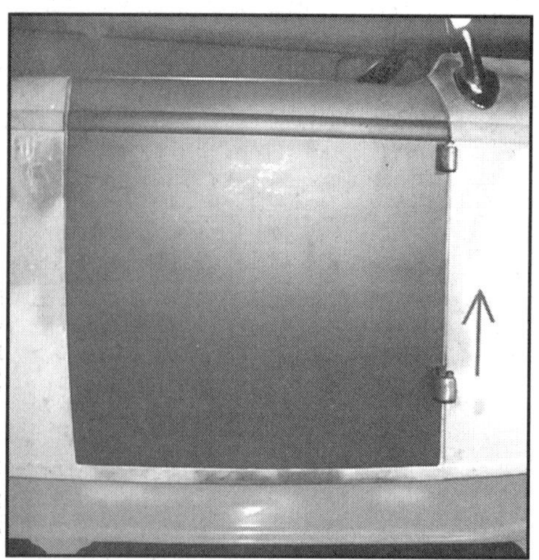

Fit door into opening aligning the raised rib with one on body. A gap 1/8-inch wide around door is ideal.

Door overlapped at bottom requiring that it be trimmed. Reproduction pieces are standardized, originals are not, so they don't just bolt on.

Door skin is carefully peeled back so that the inner panel can be trimmed.

Tape on top of inner panel serves as a guide for plastic based grinding disk. It trims inner panel without cutting into the outer one.

Edge of outer skin is folded back using a body hammer and dolly.

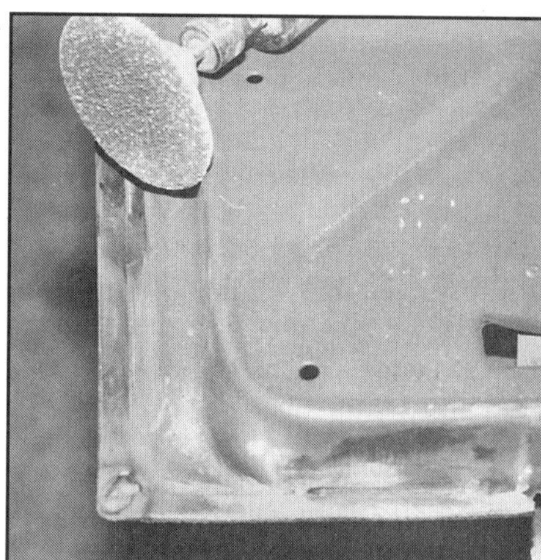

Inner and outer panels are joined by welds at corners and about 4 to 5-inch intervals. True edges with file.

Hinges are Brookville replacements, the lower being longer to allow for curvature in the body. Smaller bolts are used to align hinge then replaced with larger ones.

Reproduction hardware from Wescott attaches the hinges at both the doors and door pillars.

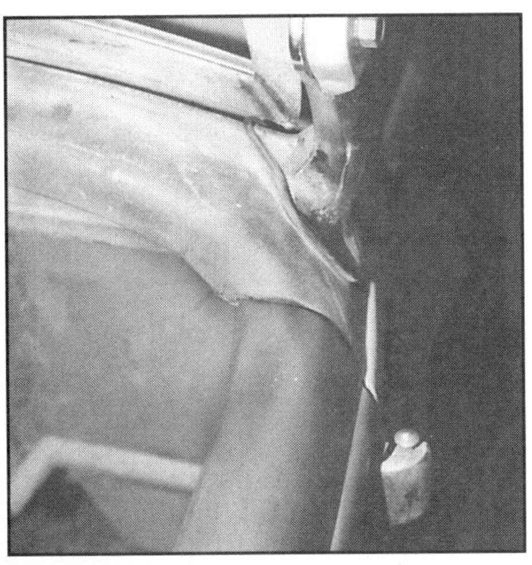

Matching the contour between the new door and the cowl required the addition of weld to both inner edges.

After grinding the door matches the contour of the cowl, creating the cockpit effect typical on deuces.

Door is square but door opening has gap where patch panel had been installed in the past.

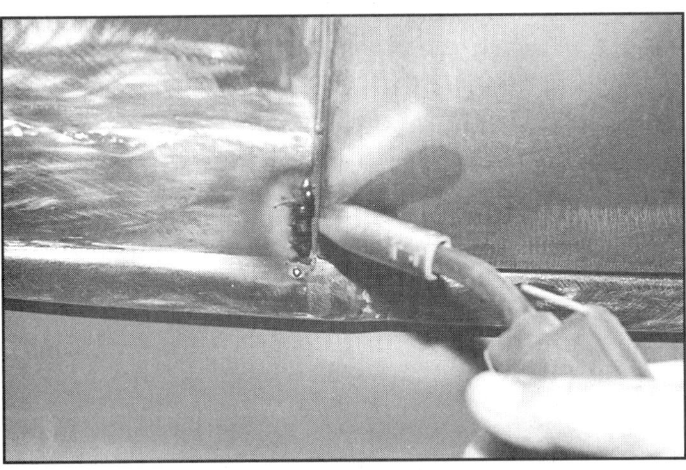

Where the original door opening is out-of-square MIG weld is added then ground down to the proper contour.

Finished door installation shows consistent door gaps and alighnment of raised rib along body beltline.

hot rod builders and painters in the business.

Over the years the car went through some moves and the doors had disappeared, so I bought reproductions from Brookville along with a correct top rear deckpanel. Carl assured me that he could install these so that I would never know the replacements from original. The accompanying photos show that he was correct. I now have one of the nicest original deuce roadster bodies. One less original piece sent to the crusher.

Over the years the car has risen in value to ridiculous levels but I wouldn't part with it for any price. However, in hindsight I would never recommend that anyone buy a car that needs this kind of restoration unless they have the talent, tools and /or money to accomplish the task in a reasonable amount of time.

Seating for the highboy

A basic hot rod may be built on a budget utilizing components from many different vehicles but building a strictly functional car doesn't mean that it has to be uncomfortable. Seats made of foam and plywood covered with an Indian blanket may fit the "rat rod" theme but offer little comfort in a car that was designed primarily as a driver.

Very comfortable seats can be adapted from donor cars without breaking the budget. However, when it came time to install one in my roadster I chose to devote a larger portion of my budget to one of the new split-bench seats offered by Glide Engineering. The split-bench allows both my wife and I to sit behind the wheel in the proper driving position even though I am a foot taller than she is.

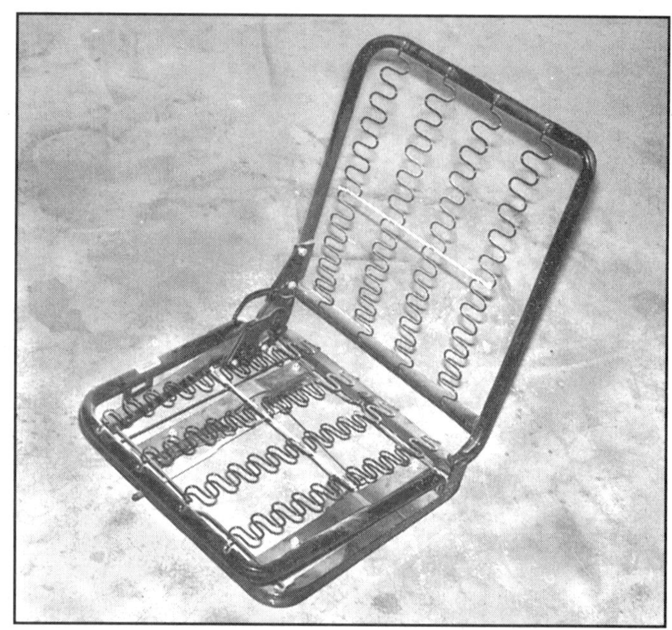

Glide Engineering's welded steel seat frame has OEM-style spring suspension and sliding tracks on the base.

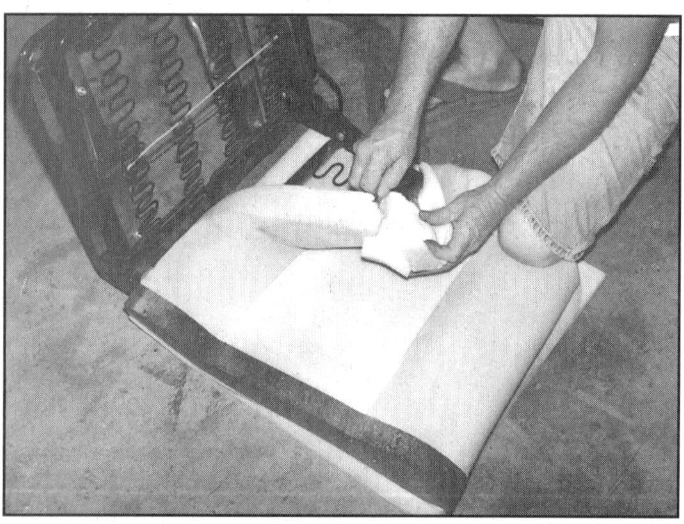

Dark colored strip is high-density foam along edge of pre-formed kit. Provides support where seats mate in center.

Pleats are laid out on foam-backed vinyl leaving an allowance for contraction of material length when sewing.

Foam and vinyl are stitched along chalk lines creating the pleats for bottom and back cushions.

Bob folds the pleats over and back-stitches them to eliminate the visible stitched seam on the front side.

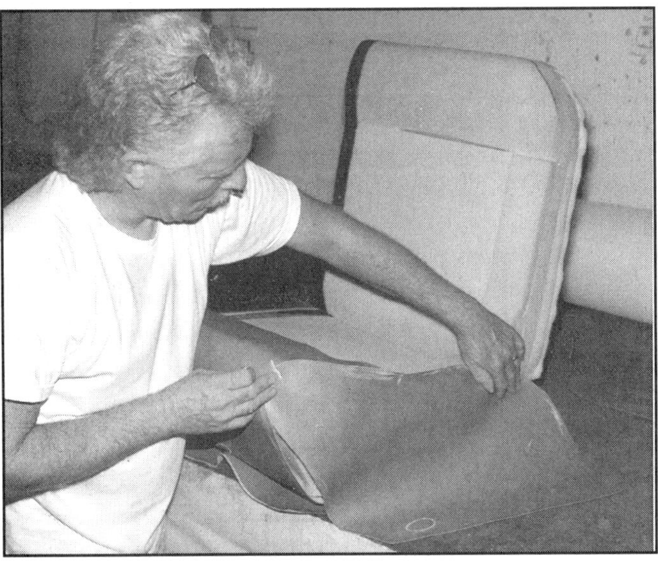

Front and side panels are cut leaving an allowance for stitching them together with the pleated inserts.

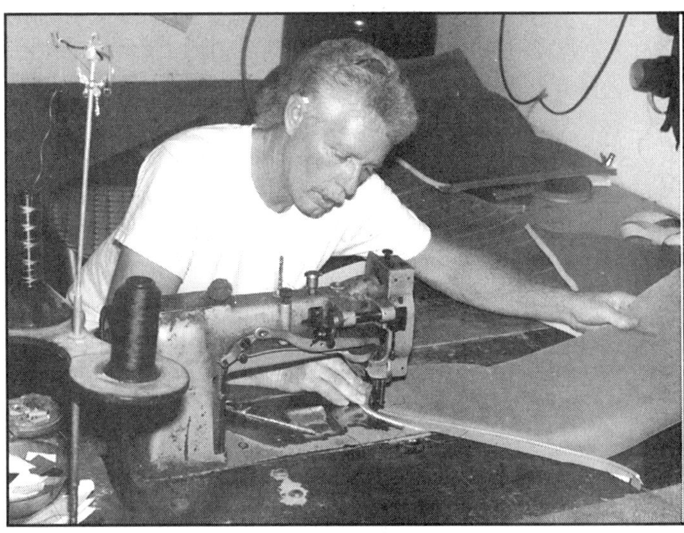

Piping pre-sewn from same material is used to join and reinforce the seam where panels meet.

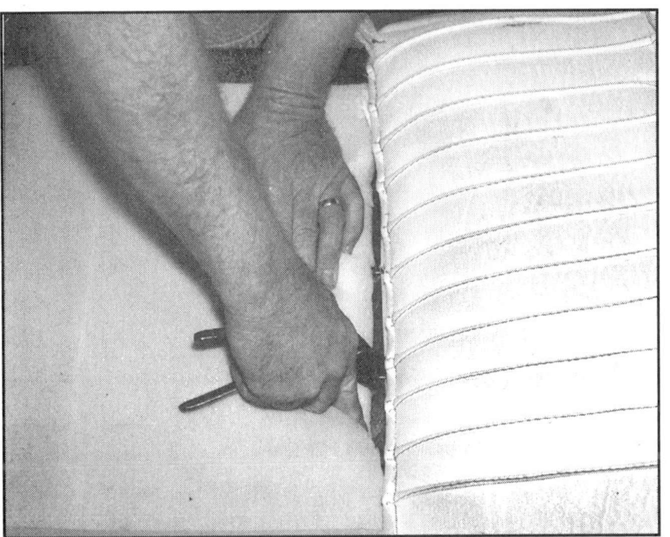

Opening in bottom cushion is there to allow hog-ringing of seat cover at intersection of roll and pleats.

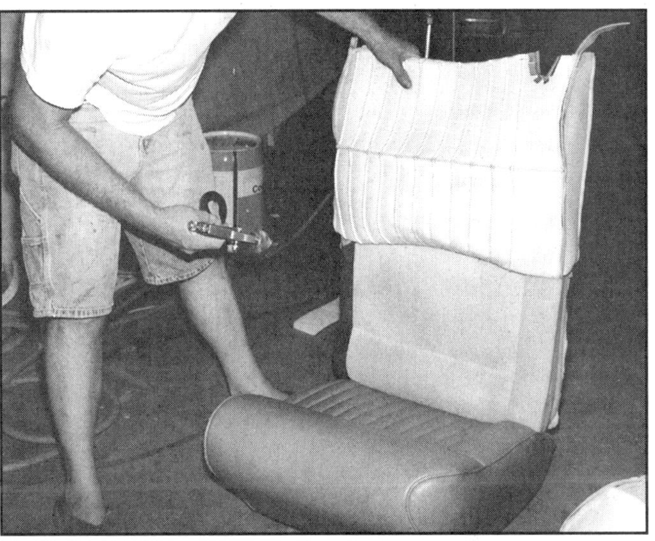

Glue is applied to foam after cover is positioned and fitted over top of back cushion.

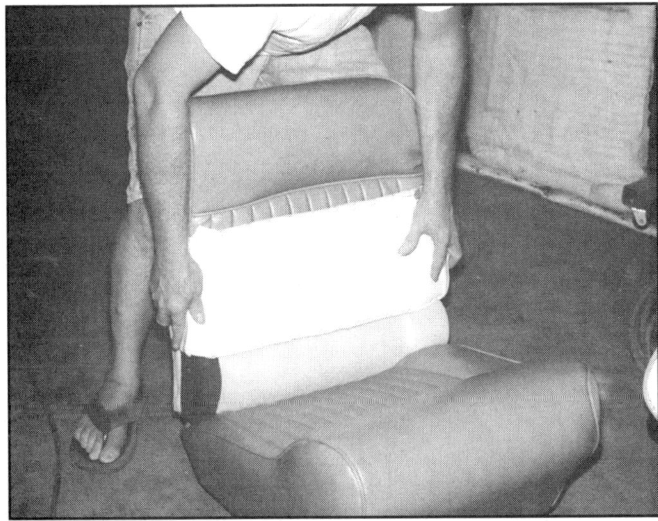

Back cushion cover is rolled down over glued foam making sure that pleated panel is aligned properly.

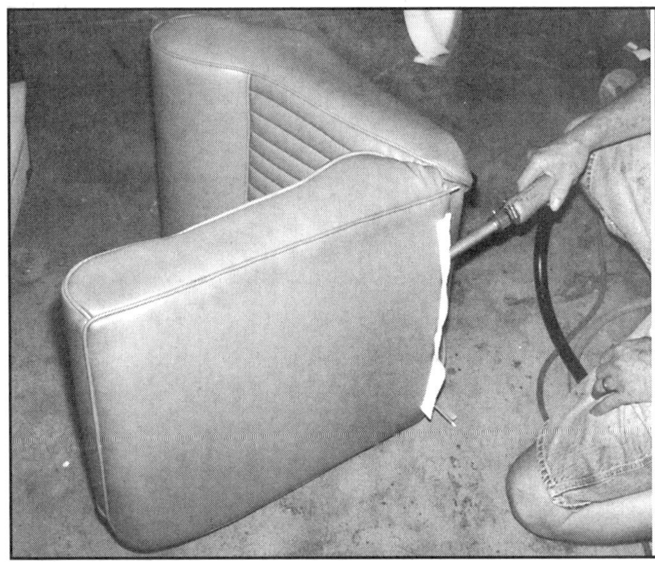

Steam is introduced between back panel and foam shrinking fabric backing and removing wrinkles.

I also purchased Glided Engineering's custom foam kit made specifically for this split-bench seat. I had neither the skills nor the tools necessary to upholster a seat, let alone a complete interior, so I took the seat to Bob's Custom Upholstery in Las Vegas, Nevada. First, owner Bob Childers assisted us with the selection of a suitable Naugahyde vinyl to cover our split-bench. We settled on a light tan to contrast with the Mustang orange that will be the color applied to the car.

Bob stitched the cover for the bottom and back cushions in a rolled-and-pleated pattern reminiscent of those seen in many early hot rods. The job took about a day of shop time and roughly $1,300, including the cost of the split-bench seat frame and foam kit.

I mounted the seats on elevated tracks utilizing a sheetmetal hat-section that is used to make wall uprights by a utility trailer manufacturer. They provided the necessary elevation in the bottom cushions and the strength of steel to ensure a safe mounting. The combination provides safe and comfortable seating for short trips or extended cruising without jeopardizing the future financial stability of my family or killing too many Naugas.

Right—Glide Engineering's split-bench seat reclines or tilts forward to afford access to area behind seat.

Fabric sleeves secure the covers when hog rings are crimped over the metal-rod reinforced sleeves.

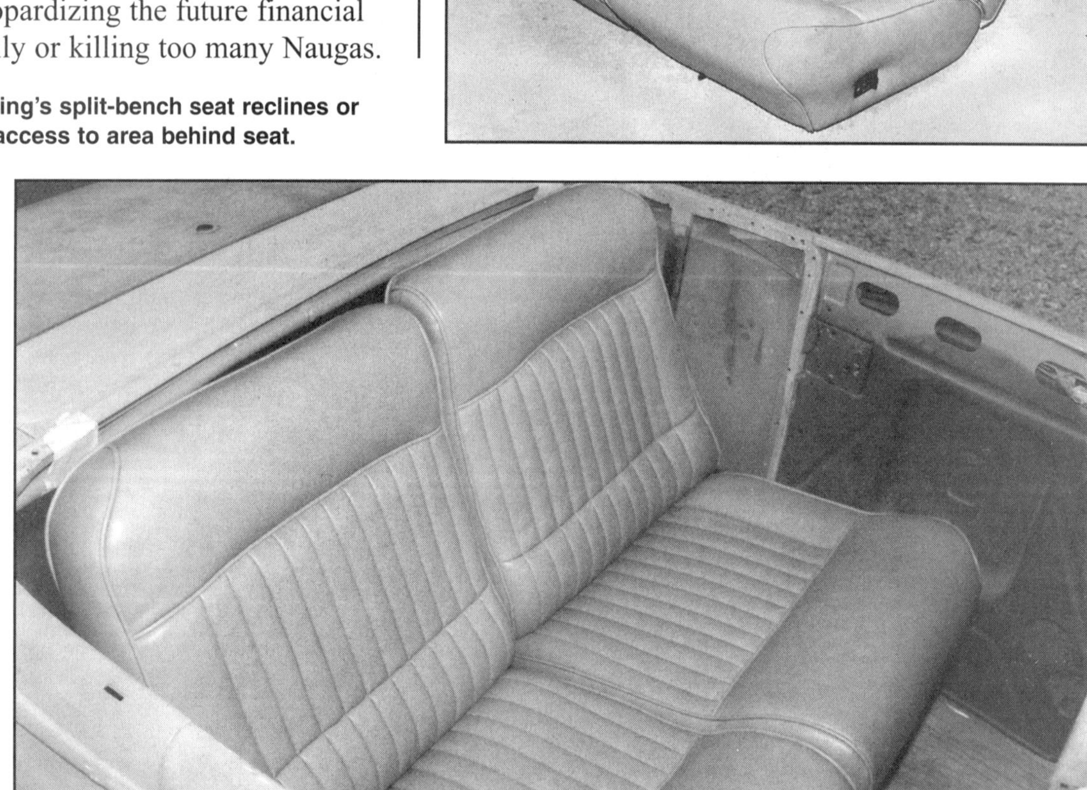

Right—Traditional look of a bench seat is retained while allowing individual adjustment fore and aft to accommodate different drivers of varying heights. The use of vinyl in addition to keeping costs down, offers durability and ease of cleaning in a car that is intended as a driver rather than a display piece.

Stamped steel hat-section, so called because of the profile, raises seat track off floor. One source for this is utility box-trailer or truck-body manufacturer.

Riser mounting holes are drilled at front of flange on both sides where they will mount to body main cross-channel.

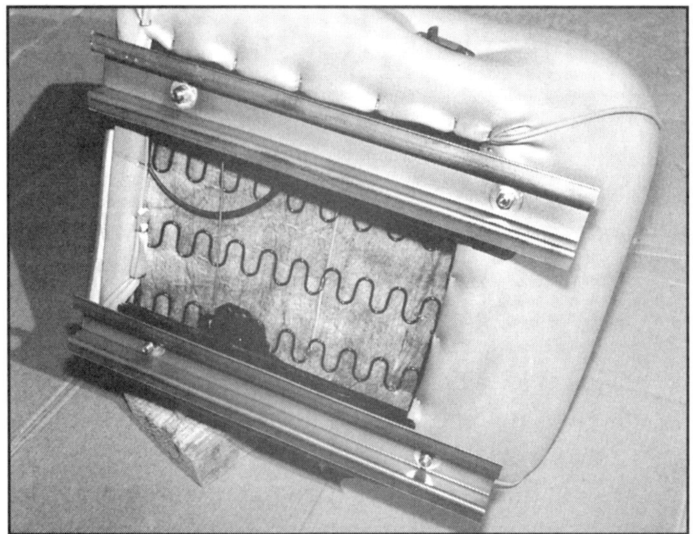

Holes are drilled and the seat track is bolted to it.

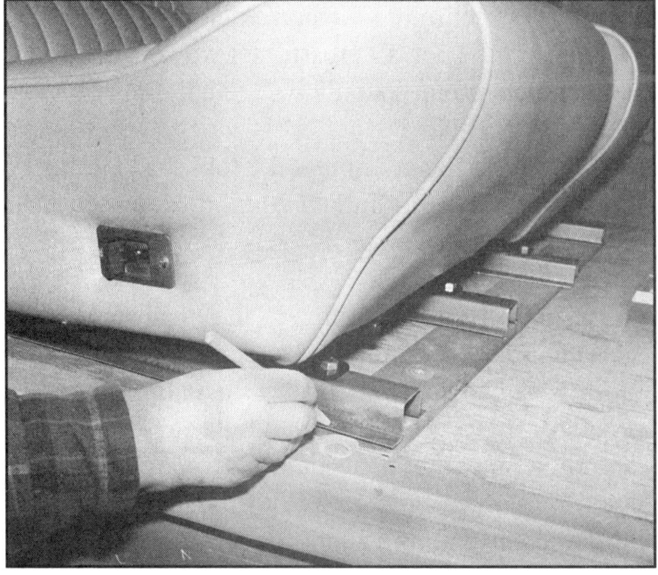

Above—Seats are reinstalled to riser and positioned in the cockpit of car. Cross-channel is marked for drilling.

Left—After the holes have been drilled for the front mounts and secured in place the holes to mount rear of riser can be drilled in one operation. Risers can be bolted in place or removed and seats attached before mounting, whichever gives the easiest access to fasteners.

Updating the Deuce steering

In the '70's when I started this deuce highboy project steering system options were limited to adaptation of components from popular cars of the time. I chose a modified '65 Mustang column connected to a Vega steering box by u-joints from a Honda 600. A spherical saddle-block style bearing supported this multiple-joint assembly.

The drag link connected the stock Vega pitman arm to the right front spindle arm, similar to the '40's style Ford cross-steering. This system worked well for the standard of the time but was a bit slow (about 20 to 1) for a light roadster and the u-joints were small with no fittings for lubrication.

To address these shortcomings I decided to upgrade the steering system with a new quick-ratio (16 to 1) polished aluminum Vega style steering box from Flaming River. It bolted to the same mounts as the original Vega box and utilized the existing pitman arm and drag link.

Flaming River's new polished stainless roadster column was chosen to replace the Mustang unit. It is offered with or without a turn signal lever and mechanism. I selected the clean unit with no signal lever.

A notch was cut in the flat firewall to allow the column to protrude into the engine compartment. It is secured to the horseshoe-shaped mount welded to the firewall crosstube by a self-centering ball-shaped mount that allows the column to swivel at the floorboard.

Securing the column at the top is a Flaming River 5-1/2–inch aluminum column-drop with a swivel mount that attaches to the lower flange of the dash.

Connecting the column to the Vega style steering box is a vibration dampening u-joint, double-D 3/4-inch stainless shaft with a slip-joint and regular u-joint. This combination allowed a straight connection between the two points. If another u-joint were necessary to route the shaft around obstructions a support bearing would have to be installed.

The original setup that I assembled from parts of various vehicles functioned well, but utilizing new components from a source like Flaming River assures the basic hot rod builder of a safe and reliable system. Steering and braking are arguably the two most important systems in a car so they are not areas to skimp on when setting the budget.

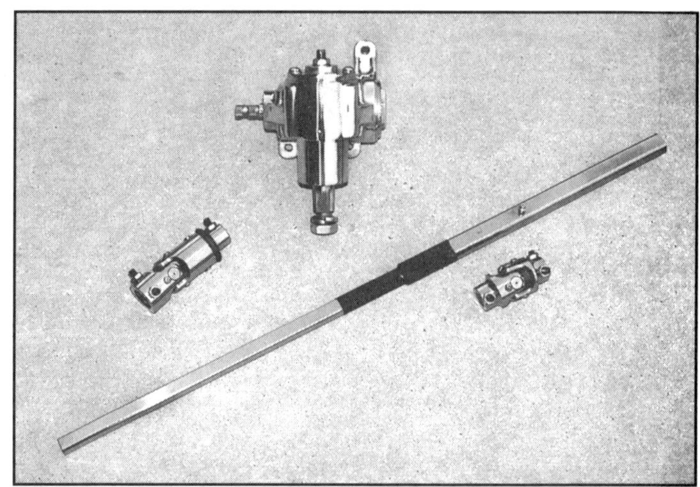

New steering setup is Flaming River polished aluminum fast-ratio Vega style steering box, slip-jointed double-D shaft and polished stainless universal joints.

Original steering column was a modified Mustang unit with a lower bearing and flange to mount to firewall.

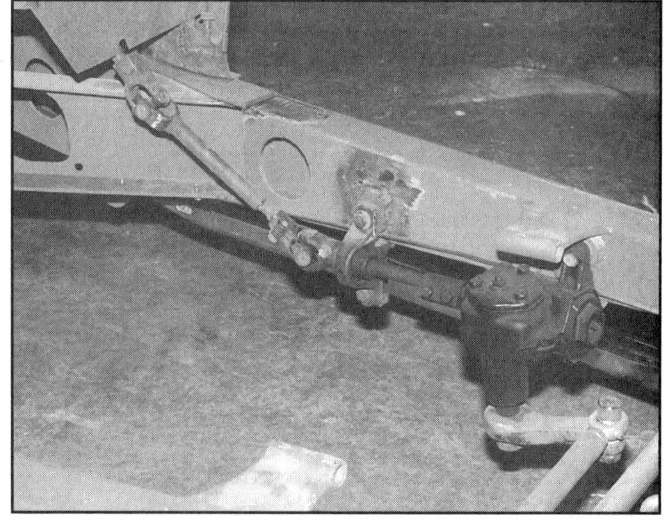

Vega box cross-steered, actuated by modified Honda 600 shafts supported by a frame mounted spherical bearing.

New Flaming River steering box bolted into the same bracket as the original, used original pitman arm.

Joint at the bottom of the steering column incorporates a rubber vibration dampener into the design.

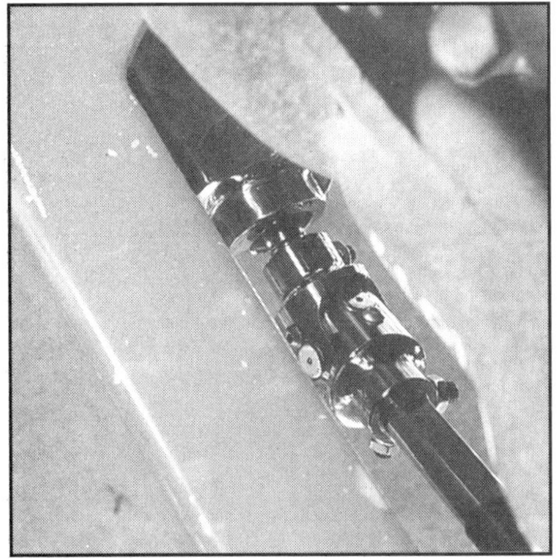

Double-D shaft connects at the steering box via a polished stainless steel u-joint.

If more than two u-joints are needed to route the steering shaft around obstructions a support bearing of this type should be used. A custom mounting bracket needs to be fabricated.

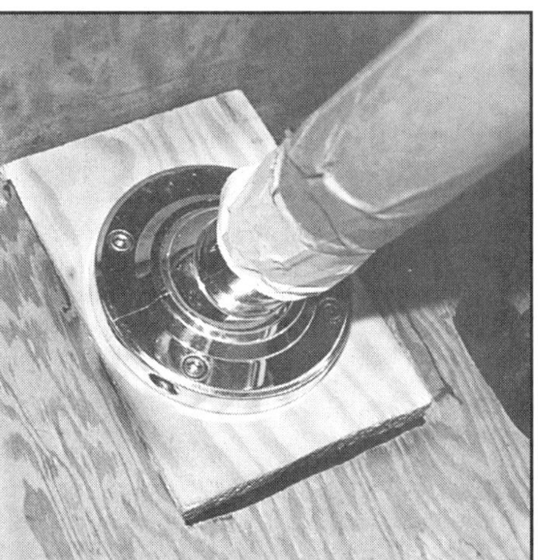

Supporting the column at the bottom is much easier with this self-centering ball-style mount.

The new column is Flaming River's polished stainless roadster column. I chose the one without turn signal mechanism to keep it really clean looking. Leather wrapped wheel is LeCarra.

Aluminum column drop is 5-1/2–inch long with a pivoting mount at the dash and split column clamp.

Direct from a barn in Ohio, Dan Hall had a great two-door, in this day it might even be fair game for a heavy patina rag rod. But like the saying goes, anyone can restore a car; it takes a real man to cut one up!

MAKE A VICKY

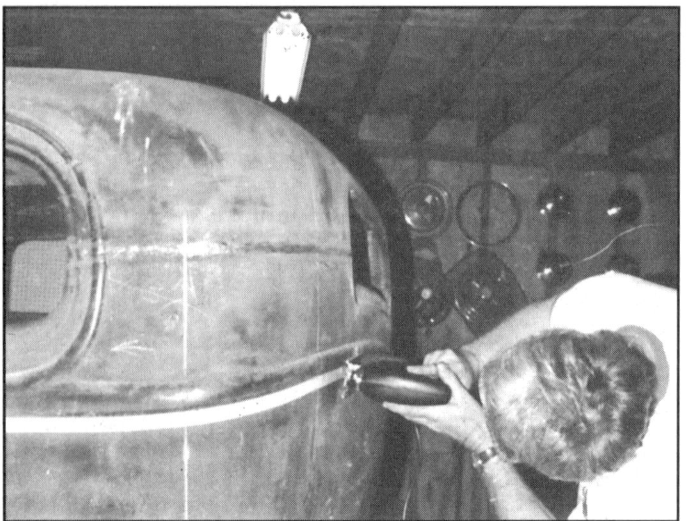

Hall started by cutting across the top, side to side, through midpoint of the side windows. This cut was extended to just below the molding line. Then a saber saw was used to cut horizontally around the rear of the body just below the molding line, about l-inch below the mold, using masking tape as a guide. This extra bit of flat metal would allow gas welding and hammer-welding later.

Interesting how history repeats. Long years ago, I met our own company's Jim Clark at an LA Roadster meeting. He had come with mutual friend Tom McMullen, and he owned a l932 Ford Victoria. Nice car, rather rare. So it was that when I saw Dan Hall's Vicky at the l986 NSRA Street Rod Nationals in Oklahoma City, my mind flashed back to Clark's version twenty-seven years prior. What I learned was that Hall was driving a flawless counterfeit.

Consider the Ford production numbers. For l932, Ford produced: Tudor sedan V8 (57,930); Deluxe Tudor sedan V8 (18,836); Tudor sedan 4-cylinder (36,553); Deluxe Tudor sedan 4-cylinder (4,077). In the Victoria body style there were only 7,24l V8s made, and 52l four-bangers. Lots more rare than for 1933-34 Vickys (26,552).

So, not many Vickys around, even in l932. Dan Hall found his future Victoria as a 4-cylinder Tudor sedan, stored in Ohio. Cost him $3500, a

People will do almost anything to get their photo in a hot rod publication, Dan Hall cut up a perfectly good Deuce Tudor so he could lift off the rear top section and prove he eats Wheaties. Yes, he did it all, alone, the old-fashioned way.

Above—Here is where things get interesting, proving that perhaps Henry Fords famous penchant for making things do double duty was still at play in 1932. Dan made a vertical cut of the lower rear panel from where the body fender bead curves around the back to where the top originally fit. Next he cut horizontally below the back panel bead. This bead is smaller on the Vicky, so some hammer and dolly reshaping was needed there.

Above Right—The rear body section is tilted forward to again touch the relocated top. It is basically the same shape as a production Vicky. Metal at the sides was trimmed for a butt-weld fit.

Right—Once the relocated panels were trimmed they were tack-welded. Satisfied that all the curves were correct, Hall started the process of hammer-welding the seams. In contemporary garages, this would probably be replaced by MIG welding.

The severed top section was tack-welded back in place, after metal was taken through the midpoint of each rear side window. Stock measurement for the two-door sedan is 20-l/4 inches, but the Vicky is only l0-3/4 inches long. The result at this stage is a severe case of underbite. All of that original overhang translates to reduced legroom in the Vicky.

With the rear panel back in place, the gas tank and fenders were repositioned to check for fit. Note how well the rear section fits, but it leaves a pie-shaped opening at the upper corner on either side.

The original Tudor sedan lines around the rear side windows is different than the lines of a Victoria, essential reversed in flow. Dan used a bit of crafty planning to get what was needed. The chalk lines on the original sedan molding area use identical curves, with the bottom line through the center of the horizontal beltline.

bunch less than a Vicky. Originally, Hall was thinking only of a chopped sedan, but soon came the urge to own a Victoria. No major sweat, since he is a bodyman by trade.

In 6 months of spare time, Dan built a kicked-butt sedan that even the pro's have a tough time telling from original.

A piece of excess sheetmetal trimmed from the rear of quarter-panels was used to fill in the pie-shaped areas.

With this area removed, the inverted T-shape is apparent. Perhaps this trick will give builders some ideas on how they can do economical changes to about any car body.

The removed beltline/windowline areas are swapped side-for-side and hammer-welded back in place. Now the windowline sweeps to the rear in stock Vicky style. Dan finished the rework with lead rather than plastic filler.

The only clue to the sedan origins is the larger area of exposed gas tank typical on two and four-door models. Only someone extremely familiar with the Vicky would know that the rear of the body covered most of the gas tank like the coupes and roadster did. This outstanding one-of-a-kind faux Vicky is what Dan Hall achieved with some careful pre-planing, patience, and some expert metal shaping skills.

Forever the highest of tech, Jake Jacobs chose a l953 Ford pickup steering box, l932 Ford spindles and l940 Ford hydraulic drum brakes. The Deuce spring now has only 6 leaves for a softer ride, with the main leaf reversed to gain a l-inch drop. Outer ends of the headlight bar have been cut and welded to bottom of the bar, making a perfect mount for headlights of unknown origin. And the perfect rake is achieved with a stock front axle. Front wheels are 4xl6 Fords, rears are 4-l/2xl6 Fords.

JAKE TECH

Photos by Burlie Burlile

I was standing near the fabled Road's End a few years ago, visiting with several grizzled Bonneville salt flats veterans, when old acquaintance Jake Jacobs pulled off the road in yet another hot rod. You will remember Jake as a partner in Pete & Jake's street rod parts manufacturing extravaganza. When I first met him, he was hanging out with Ed Roth and similar free thinkers in the midst of southern California's hot rodding legion. Later he would come on board at Rod & Custom magazine, and still later form the famous company in cahoots with Pete Chapouris.

The point is, Jake has been around the block a few times, so when he followed a long succession of cutting edge hot rods with the most basic of rides, I wanted to know more. Said he, "I needed something fun to drive." Nuff said, really. With Jake Jacobs, no more explanation is likely to come, nor expected.

Seems that less than a month before the annual speed trials in Utah, Jake took a look around the yard and took stock. Then he started dismembering all the automotive material in order to build this particular car, a l929 Ford Model A phaeton. All totaled, Jake left seven perfectly good, running vehicles in some state of not-runningness so he could assemble the tub in 28 days. By the time he reached Road's End, he had winged from southern California over to Colorado, thence to Wendover and the salt. No Upholstery (other than a Mexican

Right—The used 283 Chevy engine was once new in a car that Jake bought, it had been idle ever since. Jake doesn't know anything about the engine, except that it has been balanced and has a high volume oil pump. Edelbrock valve covers shine (sorta) alongside the Edelbrock Torker intake and Holley carb. Transmission is a l939 Ford with a modification of some new l40 weight lube. Jim Babb did up the radiator.

Left & Below—The windshield has been chopped and leaned back in the best l940s tradition. The custom dash is from "some old car" and holds early Stewart-Warner curved-glass gauges. The l940 Ford steering wheel is customized with a "necker knob", thereby enhancing high-speed control on curved roads. Or something. The wiring is experienced (used), since this is the third Jacobs car it has been in.

blanket thrown over seat springs from a Japanese import, suitably narrowed with a carbide blade circular saw), no hood, no fenders, no paint other than a hastily sprayed grey primer.

A few days at the salt flats, then it was into the sunset in search of other things to do. Which eventually found Jake and the touring at the Goodguys West Coast Nationals. Whereat while a few of us were lazing about and one of the crowd of neer-do-wells suggested that Jake's newest car really did need color other than grey. So, no sooner said that a gallon of red house paint and half a dozen stiff bristle brushes and a roller were provided. Many hands make short work, as they say, and

The custom interior is by Tony Piner's auto wrecking, which furnished the l987 Nissan Sentra front seat. Jake did the fitment by sawing off each end of seat back with a Skil saw. A length of high tech chain holds the body together at rear of rear doors, surely a point getter at ISCA car shows. A l928 Chevy gas tank fits behind front seat, along with a wooden box for Jake's personal belongings. Jake notes that Sentra seat fills with water during inclement weather.

A l934 Ford rearend has the torque tube shortened to l932 length by George Wilson, the single taillight is in tune with current safety standards. Rear spring is from a l9l5 Model T that fits a Model A humpback spring in the Deuce frame. At the car's debut, Jake assured everyone that the tub was not in contention for the National Roadster Show 9-foot trophy.

The custom hood was labored over many seconds by Pete Eastwood, trick hood latches are genuine hardware store items. Jake narrowed the frame (Pinched would be the current high-tech lingo) l-l/2 inches for better body fit at firewall.

Jake was not at all discomfited by all the brush marks in the new red paint. House paint does take a bit of time to dry, even in the northern California summer.

Whatever, the car remained en-toto for a while longer, until at a Ventura, California rod run famed striper Herb Martinez managed to add some class with lots of fine lines. All the while, wherever the car has gone, the mega-buckers stand in awe while an army of basic rodders bestow accolades on Jake The Man.

It should be noted that some time later, in a fit of boredom, Jake decided to cover the car non-bumper to non-bumper with magazine pages and covers dutifully decoupaged to the paint.

Oh, did I forget to mention that at the Goodguys Pleasanton gig, Jake's toy picked up the highly coveted Stroker McGurk award?

T PROOF

This author (Tex Smith) constantly hears moaning wannabe rodders complain about the cost of owning a hot rod. Basic don't gotta be that way, proof being this little T that a hot rodding business mogul built while attending Brigham Young University.

Kim Smith (he of The Hot Rod Works in Nampa, Idaho) did this T roadster thanks in large part to mentor Wayne Atkinson. Upon graduation from school, Kim moved to Connecticut to work for a large company, with the roadster as his only transportation. That is, until the eastern winters proved a closed car much more feasible. So, the rod was sent back to Wayne in Utah for some regular trips to Bonneville and to local drag racing. It is still around. This is what Kim says about the car's construction.

Some people may think it is impossible to build a street rod for less than a small fortune, but I did my best to do so. Not to prove a point, but because I had no choice. I did not have much money to invest. It took many hours of hard work and lots of horse-trading. Wayne Atkinson made me an area in his garage to work, gave access to his tools, and his mentoring. Without this help, the car would not have been possible.

I exchanged several weeks of part time labor for a chassis that Wayne had tacked together from some spare parts. I finished the chassis work that was needed and traded some Chevy truck front spindles and brake drums for a tired Pinto engine and transmission. All brackets and mounts were fabricated from scratch. I had access to extensive machining equipment due to the fact that I was enrolled in the Manufacturing Engineering program at Brigham Young University.

It was cheaper for me to fabricate the parts I needed. For example, I needed windshield posts and I couldn't find any that were in good condition for the right price. So I made some from alu-

minum. Making parts for this roadster is where I got most of my initial machining experience. It was necessary to be resourceful in order to keep the costs down. I had to learn to see things not as what they are, but what they can become. I made headlight stands by bending flathead Ford connecting rods. I found inexpensive steering box bearings by going to a bearing supply house instead of a dealer or aftermarket supplier. The transmission housing placed the shifter under the seat, so I had to cut the shifter housing, shorten it, and weld it back together.

Swap meets, wrecking yards, and the local scrap dealer were good sources for parts. I bought a '32 Ford grill shell and insert at a swap meet. The bottom had been cut off years ago. Nobody wanted it, but my grille was designed to fit without the lower part. I wasn't even sure it was cut off at the right spot, but I decided that the $10 price was worth the gamble. When I got it home, I found it fit after only a slight additional trim.

I bought stuff at the scrap yard by weight. I was able to find external engine parts that were cheaper than a regular auto wrecking yard. One good deal I got at the wrecking yard was the 15-inch stainless steel early Ford style wheel trim rings. They were from a Volvo and cost me $3 each. Armstrong lever action shocks cost me $5 each at another wrecking yard. The Vega GT steering wheel cost $10.

The front half of the '27 roadster body was found in the boonies of Wyoming by a BLM helicopter pilot. He, and his son, worked on it for a while before I ended up with it through some

Right—Entire front end assembly is swap meet stuff or castaways by rodders changing direction. Axle is older stretch drop unit, brakes are early Ford drum. Grille and shell cost $10.

Below Right—Model A rear spring is as traditional as you get, wheel rings are 3-buck Volvo items. Original build cost was with used tires.

Bottom Right—Originally the car had a well-used Pinto 4 banger, a later rebuild with addition of turbocharger turned this into a great performing road runner.

horse-trading. The turtle-deck was donated by Wayne. I bought a replacement panel for the area below the decklid, and got a Wescott fiberglass decklid.

After a year of hard work, the roadster was on the road with a tired engine, old tires, and no paint or upholstery. A year later I pulled it apart, did the painting and rebuilt the engine. Neat thing is, I learned paint and bodywork by doing it. The paint job cost me $120. At this point I installed a turbocharger, and it sure added a lot of bean power.

Later that summer I got engaged and decided

to take my fiancee to visit my parents in Idaho…in the roadster. An 800 mile roundtrip with no fenders, top, or upholstery. The trip was going good until we were about 2 hours from home on the return. Road construction! Water to keep the dust down, and the mud had flowed across the road. Before I could take evasive action we were both covered in mud. The whole car, including the dash and inside the windshield was covered. We were still engaged when we got home.

The next summer was time for upholstery. I prepared the panels and cut the material, Wayne's wife sewed the pleats and I installed everything just in time for the NSRA Rocky Mountain Nats in Colorado. Cost of the upholstery job was $90.

Total investment in the car was under $1300. Most of the people I dealt with were quality individuals who were genuinely interested in helping another person. They were willing to trade favors or make easy deals to see my project through. To me, that is what basic hot rodding is all about.

ITEM	COST ($)
Decklid	22.00
Clutch	45.00
Taillight lens (2)	12.00
Title	45.00
Rear brakes	15.00
Rear axle seals	10.00
Wire & components	10.00
Rear deck panel	29.00
U-joints	27.00
Steering wheel	10.00
Deuce grille and shell	10.00
Headwork & mat'ls	50.00
Radiator work	8.00
Chrome plated valve covers	15.00
Engine tune-up parts	50.00
Headers	14.00
Tires	225.00
Bodywork mat'ls & paint	120.00
Cam followers	21.00
Muffler	2.00
Steering box rebuild	13.00
Headlights	29.00
Upholstery	90.00
(2) engine rebuilds	275.00
Beauty rings	12.00
Turbocharger	traded
Body	traded
Chassis	traded work
Steering column & e-brake	donated
Radiator	traded work
Gas tanks	traded work
Exhaust tubing	donor car
Engine & trans	traded
APPROXIMATE TOTAL	**$1259.00**

SWEDE T

By Harrison Miles

I guess my infatuation with basic hot rods started back in 1967 when I saw a picture of a cute little fenderless T roadster. There was something about the early Model T body and the Model C four-cylinder that was really neat. All that got me to dreaming, but being young meant I didn't have any money. That didn't stop me.

It wasn't long until a friend donated a Model T frame to the cause, and someone else found a dropped '32 Ford axle for $20. I wanted to use a fiberglass body and small four-banger engine to get the weight under the then California law of 1500 pounds so I wouldn't need fenders. I knew I couldn't afford to build an old Henry banger, so I started looking for alternatives. Before long I found a wrecked 544 Volvo with a good drivetrain, for $75. Now you understand where the car's name comes from.

I spent the next couple of months adapting parts and pieces from the Volvo to the boxed T frame. The engine and transmission fit like they were made for my frame, the rearend was installed with two old overload coil springs. By using a couple of piston pin bushings in the '32 Ford front axle king pin holes, the Volvo spindles bolted right on, complete with disc brakes. The axle required some bending to get the correct camber. The 544 steering worked well, and I also used the Volvo shocks, seats, and various nuts and bolts.

For several months I had been searching in vain for a fiberglass body that I could afford. There weren't very many used ones available, but one evening a buddy called and said he had found a body one of the local drag racers had purchased from Ed Roth. It was used on a modified drag roadster. It was a copy of Ed's old "Outlaw" show roadster. The body was all cobbled up, but for $40 a poor man can't be picky. I had a lot more time than money.

To rebuild the body where it had been cut up, I taped some heavy cardboard across the inside and laid fiberglass matte across the outside, smoothing it with Bondo. Then I glassed a piece of half-inch plywood in for a floor. Ed had used '58 Chevy taillights on the Outlaw, but someone gave me a pair of '50 Buicks and they worked just fine. There wasn't room to hide a gas tank, so I mounted a beer keg behind the seat. It was too big.

Then one of my neighbors was about to throw away an old water softener. By shortening it a little, and reversing the concave end so they were both convex, I had a tank. A little silver paint from the spray can and the tank looked pretty decent.

I was way into the tall

Ingenuity is the name of basic hot rodding when money is tight. In this case, a pair of Model T frame rails were boxed, then kicked way up in the rear to clear a Volvo rearend. Coil springs were from some overloads and the steering was Volvo.

windshields on the magazine cars. Somewhere back in the l930s my old uncle Harley built a little workshop on his farm, and used an early T windshield for a window. To get the window to fit, I rolled the body upside down, built the cowl section up with fiberglass until it was quite thick on the inside, and then bolted the T windshield frame on. A couple of quarter-inch rods from the windshield frame to the headlights steadied the frame a lot.

The car was starting to look like something

by then, but I still didn't have a radiator and try as I might I couldn't get the Volvo unit to fit a T shell. Finally, contrary to my cheap nature, I anted up for a custom cooler. A hundred bucks, so it was peanut butter sandwiches for a month.

In time the little car was done, and I couldn't wait to take the 80-inch wheelbase screamer to the truck stop and get a weight slip. Sigh of relief when it came in at just 1280 pounds. Total I had just over $500 in the project, not counting license

Roth used Chevy taillights, author chose free Buicks, gas tank is slightly modified water softener unit.

After author sold the T, it showed up with flames and wheels in Iowa. Current whereabouts is unknown.

and DMV fees. It handled great around town and not many cars could beat it across an intersection. Of course, it did get a bit exciting when meeting a truck doing 70 mph.

About this time I decided to move from the central California coast back to my hometown of Ridgeway, Missouri. A couple of years later I sold the roadster to a man from Bethany, later I heard that he sold it to someone from Des Moines. A friend sent me some photos of the car at a rod run in Iowa, but after that we lost contact. Wonder where it is now?

This '3l A roadster with Brookville steel body rolls on Coker wide whites and racks up thousands of road miles every year. It's beautiful, but it certainly isn't pampered.

MAIL-ORDER HOMEBUILT

Now, proof that a really good basic rod does not have to be from a rusted hulk and thrown away junk parts. Neither does it need to have a junkyard price tag. It can be as new as today's mail service. This great roadster by Matt and Jayme Dillon of Newman, Illinois is a prime example. And, it is a great comparison to the Tex Smith Junkyard Dawg roadster project.

Matt Dillon is one of the younger generation of hot rodders, an industrial painter, and he is quick to point out that he has only one hobby…street rodding.

He built his first rod, a 1948 DeSoto four door when he was just 24 years old. That car took about 8-months to build; this roadster came to be in not much more time. But, he wanted a roadster,

and with the support of his wife, Jayme, he started on a '31 Ford roadster. A second-hand Brookville steel body was located, and it wasn't long before Matt knew exactly the theme he would follow, the building procedure, and even the color.

Matt wanted the car to be a link between the old and the new in rodding, so he started by fitting the roadster to a l932 Ford stage-3 chassis from TCI. The chassis was set up with an independent front end, a Ford 9-inch triangulated rearend, and power brakes. Many body mods were needed for this combination, such as a raised trunk floor to clear the frame, and reinforced body floor structures.

All the body seams were welded, and a recessed license plate area was sunk in the rear

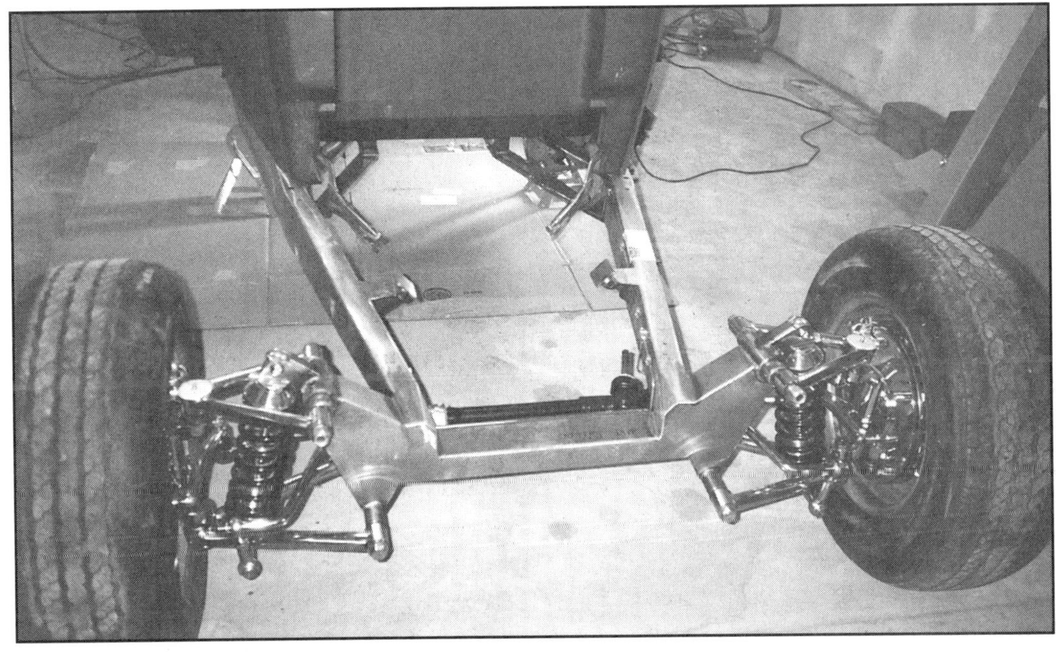

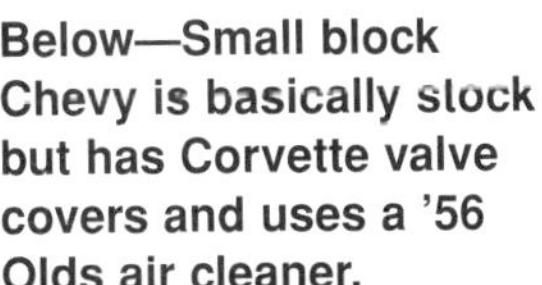

panel. The hood is from Rootlieb and grille shell is a Brookville unit. It is often overlooked that a full-on project such as this also requires a lot of incidentals, such as fuel tank, exhaust system, steering wheel and column, etc, etc. This translates to time.

Once the car was initially assembled and all the parts fit, it was taken apart for painting. From then on everything just seemed to fall in place. Total time to build was a reasonable 1-year 4-months. The result is a perfect example of basic hot rodding in any era.

Right—The trunk
floor had to be
removed, even
though it was new,
and a recessed floor
made to clear the
frame kickup.

Above—With some wheels
and tires and the body mounted the car was beginning to
impress the neighbors. Hood
and grille are aftermarket
items.

Left—Rear panel was punched
for '42-'48 Ford taillights and a
recess made for the license
plate. Large diameter
tailpipes route below the
rearend.

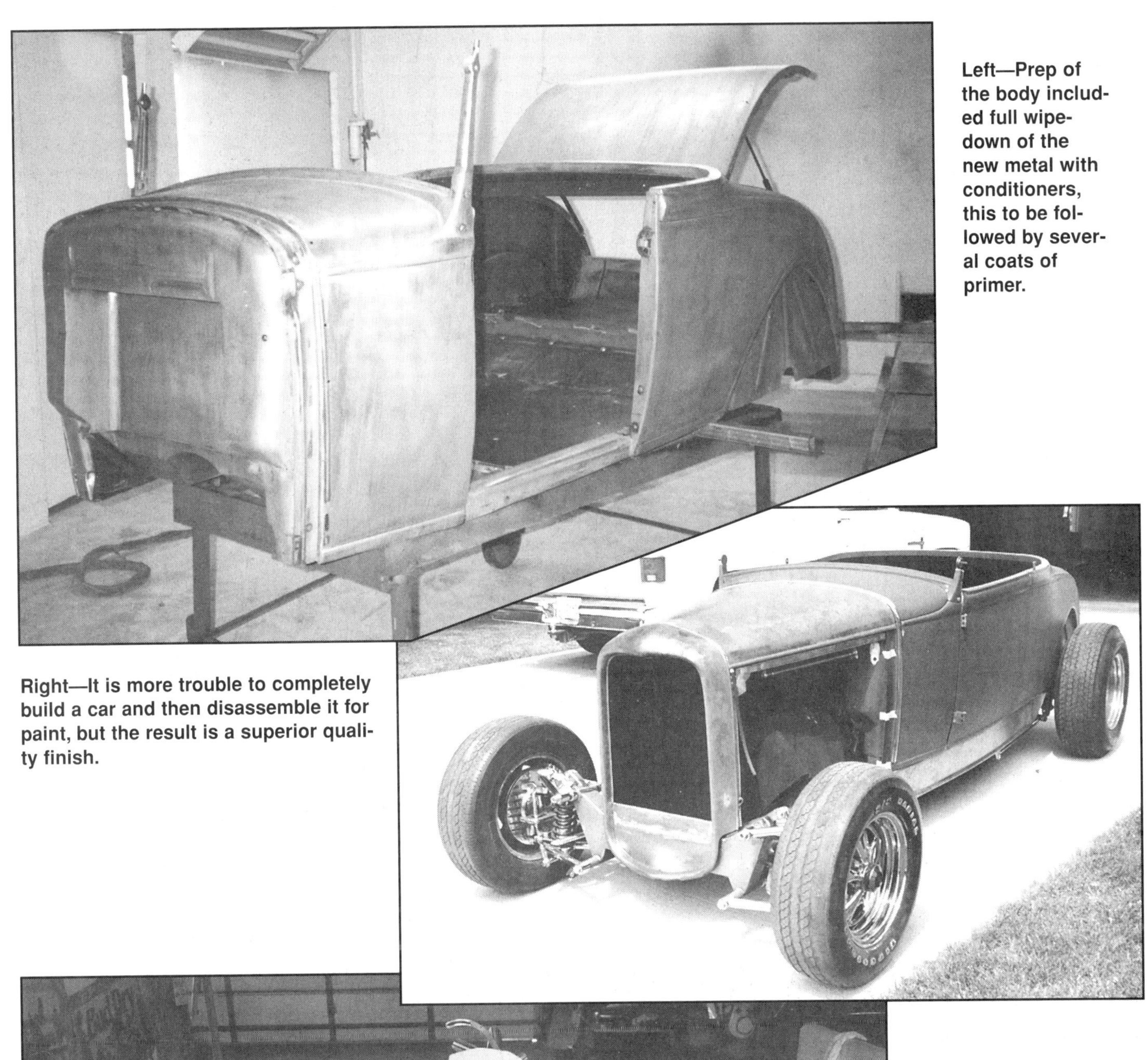

Left—Prep of the body included full wipe-down of the new metal with conditioners, this to be followed by several coats of primer.

Right—It is more trouble to completely build a car and then disassemble it for paint, but the result is a superior quality finish.

Left—The frame and rearend were painted same PPG vanilla shake color by Matt; this understated approach really makes the Dillon roadster grab attention.

Right—McElroy rod shop upholstered the Tea's Design seat and the side panels in a combination tan tweed/leather, in the rear firewall there are twin Blaupunkt speakers.

Below—The chopped windshield is right-on proportions for a basic type hot rod, as are the yellow l5x7 and 15x8 steel wheels, trim rings and moon hubcaps.

The non folding top is much appreciated in Midwestern rain storms, one of the really neat accents to keep the grey beards talking is the stainless cowl trim that is almost always removed by Model A builders.

So how did Matt and Jayme's roadster play at the Goodguys Indy run? Got the undivided attention of several judges for personal picks, Tex Smith got there first to bestow his celeb pick and to congratulate Matt.

Every hot rod project starts somewhere, in the case of a basic rod; it is often little more than a pile of rusty metal in the driveway. Here, Tex Smith takes inventory for his Junkyard Dawg.

THE JUNKYARD DAWG

By LeRoi Tex Smith

Fair enough. I have the reputation around the hot rod aftermarket business as being a junk-yard hot rodder. Kind of strange if one takes the time to study my past, but hey, being known as a scrounger ain't all that bad. Actually, I love all the modern concept rods and customs, and it was my XR-6 roadster that started the designer rod plunge. I love the pro-built rods and customs, and when I got some bucks late in life, my wife Pegge wanted me to call Roy Brizio and have a high buck Deuce built. I even toyed with the idea, but then I realized that by the time I had driven the new road-ster home I would have a list of changes a foot long. In addition, I'm now building a l932 Ford four-door sedan that is all 1-800-BUY STUFF. So I rather like it when the hobby twigs call me BASIC.

Whatever, at the risk of seeming self-impor-tant, I decided to include the full building story behind my favorite roadster, a ride that I have had on the road for a zillion miles and going on 20 years now. I include this how-I-did-it look to show how simple it is to create a basic rod with just a bit of planning and patience.

FRAMING IN THE TETONS

For me, much of the enjoyment of a hot rod is doing the building. I like to experiment, to figure ways to make things work, to feel the metal take shape beneath my hands. I sit by hours in the garage, just thinking about which way would be the best to make even the simplest bracket. I'm probably a study in the slow thinker. And then, when I'm finished, I'm off to another project, to a batch of new ideas, to a different challenge.

So back in the late 1980's, I got involved in

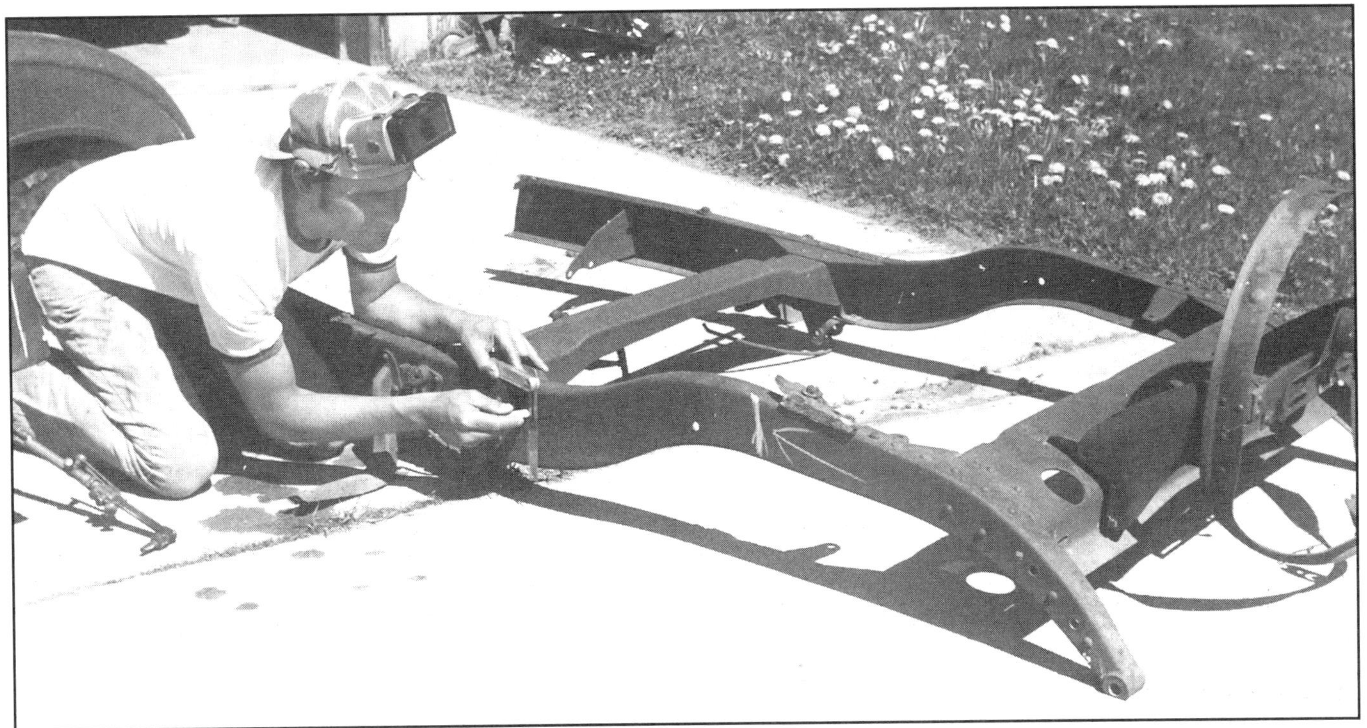

Front two-thirds of the hybrid Deuce frame was available, there was no rear kickup so a section of 20s era Dodge frame was hauled in and cut apart, with the Dodge center crossmember moved to the rear to become new rear crossmember.

With the Dodge crossmember moved aft, the Volvo rearend and coil springs were tried on for size, flooring of Model A body was cut out in trunk area so positions could be checked easily.

The Dodge frame was trimmed to fit where the '32 Ford frame rails were cut vertically just aft of the frame lower beauty lip. Everything was tack-welded and checked/rechecked with the ruler many times.

creating a street roadster for the target sum of under a dollar a pound. Assuming that a typical roadster with a steel body comes in at around 2200 pounds, that became the goal.

All this started in Dallas, Texas where I was doing the PR work on Interstate Batteries then new Great American Race for antique cars. One evening I got a call from long time friend Wayne Atkinson. During the course of chatting, Wayne mentioned that he had his "old '31 back." A number of years before, Wayne had traded his Model A roadster body and a scraggy set of 1932 frame rails to a buddy in return for a future favor. The rodders in the Salt Lake City region are big for trading back and forth, and sometimes they forget to collect on the bargain. Anyway, Wayne got to

The frame is made of 1932 side rails in the middle, homemade extensions from the front of the rail beauty ridge, Dodge kickup from the rear of the beauty ridge, relocated rear crossmember from the Dodge frame, and eventually, rear frame horns from a 1937 Ford frame.

The homemade front crossmember is flatter than a stock '32 Ford, here it has been moved well ahead of the original '32 position to effectively extend the wheelbase.

Boxing plates are welded to the frame inside lips in the same area the Ford and Dodge frames were mated. Quarter-elliptic four-bar rear spring and rearend locator can be added at a later date if desired since the unit bolts to the boxing plate.

thinking about building another low dollar roadster, and happened to remember the '31. A call to the friend revealed the body and frame were "out back" exactly where they had been deposited so long ago.

Wayne brought the metal home, and started working on the frame rails. Part way through, he decided to use a good 1927 Model T body, so he narrowed (pinched) the rails to better accommodate the T body. The front and rear sections of the stock frame were wasted, so he constructed a new set of front rails, from the firewall forward. At the rear, the frame was cut off just as the kick-up began. It was at this point that he had called me.

"Listen," I said, "I've always lusted after a '31 roadster, so if you get tired of the project, let me make first claim on the body and frame." Some time later, after I had left the Great Race and retired (lst time) to eastern Idaho, Wayne called. "You sill want the '31?" Is the Pope Catholic? You bet I wanted it, but I didn't have money, being so recently retired. "Don't worry about that",

Above—Building a lower-dollar basic hot rod starts with keeping an eye out for future building pieces, this trailer load of Ford frames came from scouring back farm roads in eastern Idaho.

Right—An abandoned and wrecked Volvo station wagon proved a donor for entire rearend and front brakes. Even the wheels were saved for the hot rod. Think of it as helping to beautify America.

Left—A badly damaged 1937 Ford frame provided an X-member that could be salvaged to work with the Junkyard Dawg hybrid '32 frame. X-member is shown in approximate location it would eventually occupy. Center had to be widened to allow transmission and driveshaft to pass through.

Wayne said. "You remember that set of forged small block pistons you gave me once? I never did give you something in return."

When the snows cleared that spring, I had a body and frame stub lying in my driveway. There was no floor in the body, and a bit of rust in the normal spots at the quarter panel and cowl panel lower edges. But the basic body was in good condition. The frame was exactly where Wayne had lost interest some time before, after he had fabricated the front frame half from plate stock, and built a lowered front crossmember. That is where I started.

The first problem was finding something to

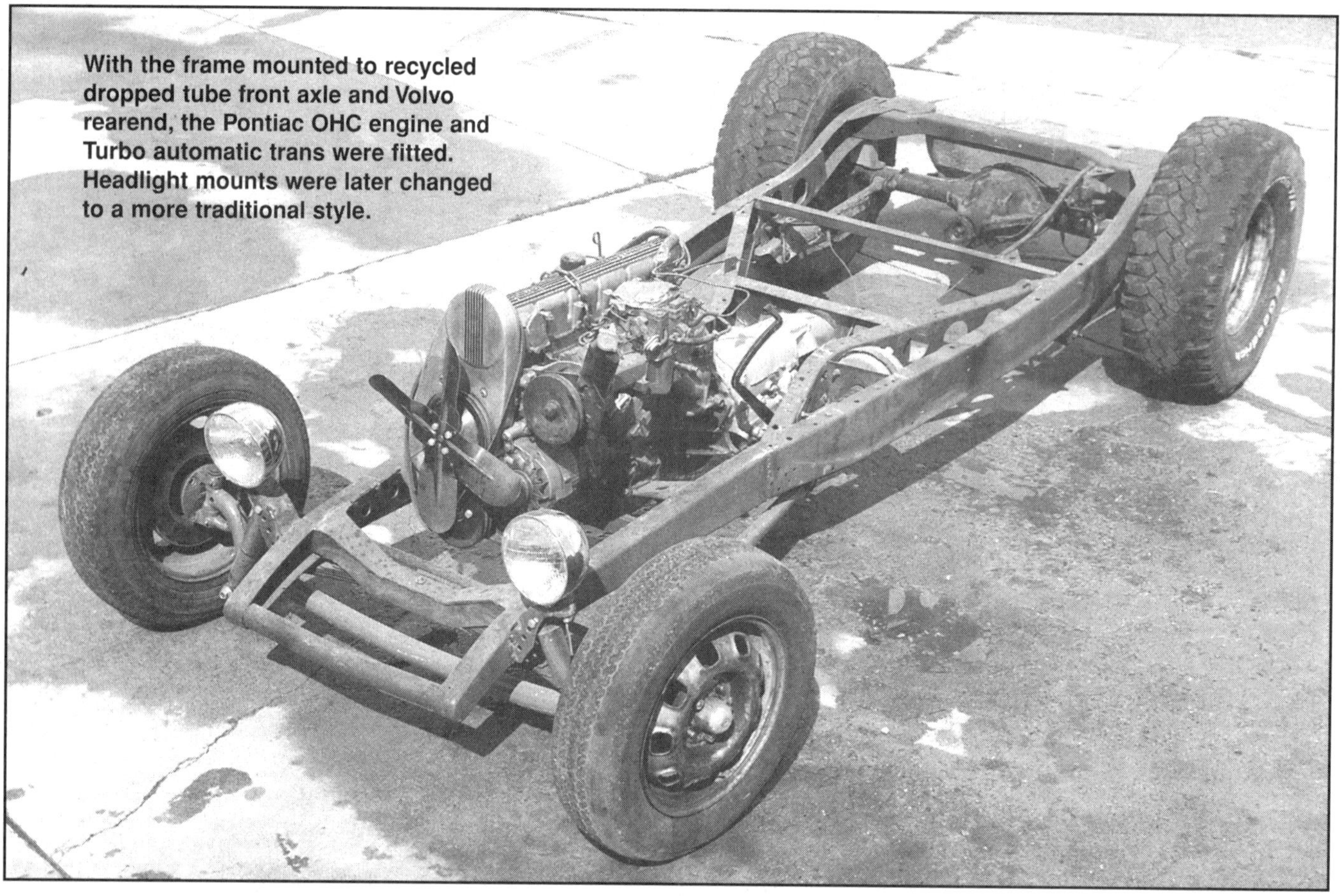

With the frame mounted to recycled dropped tube front axle and Volvo rearend, the Pontiac OHC engine and Turbo automatic trans were fitted. Headlight mounts were later changed to a more traditional style.

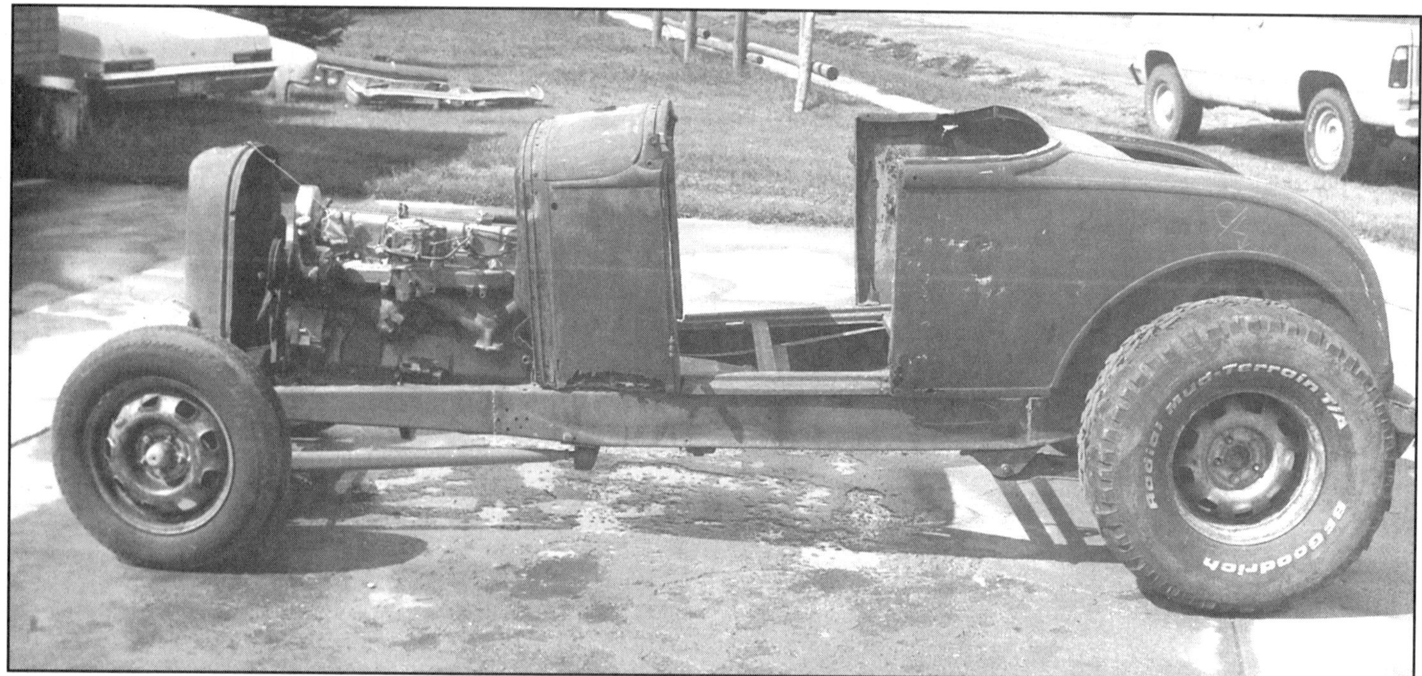

The grille shell and body in place for a test fit session shows that so far all is going well.

provide the kick-up at the rear. Just about any '30's era Ford frame could be made to fit, but at the time I didn't have anything. I did know where there was a late '20's Dodge frame rear half. Right out there in the old Driggs city dump. A bit of quick measuring tape work showed the Dodge frame to be exactly as wide as the rear of my Ford frame, at a little over 29 inches. I hauled the Dodge unit home and set all my available parts in the driveway. A quick photo and it was into the frame modification phase.

First, the rear edges of the '32 Ford rails were

Left—Since the brake master cylinder was to be mounted beneath the floor, traditional type brake pedal was required. It had to be reshaped slightly to clear the transmission bellhousing.

Below Left—Original Volvo split-system hydraulic lines to the rear include proportioning valves, the flat square pad just aft of the crossmember is top mounting point for the stock Volvo coil springs, shocks are mounted inside the coils. The Volvo rearend is quite muscular.

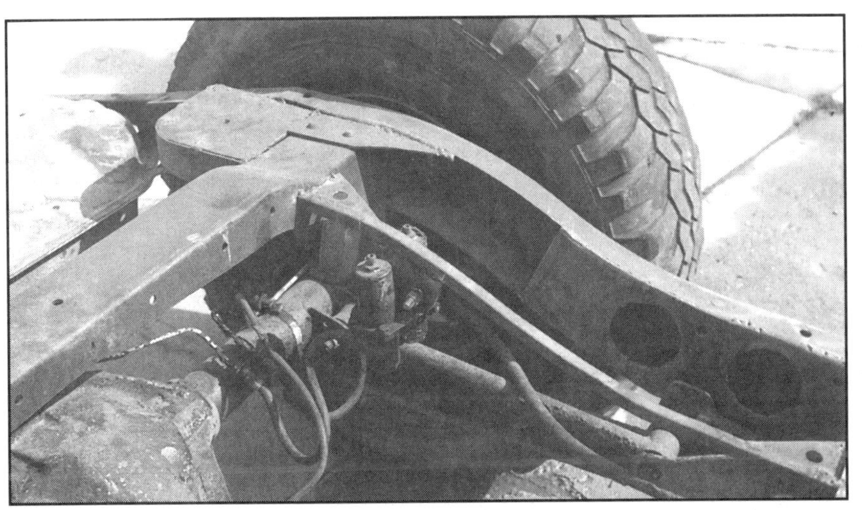

Above—Originally the stock Volvo power brake unit was going to be used, but a manual system was opted for instead. The power boost and master cylinder were mounted on Volvo station wagon firewall.

Left—The Pontiac inline-six is a long engine, the mounts are about midship and require sturdy frame supports.

trued up just where the beauty lip stops. Then, the Dodge frame was trimmed so that the highest part of the kick-up would be directly over the rear axle assembly. This Dodge unit does not have quite as high a kick as the '32 frame would have, but close enough. The Dodge unit was blocked into place on some firewood chunks, trimmed again, then arc-welded in place. With an old Lincoln buzz box. I checked and rechecked by measuring diagonally while I tack-welded everything in place. At the same time, I ran a straight 2x4 down each main framerail to get height correct as I attached the

Above Left—Recycled Super Bell tube front axle was meant to be under fat fender cars, some mixing and matching made it work fine here. Note how the shock mount has several top mounting holes so differing length shocks can be fitted.

Above Right—Gas tank from '37 Ford was set just ahead of a tubing rear-frame spreader bar, it clears the stock Volvo Panhard bar nicely. Original tank filler was cut away for frame clearance.

Left—Nice thing about an inline engine is the amount of clearance to either side.

Dodge stub to the rear of the side rails.

The 2x4's were used as a reference point. Yes, a frame table or jig would be ideal. I didn't (and still don't) have one, so I work from a level floor, measure a lot, and sometimes I get to do the job over. Whatever, it works.

I decided I wanted to make the frame look very much like a stock Deuce, so I cut the extreme rear portion off the Dodge frame, and moved a secondary frame crossmember to become the new rear crossmember. This crossmember was placed squarely over the axle centerline. Were I to do it over, I would move this rear crossmember rearward another six inches, gaining third member working room, and providing a perch for the coil springs.

What were now my frame horns would obviously interfere with the Model A body, so I cut an inverted V-notch in the frame, aft of the newly located rear crossmember, and bent the frame

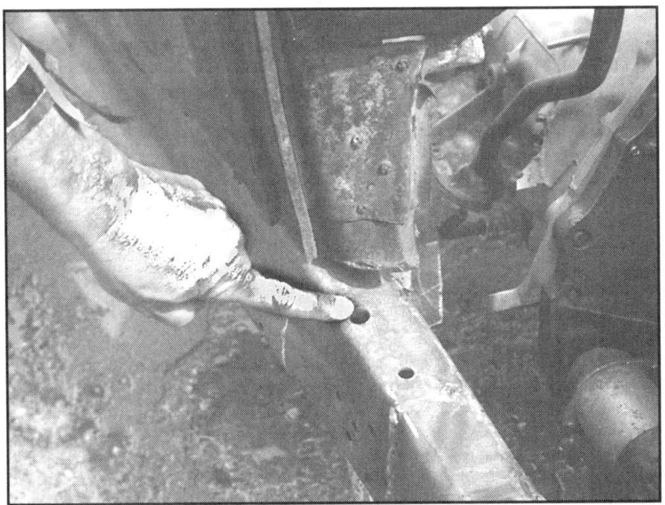

The Model A body was moved well to the rear of stock '32 cowl bolt area, this and the forward placement of the front crossmember increased the wheelbase enough for better engine room and a much improved vehicle ride.

Body trunk flooring was cut out so the fenderwell inner panels would slide down over frame. Later the panels were trimmed to closely follow the frame kickup shape.

Even though the body was moved back several inches on the frame, rear of the Pontiac engine still hit the firewall. Solution was to cut away the firewall and reshape it for head and block clearance. Original Model A footboard area was retained however.

horns downward slightly. I didn't weld the notched area yet until I had a gas tank to try for location and body clearance.

Now, I had a frame with complete side rails, and front/rear crossmembers, but nothing else. Carl Brunson, a well-known custom painter, had his shop in my little hometown of Driggs, Idaho at the time (he has since relocated to the huge speedway in Las Vegas). He had some frame pulling equipment in his shop, so we chained the frame to the floor, got out the hot wrench and went to work tweaking the frame until it was exactly right according to some TCI frame measurements. There was surprisingly little tweaking necessary, since there was no center crossmember in place.

Back in my driveway attention was turned to this crossmember problem. I opted to stay away from a round or square tubing crossmember; instead I looked for an old Ford frame to scavenge, preferably something 1933-1940. I cut the X-member from a badly damaged Ford frame, a '37 I think, and trimmed away the middle saddle. Then the sides were trimmed to fit the Deuce frame. I boxed the framerails where the X-members would intersect each rail, front and rear, then tack-welded the X-member into place.

While doing the frame, I had attended the annual auto swap meet in nearby Idaho Falls, where there is usually a half-dozen hot rodders hawking spare stuff. There I ran across a local mechanic/rodder who had been using a Pontiac OHC six as power in his street racing late Chevy

The '37 Ford gas tank had a rusted bottom, before repair was possible three large diameter access holes were cut in the tank top. This gave room to tack-weld the tank baffles to the new bottom.

A disc grinder was used to clean off the grunge on the gas tank bottom, so original spot-welds could be located and drilled clear to release bottom from the baffles.

The bad portion of tank bottom was marked off in chalk and cut free with an air-powered cutoff wheel.

truck. He was switching to a big block GM, so I got the freshly rebuilt six for $350. In addition, a just rebuilt Turbo 400 was part of the deal for an extra $50.

Problem is, a six-cylinder engine is longer than a V8. I had been toying with a big block Pontiac at the local wrecking yard, but the six was just too interesting. To gain engine room, I cut Wayne's neat front crossmember loose from each side rail, moved it forward 4-inches, and welded it back. Not quite enough engine room, but the remedy was in mounting the body rearward a couple of inches.

About this time I was riding through the high mountain Teton country with Brunson on another VT hunt, when we spotted an abandoned Volvo station wagon, in the 1974 era we thought. The wagon had been wrecked, then abandoned on a remote county road. Up in this country it is finder's keepers, so we hauled the hulk to Brunson's shop and pushed it on its side. I removed the entire rearend assembly including the dual trailing-arm links and coil spring body pads. The front brake assembly came off as well. This way, I had four-wheel disc brakes.

With the front crossmember now relocated

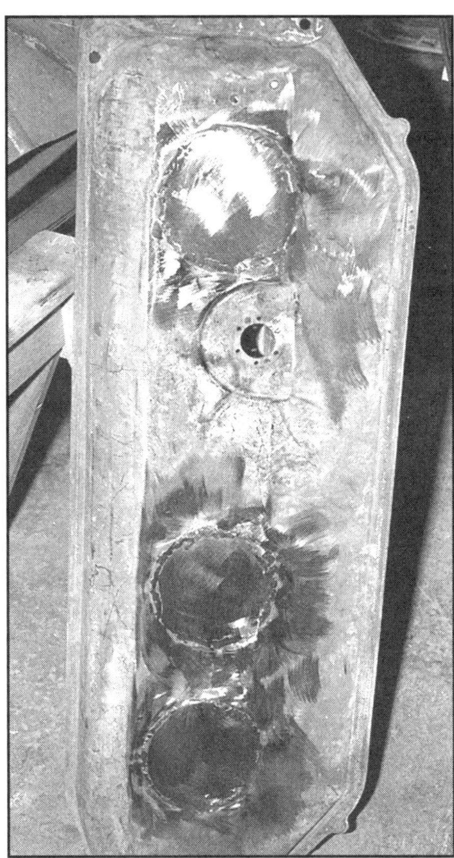

Above—Filler neck from some unknown tank was cut off and welded into the left rear tank corner to approximate location of '32 filler.

Above Left—The round hole edges were flanged with an Eastwood tool (made to flange metal panels for patch panel repairs) then new inserts trimmed and welded in place. By tack-welding with the MIG it was possible to keep distortion to almost nothing.

Above—New bottom plate in l8-gauge metal was trimmed to fit and MIG welded to the recycled tank. Using access through the top holes made previously, baffles were spot-welded from inside to the tank bottom.

FIGURING RAKE

The problem is trying to determine exactly where the frame will eventually take a "set" relative to the tire centerlines, while you are in the early frame construction stages.

In essence, you are trying to guesstimate what the final frame rake will be. This will determine the final hot rod stance. The professional shops already have this figured out, but the homebuilder doesn't usually have this information at hand.

I determine what the rear tire diameter will be within a couple of inches. On this '31, the rear tires will be between 29 and 31-inches depending on what rubber I settle on. This is a fairly constant size unless you get into the large diameter wheels now available. At the front I would use a 24-25-inch diameter tire.

With this information, I set the frame on blocks temporarily and slid the rearend into position with the axle centerline at exactly 15-inches (half the rear tire diameter). Next, the dropped front axle was positioned, with the spindle centerline at half the tire diameter of cither 12 or 12-1/2-inches.

I determined that I would need from 4-5-inches travel between the rearend housing and the frame, figuring the car loaded with two people, some minor trunk weight, and half a tank of gas. I made up two pieces of wood 4-1/2-inches high and placed them between the frame and rearend housing.

A call to several pro builders, including Magoo, Brizio, and Weedetr, for front clearance between frame and axle proved my normal use of 4-inches to be just right. This is the "loaded" distance, of course. You measure from the spring centerbolt end to the axle if they are perpendicular. This gives a slight down in the front rake to the frame, about 2-degrees is common. Extra frame kick-up at the rear will change this, of course, so plan accordingly.

In place, the tank rests on modified '37 Ford frame horns that don't look much like a stock l932 Ford, but the result is plenty good. Larger capacity provides much increased driving range over stock deuce tank.

forward, the rearend was set in place to see how things would fit. By moving the body back for more engine bay room, the rearend would be an additional two inches aft to center the rear wheels in the body wheelwells. More wheelbase equals a better ride, in this case I have ll2 inches. I also got a 6-inch longer hood, which immediately shows in a side view.

When Wayne had been doing the project, he had a big engine in mind. He had built some trailing-link quarter-elliptic rear springs, including traction arms. The assemblies would bolt to the frame ahead of where I trimmed it to accept the Dodge kick-up. I drilled the frame boxing plates to accept these springs in case I decided to go big power at some later date.

Then, I made mounts for the twin trailing arms that are stock on the Volvo rearend. The

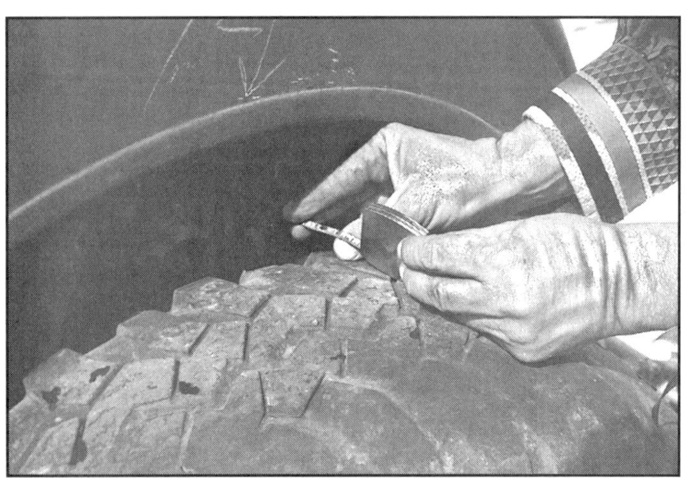

Scraggy truck tires were used in early building phase, body to tire clearance was made equal on each side before the Panhard bar was attached to frame left side.

lower locating arm frame mount was a part of the Volvo unit construction; I cut it away with a chisel and bolted it to the bottom of my Ford frame. The upper control arm had a triangular bracket as stock, this I used to get an idea of where my frame brackets should be. Location of the upper trailing arm mount would determine the pinion shaft angle, and this had to coincide with the universal joint angle at the transmission tailshaft. I could have made adjustable upper control arms had I wanted.

The Pontiac engine was slung from the garage I-beam and jockeyed around on the Come-A-Long until it was right. The floor jack finished getting the engine/trans in position. The front part of the frame had been boxed, so I made up a lx2 inch drop center crossmember to tie the frame rails together directly below the engine mounts. This keeps the frame from twisting due to engine weight, and it clears the oil pan by two inches so the pan can be removed without lifting the engine.

Engine mounts were made and tack-welded in place, and the engine set in position. The transmission tailshaft was jacked up until the four-barrel carb manifold base was nearly level. The frame had been placed on blocks at the approximate ride height and rake, front to rear. Then I made a transmission plate that attached to each part of the open center X-member. With the engine/transmission in place, I could then adjust the rearend pinion shaft flange angle to coincide with the transmission.

I decided to retain the stock Volvo rear coil springs, but I did not know their rate or weight of the wagon they were in. So, off to local wheat silos, where they had an old-time feed store platform scale. I figured the car to weigh a bit over 2000 pounds; the weight should be about 50/50 front to rear, so about 500 pounds at each wheel. I set a coil spring on the scales, then carted in some 90 pound bags of cement mix. I stacked cement bags atop the spring until I got 500 pounds and measured the difference in spring height with and without the cement weight. Rough and dirty, but it showed me that the station wagon had about the same weight as the roadster would have at each rear wheel. Ultimately, this proved to be smack on. Stock coil springs from a Volvo work dandy on a Ford basic hot rod.

However, these Volvo springs mount vertically on the Volvo lower pad, the pad being an extension on the rearend lower control arm, very similar to a Fifties era Oldsmobile. The top end of the spring hit the bottom of the frame. To cant the top of each spring inward so that the top frame mount would be at the top lip of the frame, I cut the lower control arm pad loose and angled it slightly. The Volvo shocks mount ahead of the axle, to the lower control arm, but I opted to mount shocks inside the coil springs. The stock Volvo Panhard bar was lifted to the left frame rail and I found it fit perfectly with a simple off the frame bottom lip.

Why the Volvo rearend? First, it was free, but lots of rearends were. I liked the brake flange-to-flange measurement of only 51-inches, which meant the tires would tuck close to the body. Secondly, it had a 4.10:1 final ratio, with lots of different ratios readily available. Since I would use 30-inch diameter rear tires, the pavement ratio would actually be much more friendly. Third, this particular rearend had a dual brake safety system, which means there is a separate hydraulic line for each rear wheel (with two lines to each front wheel). Fourth, the disc brakes at the rear. But finally, it was different and I wanted to see how it would work.

I knew that this Volvo combination has been a part of European rodding for years, and the rear axles are huge, meaning I could even go to a big engine and keep the rearend.

To complete the rolling chassis, up front I used a spare Super Bell axle I had, plus a few other leftover project parts. So far, I had under $500 invested, including a '33-34 Ford commercial grille shell.

THINGS ARE ROLLING

To get the chassis rolling I had to make up some wider rear wheels. Someone mentioned that the Volvo bolt pattern is the same as late Ford Mustang and a couple German cars, but I have never checked. I wanted to use the stock Volvo wheels because this would keep cost down, and I think they look kind of funky. Very mechanical. They have a rather deep offset to the inside, which helps with front tire/road geometry. If you draw a line through the Ford kingpin to the ground, ideally this line would intersect at ground level with a line drawn through the tire tread width centerline. Neutral scrub, and it would leave some margin to manipulate vehicle handling by later wheel offset.

At the rear, however, the wheel width would not be enough for bigger rubber. To the machine shop where the outer lip of the Volvo rims were cut off and mated to wider lips taken from a set of scrounged 15-inch white spokes. Result is a rim of 7-1/2 inches. The Volvo wheel spider is just different enough from common American rims that making the more common rim/spider combination wasn't readily feasible.

The front axle is a Super Bell unit left over from a '35 Ford project. It was designed to be used in the spring-ahead-of-axle design that Ford adopted from 1935-1948. I whacked the portion of the radius rods off that extend forward of the axle spring perch and used a set of old 1932-34 spring perch bolts that were laying about idle. The radius rods had earlier been split to work with a Chassis Engineering kit on the '35 project, so I just pulled them farther apart to fit brackets off each frame rail and stubbed in threaded inserts to accept Ford tie rod ends.

The '35 spring fit into the front crossmember, so I removed every other leaf to end up with a total of 6-leaves. This spring tuning is a trial and error jig, but I lucked out the first time. The main leaf was discarded in favor of a reverse eye unit made by a local spring company, which gives an extra 1-inch front end drop to the chassis. Strips of Teflon were inserted between each spring leaf, at some later date this will be replaced with the neat Teflon buttons now available. Finally, the spring was wrapped in vinyl tape to keep out road dust. This tape job lasts about one year before it is wasted.

The front spindles were then ready for the Volvo disc brakes. Some years ago, Bill Brutsman of the Kansas City area discovered that Volvo disc brake hubs fit the Ford spindle—If the Volvo hubs are spaced outward on the spindle bolt by 1/2-inch, or if the spindle bolt is shortened by the same 1/2-inch. You either make spacers for the spindle, or cut the spindle off. Finally Wayne Atkinson made up some caliper mounting brackets from plate stock. Now, I had a rolling chassis.

At first I planned on using the stock Volvo power brake booster, but later I discarded the idea. I should have stayed with the original idea because the four-wheel discs need just enough extra leg muscle that I plan on using one of the new aftermarket small diameter boosters anyway. I had an old Pete & Jake's brake lever from a '34 Ford project. Using a piece of round steel bar stock as the

Work on the modified front axle system began by cleaning the axle and all the parts and fitting a Ford front spindle with new kingpin bolts and bushings.

The objective was to get the tie rod above the radius rods without having to bend the spindle steering arms. The original front-mounted spring was used after the main-leaf shackle eye had been reversed to gain an extra 1-inch drop.

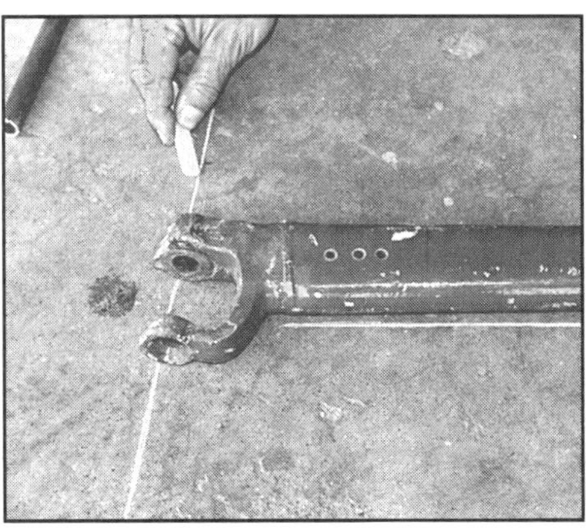

The spring forward design used by Ford from l935 through l948 can be overcome by cutting off the radius rod spring hanger that protrudes ahead of the spring perch bolt.

After the radius rod spring perch was cut off, holes were drilled in the rod tubing to locate where the original casting ended in the tubing. A line chalked on the floor is for reference when the tubing is notched to get a usable angle between spring perch holes and the frame mount end of the radius rod.

Lines chalked on the floor show the angle the radius rod end should be in relation to the rod tubing.

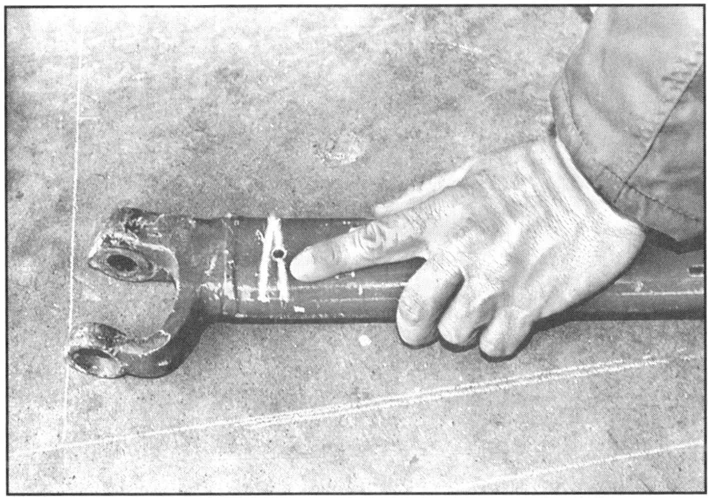

A pie-shape cut made in the tubing just behind the casting will allow the radius rods to tuck up toward the frame.

If there is no tie rod clearance problems a radius rod can be cut adjacent to the end casting. Make sure the ncw weld has maximum penetration.

The unmodified radius rod end compared to the much more angular end.

Spring perches may require shim washers between tie rod yoke and the axle for a snug fit.

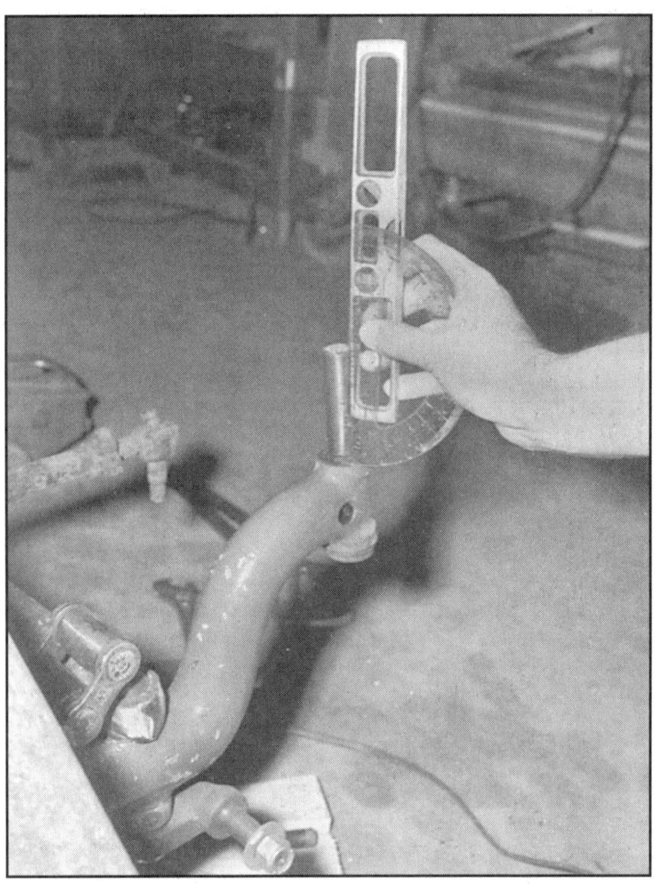

With the frame blocked at ride angle (rake) and the front axle blocked into place, a protractor and level or an angle finder can be used to make sure the eventual kingpin inclination of between 6 and 8-degrees is near.

fulcrum mount, I made up a bolt-in pedal mount that tied the X-member to the frame rail as part of the left side radius rod mount. The stock Volvo master cylinder pushrod was shortened slightly. The rear brakes are served fluid through a pair of stock Volvo adjustable regulators that were on the wrecked wagon.

BODY TIME

When the body was set on the frame again, the engine and firewall clashed. My initial eyeballing had been off a tad, so I made a vertical setback in the firewall. At the rear, the centerline of the rearend was carefully aligned with the exact center of the body wheelwell. Some scraggy rusted metal on the inside of each wheelwell was torched away so that the wheelwell panels would just barely slide down over the frame kick-up. Remember, the Model A has a flat floor in the trunk area while the '32 and later Ford frames have a kick-up.

The frame extensions that were bent downward behind the rear crossmember were then posi-

tioned to clear the lower edge of the body back section, but not welded yet. The gas tank would have to be positioned so it would clear the body.

I wanted to make this look somewhat like a 1932 frame out back, so out to Carl Brunson's place where he had a stashed 1937 Ford coupe (conveniently laying on its side). I took the gas tank and from the bent frame that had contributed the X-member I scavenged the rear frame horns.

With the body in place, I used the floor jack to get the gas tank in place; it turned out that with the rear 1/3 of the tank sticking back beyond the body the front edge of the tank just cleared the Volvo Panhard bar. Dumb luck. With the tank clearing the body by about 1-inch, those '37 Ford frame horns were aligned so that the gas tank mounting holes fit the tank. The horns were trimmed to fit the bent-down Dodge frame extensions and everything was tack-welded. Turned out the Ford horns were slightly deeper than the Dodge frame, so they were narrowed to fit.

In keeping with the tongue-in-cheek attitude of a fun time basic rod, I made little "beauty" ribs along the lower length of each frame horn. Used some 1/2-inch pieces of half-round steel bar. It has worked very well, as I watch knowledgeable rodders carefully inspect the frame horns and conclude that it must, indeed, be a deuce frame.

Now, we had a larger capacity gas tank, but the filler inlet was directly into the left frame horn. I cut the filler neck out and relocated to the aft position of a '32 tank. No big Whizzer Bike! A spreader bar was made from some heavy-wall round tubing found at the local airport, with end plates matching the mounting holes in the '37 frame horns.

From some 3/16-inch steel plate I made up the front shock mounts, made to swing up and away from the frame so the shocks can mount somewhere near the optimum 35-degree cant. I included several holes in these mounts to accept different length shocks, just in case. At first I made headlight mounts atop the shock towers, but decided I wanted to position the headlights forward of the grille as viewed from the side. I'm from that old school that wanted the lights well forward, just a quirk of old age I guess. I used some old dune buggy sealed beams at first, but at a swap meet I found some old truck headlamp buckets that had small park lights on top. I had used some headlamp buckets like these back in l949. Paid two bucks for the pair and no sooner had they appeared in Hot Rod Mechanix than rodders everywhere were onto the trick. Overnight the swap meet prices leaped.

MAKING VOLVO BRAKES WORK

I knew the Volvo discs could work on the Ford spindles, thanks to lots of pioneering hot rodders before, and I had an old magazine with a story on the swap, and it included a caliper pattern. Some machining work was required on the Ford spindles, capably handled by buddy Wayne Atkinson, and acquaintance Mark Bauer of southern Idaho flame cut the calipers…only to find they were intended for the earlier Volvo single brake line calipers. Atkinson redid that pattern to come up with the pattern I give here, which is for the later dual line calipers.

Atkinson shortened the spindle bolts l/2-inch. Then, at the Oakland Roadster Show met up with Glen Chambers of northern California who told me how he had done the same procedure a few years earlier, and how he did it. So, I'll just include his information.

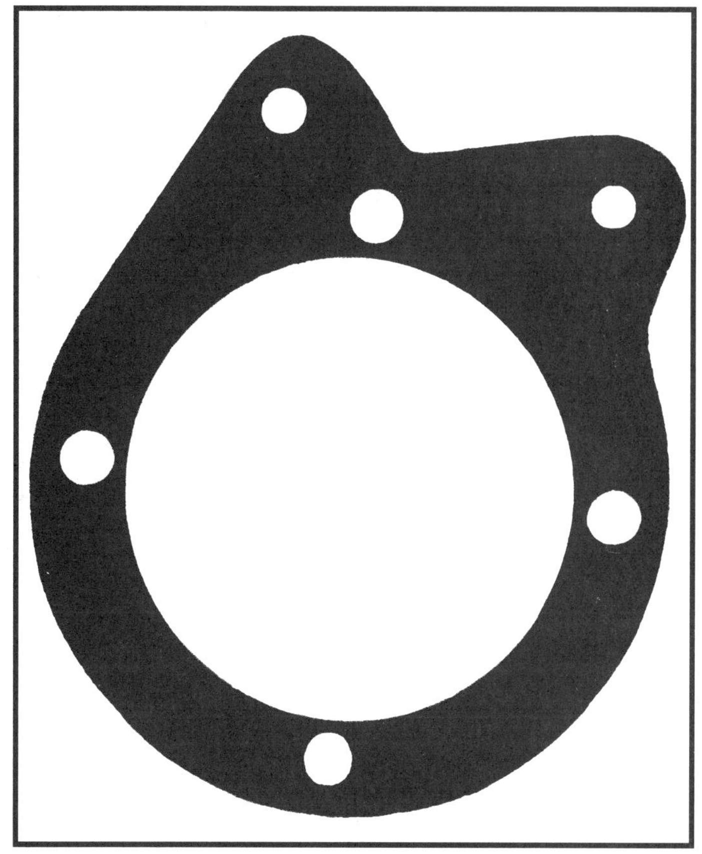

This is the Volvo to Ford spindle brake caliper mounting bracket pattern. It is for the twin hydraulic line system. Just enlarge on copy machine to proper center hole size.

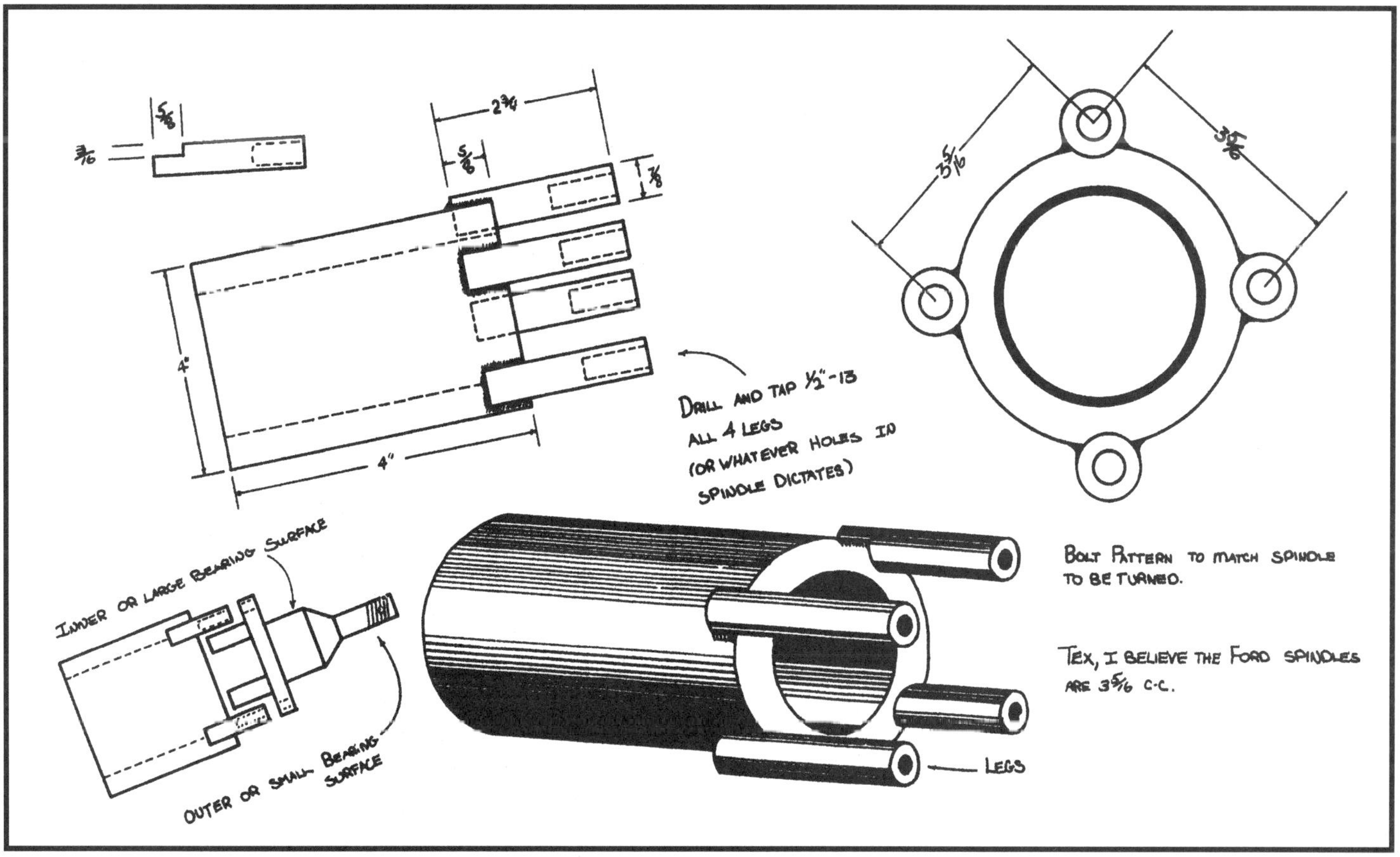

Homemade jig to hold Ford spindle in lathe so spindle bolt can be shortened and threaded.

Above—Once the Ford spindle was modified all the Volvo parts shown were gathered and cleaned, painted and assembly of the Volvo hubs started.

Right—The Volvo rotors and hubs are slightly lighter in weight than the commonly used GM or Pinto units, the rotor separates from the hub and bearings/races are mixed to make this swap work.

The problem Glen found was holding the spindle securely in the lathe so the spindle bolt can be cut off and the threads extended. Glen did this just for the early Ford, but the same fixture could probably be made for any spindle.

Glen cut 4 pieces of 7/8-inch diameter hot-rolled steel round stock, 2-3/4-inches long. The ends were faced to make them square, then each was drilled and tapped for l/2xl3 bolts. These were bolted to the spindle backside, then the spindle was chucked in the lathe, using the big inner bearing race to grab hold of. He then took a cut on the inside diameter of the four pieces of tubing. This was done to give a little more surface for welding to a big diameter "hub". The cuts were only about 3/l6-inch deep and about 5/8-inch long.

A secondary "hub" was made from a chunk of 4-inch diameter, 5/8-inch wall hot-rolled steel tubing, about 4-inches long. This hub would become the base for the four tubes that bolt to the spindle. With the spindle bolt ends center drilled slightly (some Ford spindles have this center drilled feature), one end of the spindle was held by the lathe

center point, the other end by the new fixture.

After the spindle end was shortened the needed l/2-inch, it was threaded the additional same amount. Then the spindle was mounted in a Bridgeport mill and the bearing retainer washer slot was cut the same additional 1/2-inch, then a new cotter pin hole drilled through the spindle bolt. With the new caliper brackets and Volvo hub/disc in place, the Ford spindle kingpin area may need to be ground slightly for caliper clearance. Or the caliper bracket can be ground. Spacers will be needed to space the caliper from the bracket for rotor disc alignment.

To use the l964 and later l22S or similar Volvo hubs on modified early Ford spindles, you must mix the Ford/Volvo bearings and races. The early Ford bearing is a Timken l5ll8; the Volvo race is an SKF 15245. The stock Volvo outer race is Timken 09195 and the bearing is 09074. Use the stock Ford bearing washer and spindle nut.

The stock Volvo uses a splash panel behind the rotor, and a bit of eyeballing indicated it just

Caliper bracket to mount Volvo caliper to Ford spindle is rather simple to make, especially since we include the pattern here. Caliper is aligned with rotor with shims between bracket and caliper.

Volvo hub and rotor assembly is small enough for l4-inch wheels and has no interference with Ford steering arms.

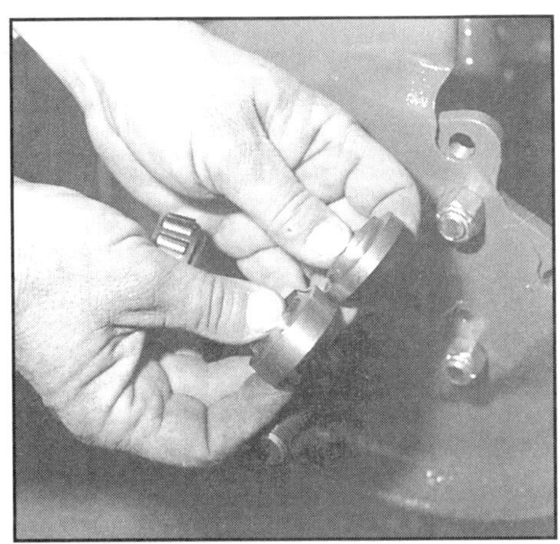

In addition to shortening the Ford spindle bolt, it is necessary to make an inner bearing race and seal spacer. If the spindle bolt is not shortened, a wide spacer is needed.

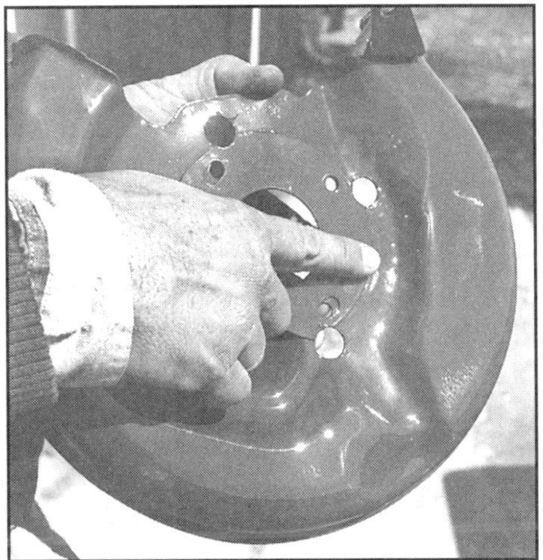

Stock Volvo front dust shields can be used by adding the Ford spindle bolt pattern and slightly dinging the metal for clearance where shown.

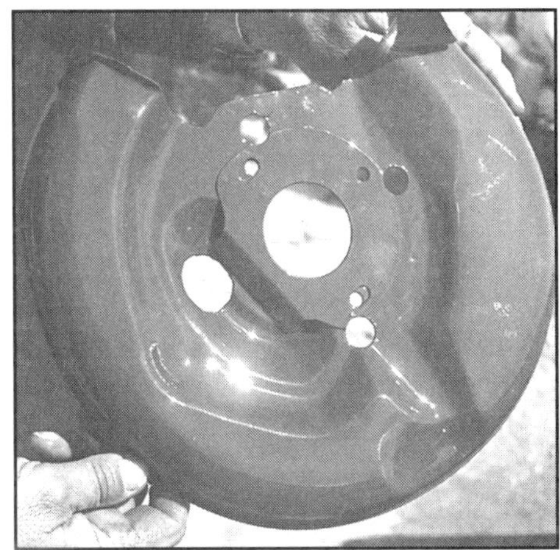

Three holes of Ford bolt pattern easily transfer to the dust shield, fourth is inconvenient so it is opened up to allow access to bolt. Thus only three bolts hold shield to spindle.

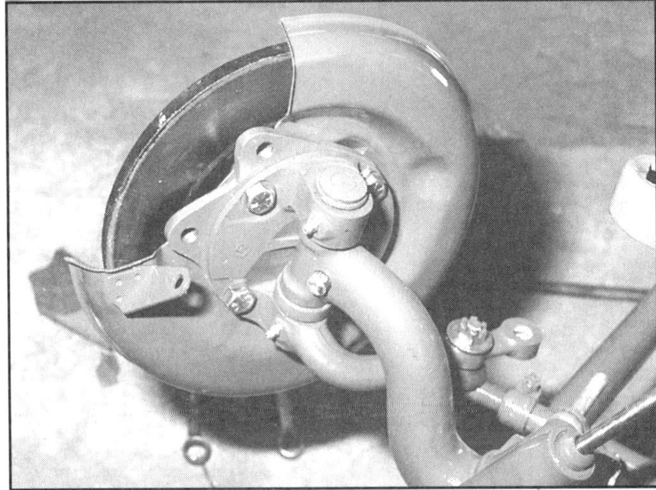

In place the dust shield is a very effective way to keep lots of road stuff from the rotor.

Caliper bracket mounts between the spindle face and the dust shield.

It may be necessary to grind a bit of metal from either caliper or spindle at area shown, but this is minor.

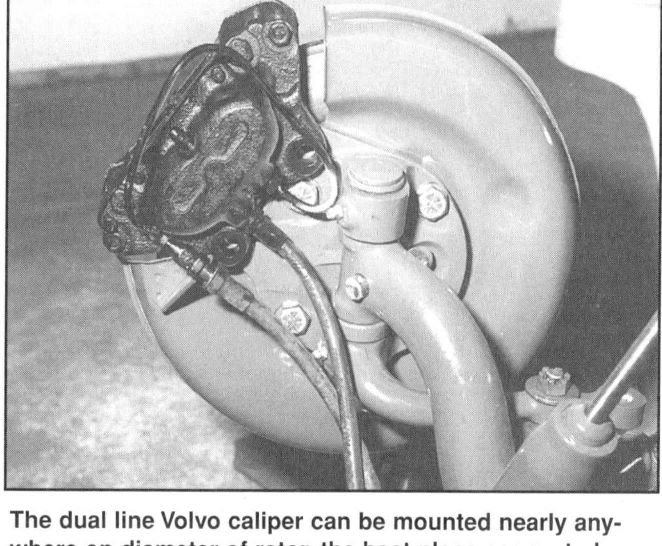

The dual line Volvo caliper can be mounted nearly anywhere on diameter of rotor, the best place seems to be ahead of the spindle.

New bearings and races are always a good bet when doing any rod front end work, the cost is small for huge benefits.

The Volvo power boost was left off final version with the master cylinder being a Corvette unit to include pressure residual valves for both front and rear lines.

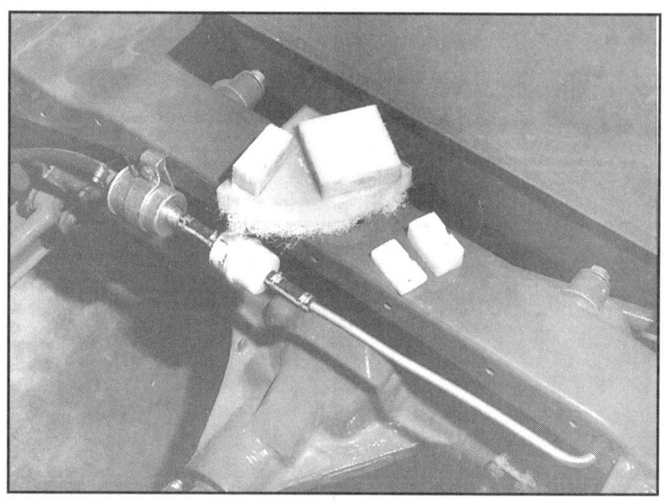

Fuel line routes through the rear crossmember with a filter ahead of the electric pump and another filter at the carburetor. Line clamps were made from some neat plastic material found at local machine shop, for free.

might be adaptable to the Ford spindle backing plate. Sure enough it could be made to fit, and while I painted it red, the sheetmetal is neat enough that it could be chromed nicely.

BACK TO THE BODY

With the project rolling so I could push it into/outta/around my small home garage, it was time to get serious with the body. First off, I discovered the deck lid Wayne had supplied was actually for something else, perhaps a Chevy. So, I tracked down a reject second from somewhere,

It is by rebuilding a wasted hot rod body that the homebuilder can save huge amounts of money, but planning and patience must be observed every step of the way. Here the Dawg Model a body is upside down for tack-welding after making various new floor panels.

Three sheetmetal panels were cut by a metal supply; edges were bent 90-degrees to make installation and welding easier.

Large expanses of sheetmetal will flex (oil can) unless beads are rolled into the panel; here a couple of friends supply the manpower to bead the trunk floor.

Once beads were rolled a metal shrinker/stretcher tool from Eastwood curved the folded over lips of the floor to fit over the frame kick-up.

Installed with the lips faced down and curved to match the trimmed fenderwell panels, new floor can be tack-welded in place.

With two of the three new floor sections in place, attention can be turned to the cowl and quarter panel bottom pieces, which were completely rusted away. Where the body panel subframe was rusted away new l8-guage pieces were hand formed and welded to the original subframe to give a place where the patch panels would crimp along their bottom edges.

Above—Friend Andy Thacker helped remove some lx2-inch tubing that was initially installed to hold floor subframe in place while new hat section crossbraces were fabricated, all this to hold the new steel floor in place.

Right—Tubing is added below the rusted subframe to provide even more strength to an area that is vital for integrity of the roadster body.

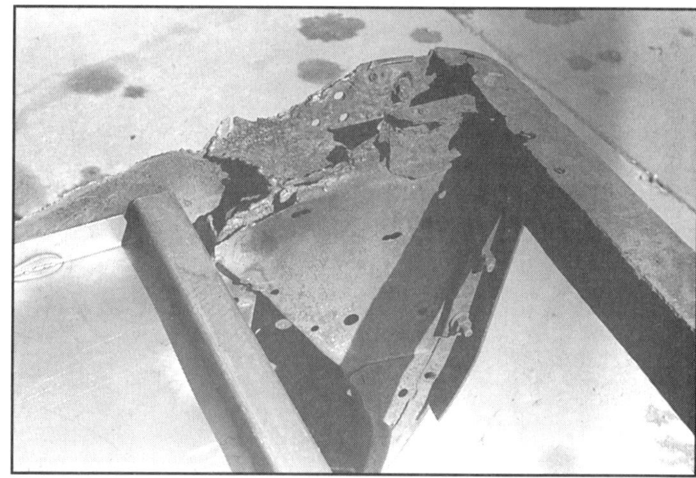

Almost the entire area at each body rear corner was rusted so badly that it was all removed so new subframes could be built.

In the floor subframe area where repairs were needed it was sometimes better to make supports from square tubing and then add sheet stock.

and with a little bit of tweaking got it correct. Mounted the metal deck lid as a rumble lid. Also ended up with an extra outer skin.

Gary Wescott found a fiberglass deck lid that needed some attention, and sent that along as well. I found the Wescott lid actually fit the body better than the metal unit, and the extra metal skin would slip onto the fiberglass unit perfectly. Hmmmm. Punch the skin with a bunch of B-ville louvers, put it over the fiberglass Wescott unit, and you have the best of both worlds. But that was saved for a

Sheet steel is cut to length and folded into a hat section by steel supplier, then it is welded into place to the subframe.

When an early Ford body floor area is rebuilt the body becomes much stronger and resistant to flexing.

It is not necessary to fully weld in flooring panels, a full series of tack-welds will do the job, the seams are then filled with sealer from the cabin side.

Rust rot had destroyed the subframe rear crossbar, one from a Model A coupe was used as a replacement. A piece of square tubing could have been used.

After the body rear corner had been cut away some 1/16-inch steel plate was welded in place, along with extra side gussets that could be trimmed to match the frame kickup.

The repaired subframe rear cross bar area was then welded to the quarter panels.

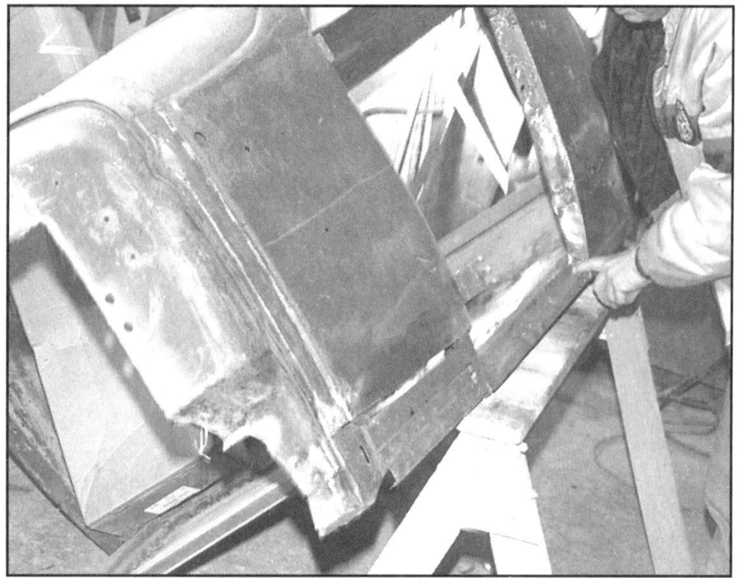

Repairs of the cowl and quarter panels can be started only after the floor subframe is repaired, since the panel bottoms will crimp under the subframe.

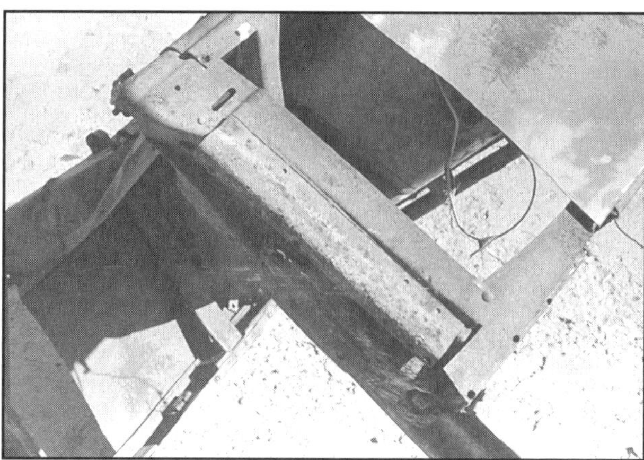

On older metal bodies, rust is usually present on any inner body panel substructure, this is exposed after the Model A cowl panel was trimmed. Now is the time to do some spot sandblasting, if possible, or at least wire brush the rust scale and use one of the good rust killer chemicals. Once the patch panels are installed, it is a good idea to liberally soak the area with the same rust killer.

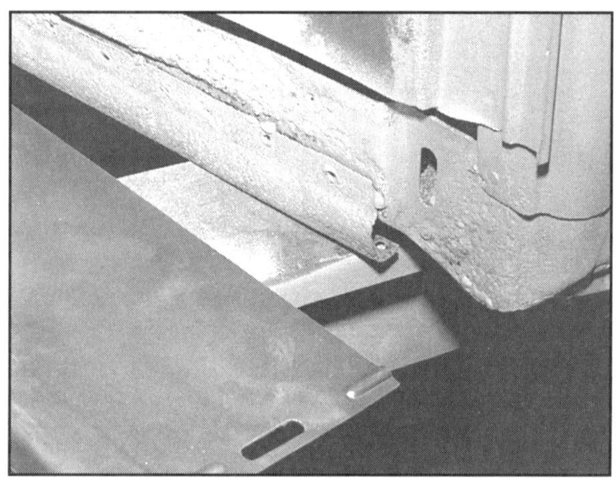

Most patch panels come with plenty of meat so they can be trimmed to fit, note that the slot in the cowl patch panel aligns with slot in the subframe.

Make a straight chalk line on the rusted panel, then cut away the bad metal.

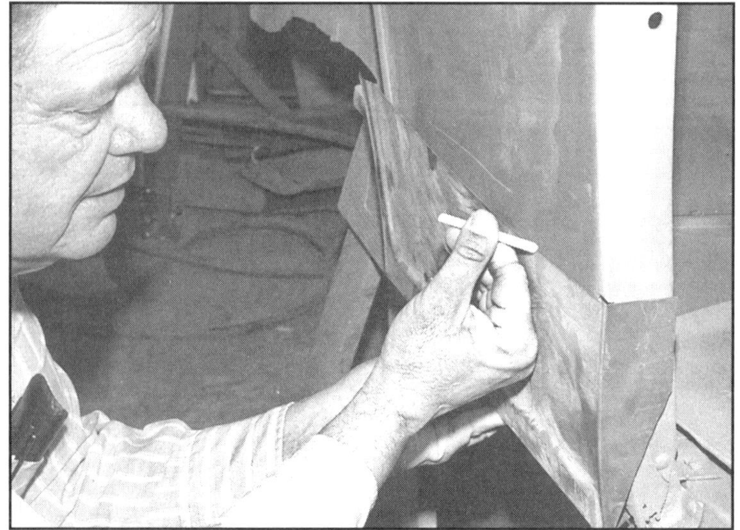

Trim and fit the new patch panel to the original panel, once the panel fits it can be trimmed for butt-welding or flanging.

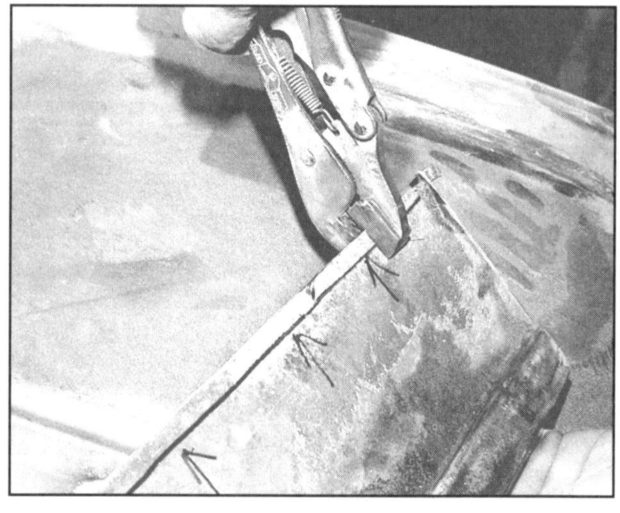

In this case, cowl patch was flanged so it would slide inside the original cowl metal. Simple flangers are available from Eastwood and/or body shop suppliers.

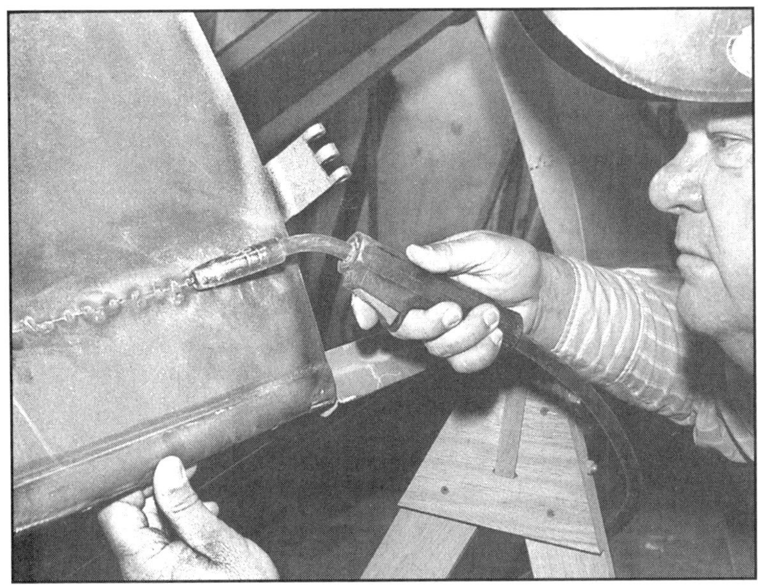

In place, the cowl patch panel is tack-welded with the MIG machine. It is also possible to glue the panels together with modern body adhesives.

Sometimes it is necessary to do repairs to the body substructure; here the firewall flange needed to be repaired before the patch panel could be attached.

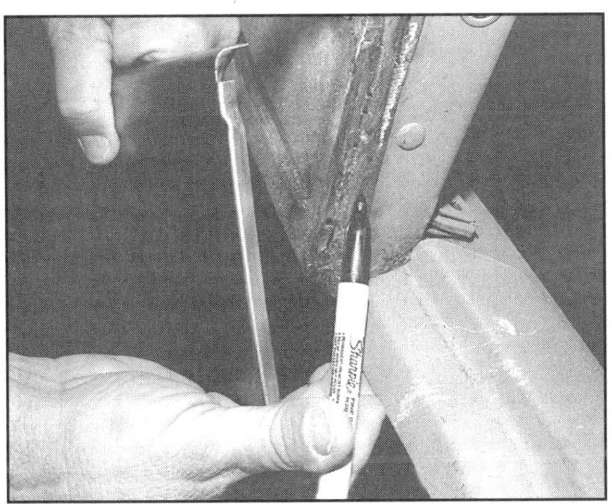

Some repairs were also needed where the sub-structure attached to the doorpost.

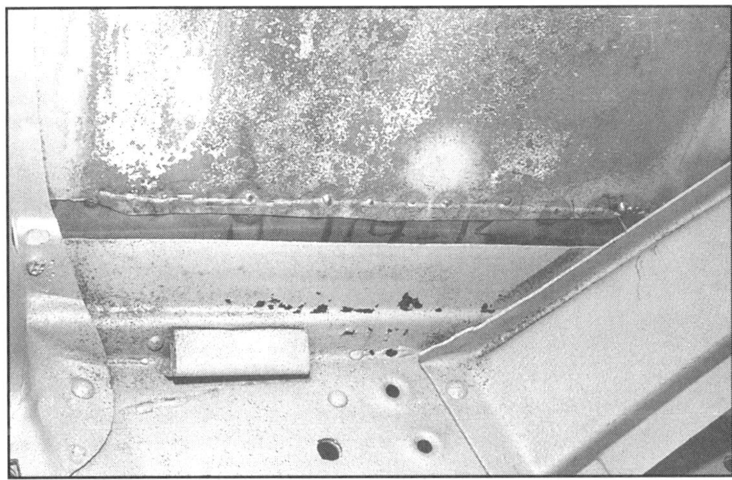

The inside of a lapped panel with the lap edge facing downward. This will prevent moisture buildup in the future.

The quarter-panel patch was installed same way as the cowl patch, but it wrapped around the doorjamb and into fenderwell.

Once welded in place, inner lip of the patch panel was bent around doorpost frame and tack-welded.

The tabs along bottom of patch must be bent over the sub-frame; this area is normally not welded.

Patch bottom flange must be trimmed to fit around any interference, in this case the hat section cross-pieces of the subframe.

Once the panel is fit at the doorpost and the fenderwell, and secured along the bottom, the MIG welds can be dressed down with a body grinder.

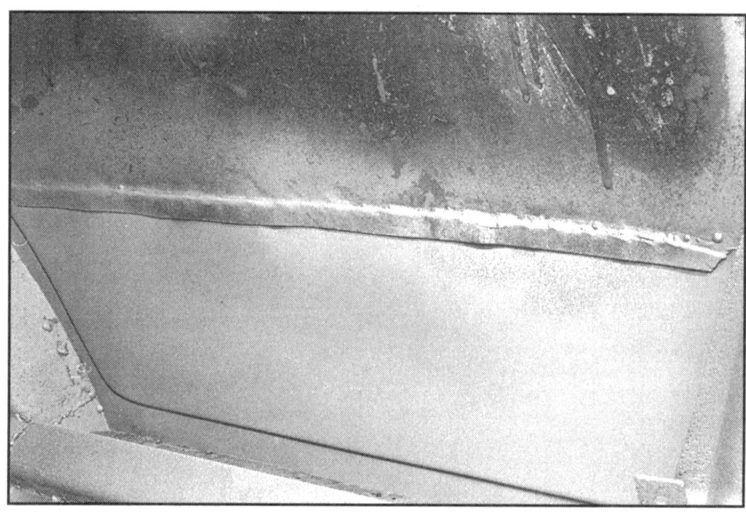

Again, the flange has been put in the original panel so that it faces downward and keeps water from accumulating.

later maybe re-do when updating is in order.

Next order of business was to make up a new floor. The original cross channels were still in usable shape, but I removed them and installed temporary 1x2-inch rectangular tubing anyway. Tack-welded for later removal. This left a bunch of sheetmetal flooring to be made. I measured each floor opening between the body side rails and between the new crossbracing. Originally there was a dropped pan beneath the seat, and I had cut the trunk area clear for frame clearance. Originally, the A used a wooden removable insert for a floor ahead of the seat.

With the body set on the frame and measured/tweaked for alignment, then I made measurements and cardboard patterns for the flooring.

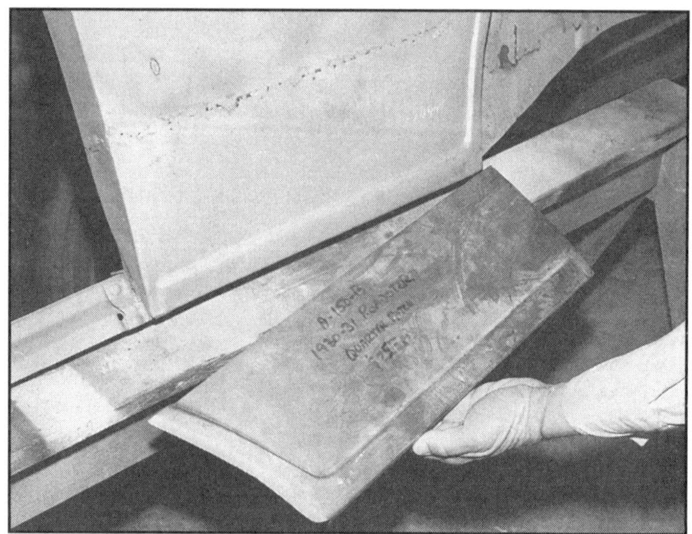

This is the opposite side patch panel held against the new repair.

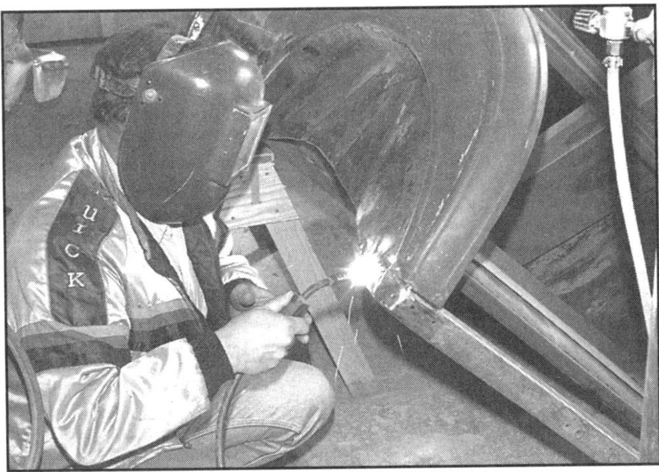

Some final welding done at all the critical crossbraces will ensure that the body does not separate in areas that were spot-welded or riveted by the factory.

The body grinder cleans all welds, and filler will smooth the area, Tex Smith prefers to use lead in critical areas but is not averse to plastic fillers.

Where two metal panels have been welded together, either with a lap- or butt-weld, it is probable that some metal shrinking will be needed. This is where an amateur needs to call for pro help, or at least practice a lot before attempting the real thing.

John Courier, left, and Andy Thacker working over a thrashed '34-35 Chevy grille shell for the Junkyard Dawg. Radiator filler opening was trimmed and shaped before a metal insert was welded in.

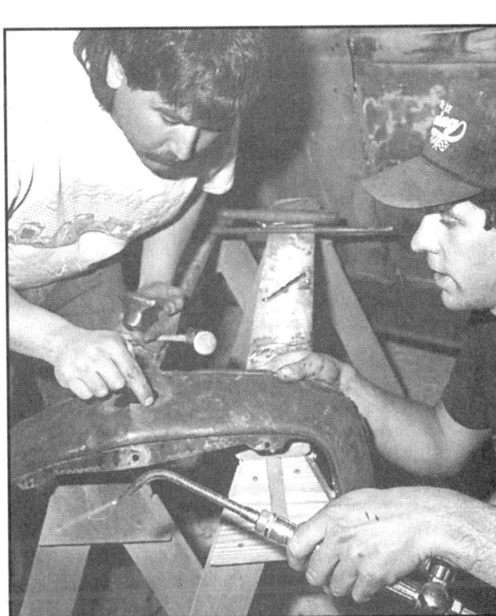

Badly damaged shell corner needed minor bit of metal shrinking to make it usable.

Tex starts process of rolling edge of the Model A dash area by tack-welding length of half-round steel at the center point, then bending the bar to fit dash curve.

The half-round was tack-welded every inch or so as the curving process continued.

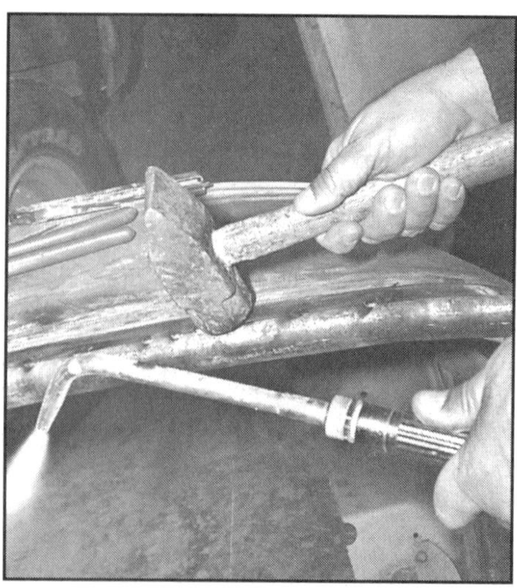

Sometimes just a little extra persuasion was needed to get the half-round aligned perfectly.

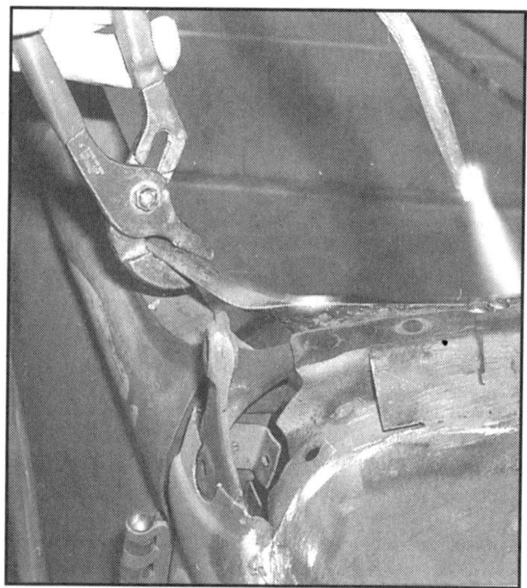

The extra sweeping curve down and to the rear at each end of the dash area took a bit of patience.

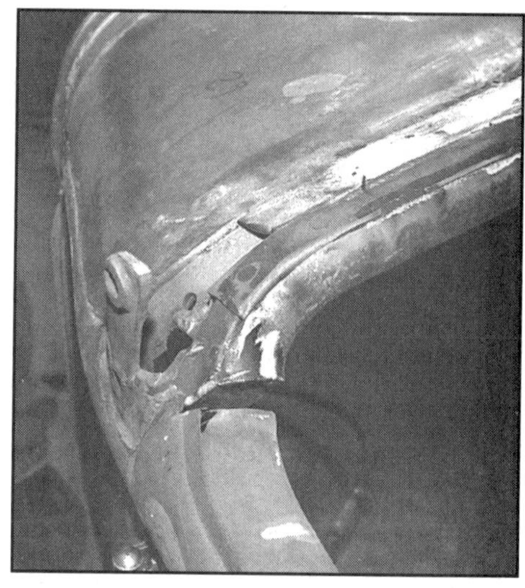

Excess from end of half-round was cut to fit angle of the body where it met the door.

Very little filler was needed where half-round was welded to body.

What little filling needed was supplied by lead, a better choice in high-stress areas. Shaping is done carefully with vixen files.

Then, down the road 75 miles to the nearest metal supply house where 16-guage sheetmetal was trimmed, with the edges bent with a lip. Back at the ranch, the metal pieces fit perfectly, with the trunk floor bent to fit the frame kickup. I used an Eastwood metal shrinker to run along the "broke" edges of the trunk panel, effectively curving the panel as I progressed. Took about 5-minutes and the 'broke" edges then fit snugly to the wheelwell panels.

With the pieces in place it was apparent there was going to be some 'oil canning' of the large flat panels. So, I also have an Eastwood bead roller (most any sheetmetal shop will have such a roller), with this I rolled some beads in the panels to make them stiffen. With everything in place, I then went back to the metal supplier and had some hat-section cross braces made up. Everything was then tack-welded to get it solid.

I don't know about you, but I absolutely hate the grunge work on anything, but I particularly dislike it with metal. Probably a holdover from my teenage years in my dad's body/fender shop. But this is stuff that must be done to have a rod body right, even a daily driver. Not the surface stuff, like the major body panels, but the down and dirty gunk such as the body framing. It has to be right.

In the case of my '31 Model A body, about half the framework lower side rails were savable. I couldn't find better ones anywhere, and I couldn't make new ones fit the projected budget. So, I

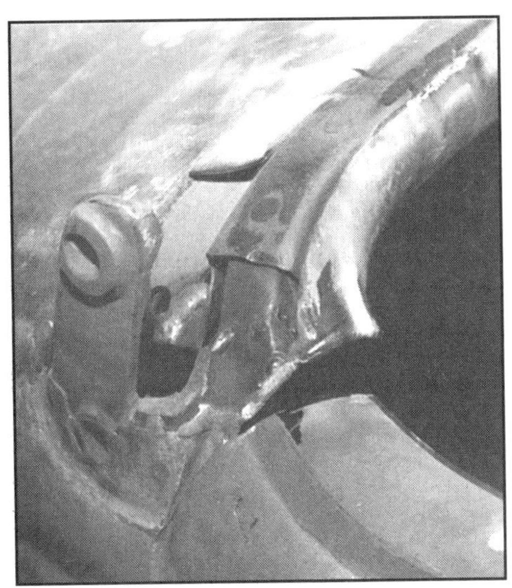

With the cowl rolled, a big gap remains on the door front edge.

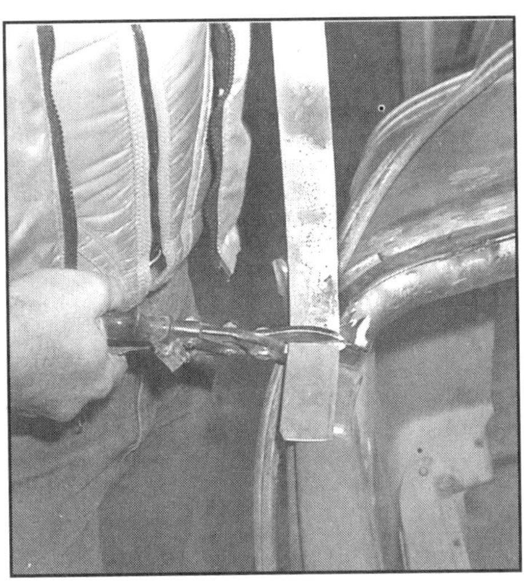

Strips of sheetmetal were trimmed to fit the door gap, then tack-welded in place until the desired shape was attained.

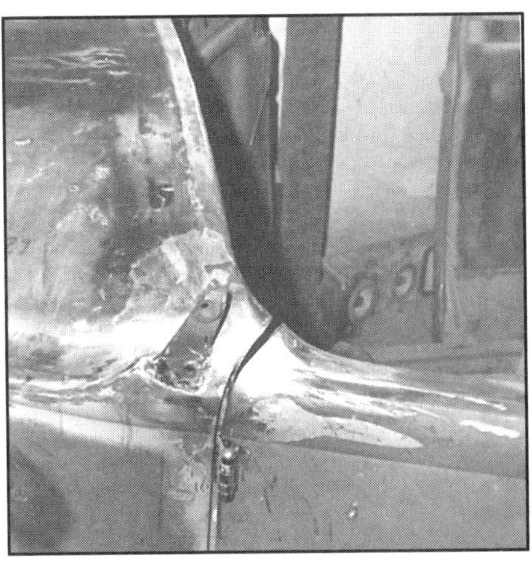

Again, small amount of lead filler added to the sheetmetal buildup and the door edges swoop up and into the cowl roll.

patched the rails together with 14 through 18-gauge metal.

The lower body sections were rusted so that a complete set of patch panels would be needed, cowl/door/and quarter. I found a discarded coupe on a nearby farm, but the coupe panels are different. Besides, they were rusty as well. On the phone to Wescott again and they sent UPS by with a complete set of patch panels for under $100. A bargain.

When doing panel patch work, you will learn how to do it, but not rapidly. When I did these repairs, I had been working metal sporadically for 50-years. Had I been doing them today, I would have opted for the new metal panel glues that bodymen are using. Makes much more sense on a driver, maybe even for top-drawer show cars. Anyway, I used my Daytona MIG to do two different types of repairs. One would be the common butt-weld, the other the flange repair.

To control any distortion when welding, use a series of spot-welds, and this is much better if you use the MIG. A trick I learned from Cincinnati customizer Larry Kramer is to make the spot-tacks, then weld from the panel rear. This way the weld penetrates the butt-weld gap, but leaves the larger bead build-up on the backside. Not as much grinding required. Of course, not so much a concern with the lap-weld. In the accompanying photos I'll spend a bit more time on this because so many rodders fear making patch repairs, yet it is only a matter of patience.

Once the patch panels were all final welded, there remained some metal shrinking to do. I won't even go into how this is done here, that is covered in length in some metal fabricating books. But I'll include a couple of photos showing a few places the '31 body needed massaging. Oh, the body needed thorough massaging everywhere, but it started with some metal shrinking.

Then I started to get cute. I wanted a rolled cowl lip, more like a '32 Ford. Let me digress a moment. Years ago, during the stone ages of WW II, I worked in my dad's body shop in northern California. He did a lot of custom and race car body stuff, and he flush mounted a number of Model A doors so that the door fit into the body at the rear door edge. I started to do this with the Dawg, then decided I would rather leave a tattle-tell or two just to smooz the troops. Just enough little tips that this was a Model A, not a '32. But I did want the rolled cowl.

Off to that far away metal supply store for some 1-inch half-round bar stock. The Model A cowl dash flange is flat. I welded the mid-point of a length of half-round to the mid-point of the dash flange, then with a humongous gas torch flame I began heating the bar stock and bending it in a curve to match the cowl. At either end, I then made a nice little bend toward the door, which gives a flowing curve much like the deuce cowl. Pieces of sheetmetal were used to fill the gap between half-round and the cowl lip.

The top front area of the doors is straight on the Model A. I snipped up lengths of sheetmetal and fashioned a curve so the door tops flowed into the curve of the cowl lip. All of this took about 2-hours. No biggie, it really improves the dash area, and it is just another little tweak to fool the experts. Oh yeah, I had cut out the Model A gas tank and filled the cowl filler neck hole.

A SHIELD IN TIME

I won't get detailed about building the Junkyard Dawg windshield. It is something that might be more of a pro job, but with patience anyone can make a frame. If you go back to the earliest photos of hot rods, you'll note that a common practice of the Thirties and Forties was to lean the roadster windshields back. Later, the same practice was applied to closed rods running at the lakes and Bonneville. Reason: a barn door sheds more air if it leans away from that wind. At the same time, this lends a rather rakish look to the vehicle. Makes it look faster.

I am not a particular fan of the stock windshield rake on any of the earlier rod-suitable bodies, so I didn't even consider a stock windshield for the Dawg. At first I mocked up a split motorboat-DuVall type 'shield, but that just didn't seem to do the job. Then, at an Oakland Roadster Show I saw one of the really neat high-buck cars with a one-piece curved and reclined windshield. Got me to thinking of the windshield on my old l954 Austin Healey. That was the shape I wanted.

So, I started on my cardboard mock-up again. This time I made a cardboard pattern of the center portion of a mid-'70s GM pickup. It seemed to be

Left—At first, a split-style windshield was anticipated; some post mock-ups were fashioned.

The final windshield frame was more like what some contemporary aftermarket roadster windshields are. Glass is cut down mid-section from 70's era GM pickups; posts are made from sheet stock.

Tex Smith, right, shows exhaust Guru Jerry Jardine how the new tubing lakes-style header must exit over the left framerail. Tex was smart enough to then walk away while Jerry performed his magic.

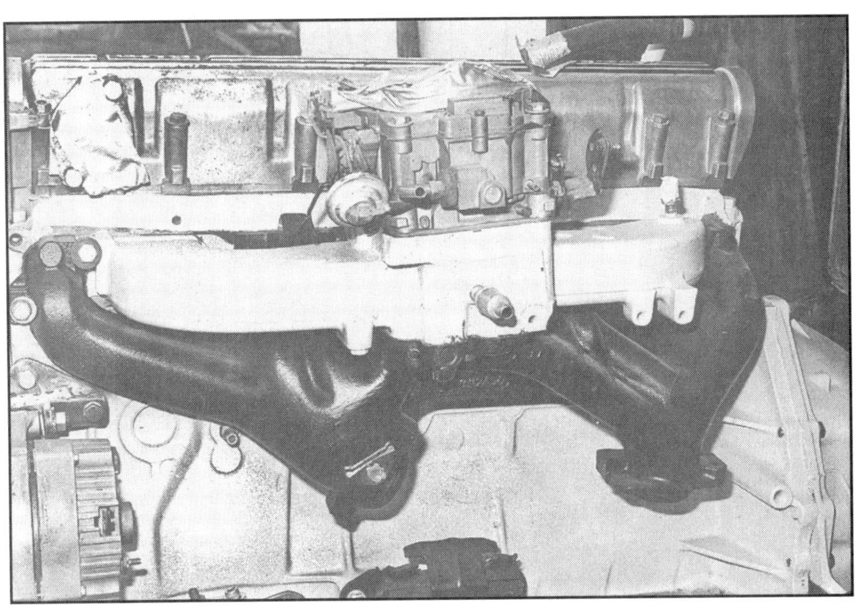

The high performance 1969 Pontiac OHC inline-six engine used a four-barrel carburetor and cast-iron split exhaust manifold.

Jardine started the program by looking through Inventory of tubing to get pieces needed. His decades of experience made short work of a tricky job.

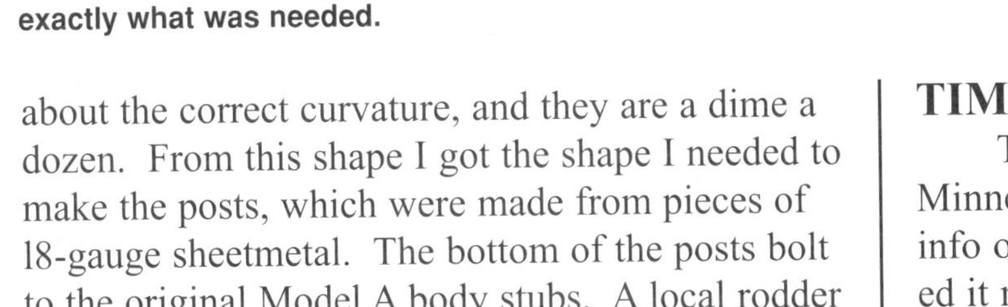

Right—Perhaps the most difficult part of the header build was finding an aftermarket head flange, turned out that Headers by Ed in Minnesota had exactly what was needed.

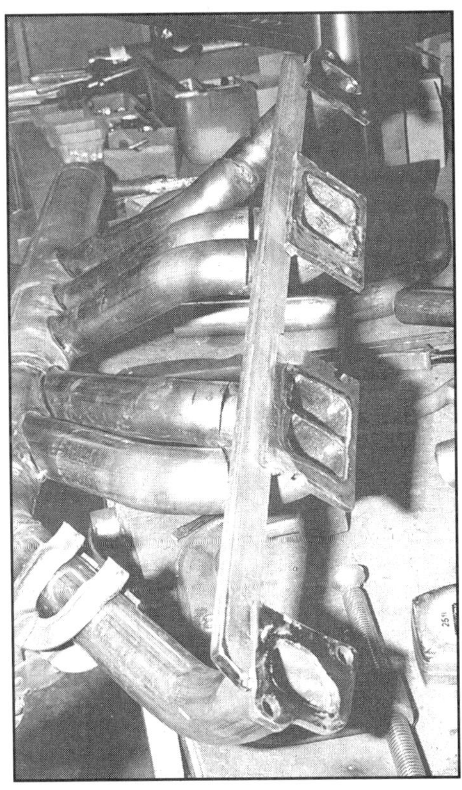

about the correct curvature, and they are a dime a dozen. From this shape I got the shape I needed to make the posts, which were made from pieces of 18-gauge sheetmetal. The bottom of the posts bolt to the original Model A body stubs. A local rodder who is a windshield fixer-upper whittled out the GM pickup glass center section, and I had a shield that really works great. It cuts air turbulence in the cockpit tremendously and it is far and away superior to the stock flat screen.

TIME TO POWER UP

That year, I talked to Dave Ubl from Minnesota at the salt flats. He was a fountain of info on the inline Pontiac engine, just when I needed it most. When I was hanging around the Hot Rod Magazine offices in Hollywood, Ray Brock came in one day with an article about the then-new Pontiac overhead-cam inline-six engine. I have always been a fan of six-cylinder inlines…and four-bangers, and V12's and radials. You get the

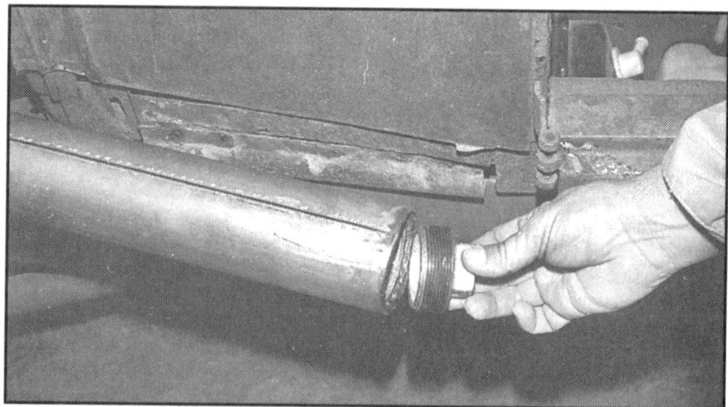

Above—Concerned over what to use for the collector end, Tex said to use an ordinary plumbing plug!

Left—Head-pipes needed to sweep downward immediately after exiting the head, then roll to rear for entry into collector pipe.

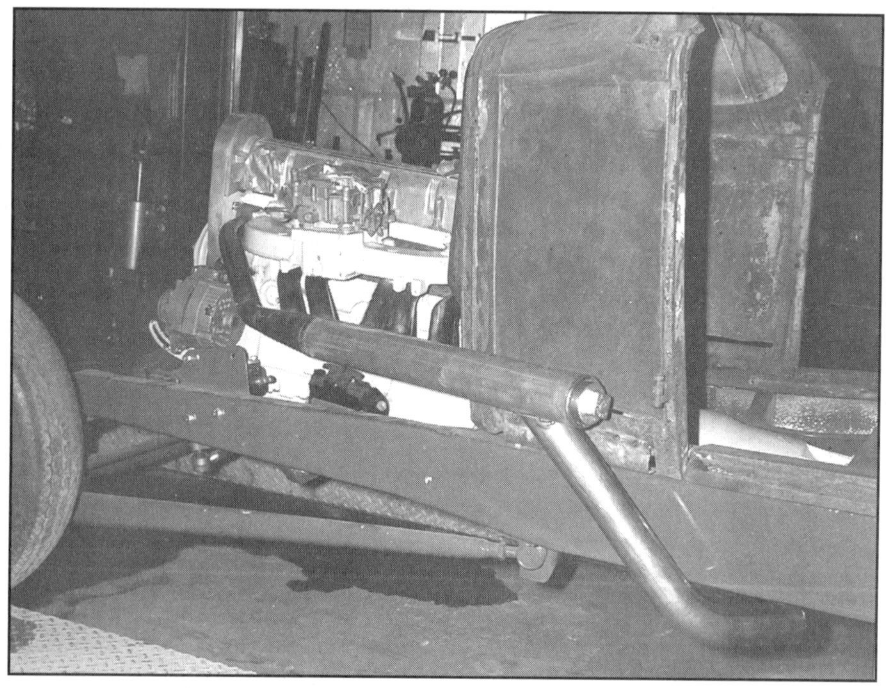

Above—A bracket was made to hold the alternator low and away from the header yet high enough to clear the Vega steering box.

Left—With collector plug installed, exhaust is diverted to pipe sweeping under the frame into a turbo muffler.

idea. I'm an engine dude. Any kind of engine.

Even so, I wasn't blown away back then by the Pontiac OHC. Just a Chevy six with the cam on top. So, when I got a chance to buy a swap meet six for the Dawg, it was more out of curiosity and finances than expectations. Turns out I was way wrong on that last bit.

The engine I bought was the high performance model, with four-barrel carb and factory split cast-iron headers. It would probably have worked fine, but in talking with Jack Clifford (the inline-six Chevy Guru) before he died, he said to get the best performance I should use tubing headers. Hey, cool, because it just so happened that Jerry Jardine of Jardine header fame had recently moved to my neighborhood of Jackson Hole, Wyoming.

I had done some of the first stories on Jerry's trick exhaust while at Hot Rod Magazine way back when. The perfect guy for the roadster project. All of his work is covered in the photos included here. Except for the HPC coating that was sprayed on in Salt Lake City. To date, after all these thousands of miles, the exhaust is just fine.

As for the engine and transmission, I have changed to a 700-R4 automatic trans, and this is great for getting better highway mileage. If I keep below 75mph, I get as high as 26mpg, but if I go above that mileage can drop to around 20mpg. Top speed, taking into account the 30-inch rear tire diameter and 4:10 rear gear and the approximate

25-percent overdrive, is just a bit over 100mph.

Is there more grunt in the beast. Oh yes. Clifford wanted me to use some of his stuff to bring the engine up to 294 cubes. Nah, fun where it is. But that four-barrel carb is kind of dorky, so last time in Australia I found a triple Weber side-draft setup from a Ford inline-six. These are very common performance items over there, on Ford, Holden (GM), and Mopar. Turns out Clifford's company used to make a three Weber manifold for the Pontiac OHC, and they found one lurking on a back shelf. So, still playing with the engine.

TOPPING IT OFF

I had painted the chassis Porsche red before installing the primered body, and the seat was found in the back of a VW sedan (at the local dump). I made up a dash from some swap meet stuff, and the steering column was from an abandoned Mopar big thing (same tilt/tele as GM products), connecting to a Vega gearbox. One of the very first Painless Performance wiring kits was used, but I had to rely heavily on buddy Ron Ceridono to get all those wires in place, because I am an idiot with electronics.

I made some nerf bars front and rear from solid steel round stock, as well as an old "shaker screen" headlight bar. I cut the original light mounts off the shock mounts, then I had a handful of things chrome plated. Not much, because of cost.

Along the line I had changed the grille shell from the Ford commercial unit to a '34-35 Chevy unit I found in a farm field. Kinda looks more funky. A local potato-truck radiator guy made up a great radiator with a 4-inch core he had laying around, using Model A tanks that I had. One day Ceridono helped me bend up a hood top using a 6-inch pipe that was embedded in cement to keep truckers from knocking over our shop doors. The hood sides were fit, with the left one being cut away to clear the lakes type header. Then I measured up where I figured the louvers would go, and metal genius Chris Boggess from Salt Lake City only laughed at my efforts for half an hour before fixing the lines and punching the louvers. Apparently I'm not very good with mechanical

A set of swap meet top irons has been constructed with after-market wood bows and windshield header. Note how far ahead of the custom windshield stock header bar is.

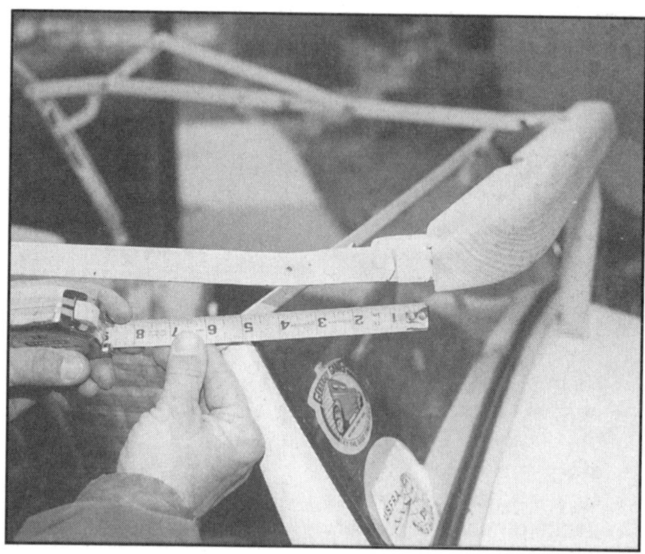

This is an indication of how much rear rake is in the windshield.

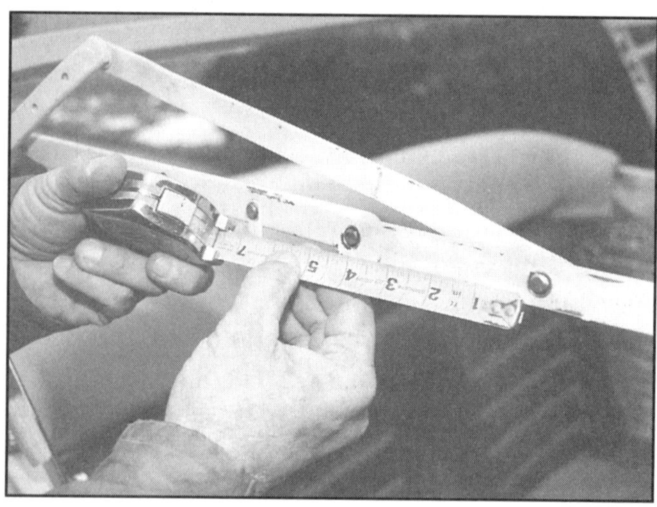

The extra length was taken from each forward side-section where it attached to the folding mid-point.

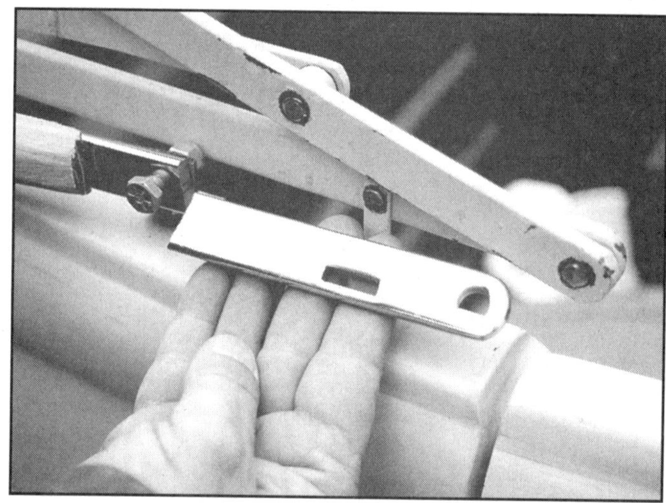

This much of the main bow upright was removed during the chopping process.

It was cut-and-try engineering all the way to have a chopped roadster top that would still fold with the bows and header fitting behind the seat California roll.

Part of the cut-and-try is making sure the top profile remains what is wanted, in this case Tex insisted that the back panel had to lean forward slightly, so for the unit to fold the body pivot point had to be carefully determined.

Once the top mechanism was correct, masking tape was run lengthwise to get an idea of the top shape, then everything was rolled into the Idaho spring sunshine and a fabric cover started. Industrial sewing machines can often be rented.

First order of business was to make up top patterns from heavy paper, then the fabric was cut slightly oversize and trimmed for best fit.

Above—Rear of top was sewn and installed between body and rear top bow first, then side panels were trimmed and put in place.

Right—Big top panel was cut and rolled edge sewn in place, then the top and side panels were marked with chalk so alignment during sewing would be correct.

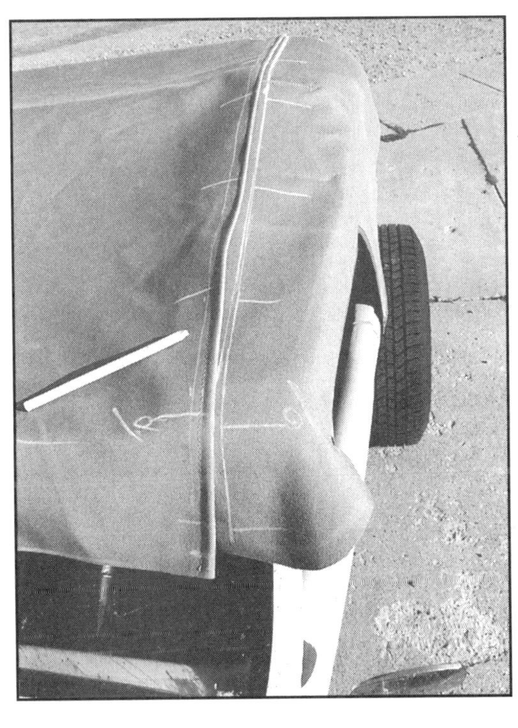

drawing, either.

To this point in time I had a genuine, running and funning titled as a 1932 Ford roadster at the total cost of $1980. Plus a bunch of personal labor and help from friends. The tires were sorta new car takeoffs, the red VW seat upholstery had been repainted to a tan, and a local upholstery shop had stitched up a California roll around the passenger compartment rear section. The body was in light grey primer and I was having a ball driving everywhere in the country.

But my wife Pegge wasn't having as much fun, because in our advancing years the sun was beginning to take a toll. Thus, one year at the Portland, Oregon swap meet I lucked on a set of late '31 Model A top irons for a pittance. These I cut down to the correct height and made up a wooden header to fit my windshield. Found two rear top wood bows, and started to stitch up a top. That's when I phoned buddy Tom Medley (you know, Stroker McGurk. My best fishing pal. Rod & Custom Guru. Great custom upholsterer.

With Tom's phone directions, I went about cutting and sewing some tan top canvas, using an old Phaff industrial machine I had located for only a few bucks, right in my hometown. Some side

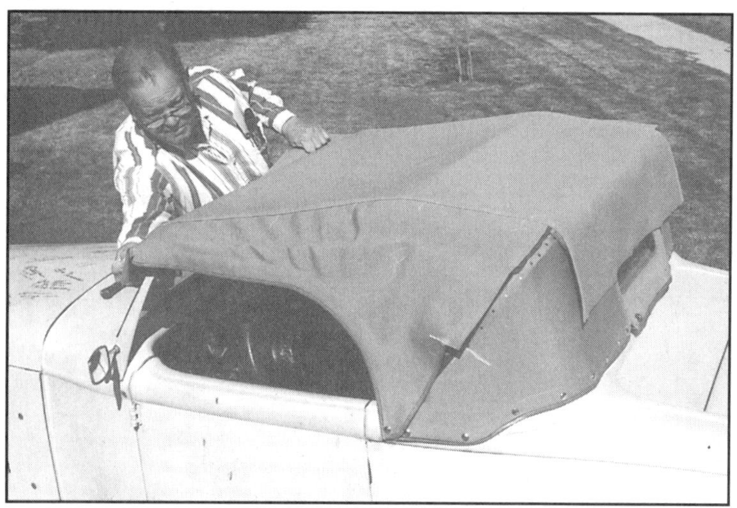

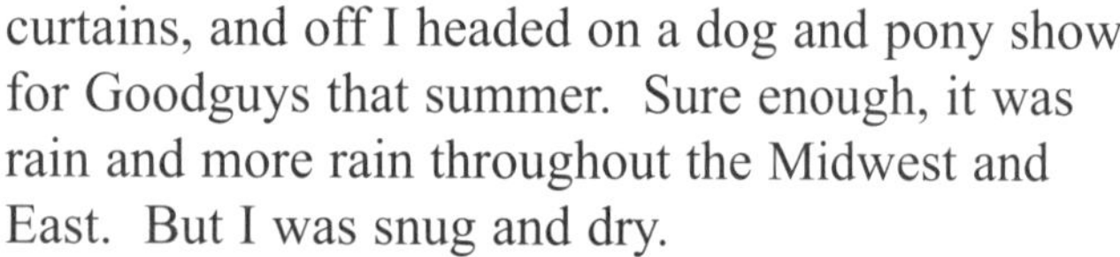

With top panel sewed to side panels, window opening was rolled and sewn, then top piece was put in place and tacked to the rear bow. The fabric was then pulled taut over front lip of windshield header and tacked in place. Tacks are copper so they won't rust. A piece of Hide-em welt is then used to cover the tack strips.

Above—The acid test was to see if the completed top would fold as intended. Yep.

Below—Next test was to see how hard it would be to enter/exit with the top up. Hmmm, a study in contortionism, but with side curtains it's dry and snug.

curtains, and off I headed on a dog and pony show for Goodguys that summer. Sure enough, it was rain and more rain throughout the Midwest and East. But I was snug and dry.

Then, I started making some running improvements, which is the way any bonafide basic hot rod should evolve. I replaced the stock Vega steering box pitman arm with some kind of longer arm from another GM. Made the steering ratio much quicker and a ton better to drive. Brand new radials all around helped another ton, and I decided that my swap meet wheel covers

Dressed in light grey primer and red chassis, the Junkyard Dawg did several years of service with little more than oil changes. Note the hubcaps in this photo.

For a proposed summer trip to Americruise with the ailing missus aboard, a Vintage Air A/C was installed.

Pilot quarters in the Junkyard Dawg are traditional to the extreme, with flat aluminum panel holding Moon gauges, small-diameter Champ car steering wheel. The collection of windshield stickers says it all about heritage.

On a trip to Australia, the intrepid Tex found a set of triple Weber carbies for a Ford inline-six. Webers are quite common at swap meets downunder, stateside Jack Clifford's company supplied the very last Pontiac OHC Weber carb manifold the company produced, this combination is in place now.

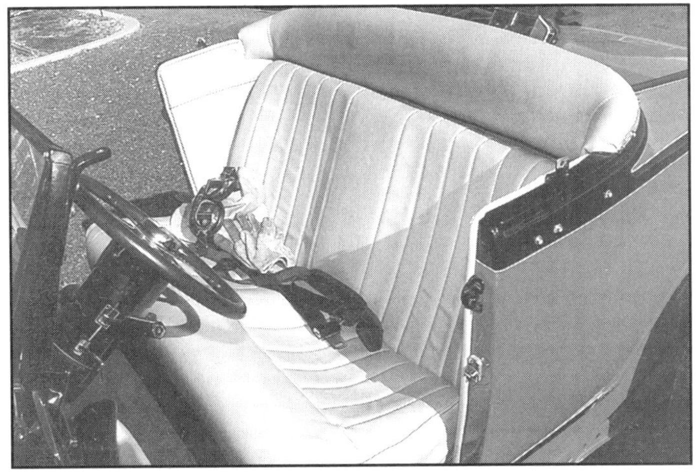

Seat is a cutdown rear seat from some kind of VW sedan; goggles and flight helmet are required wear with top down.

sucked. I had been striking out on anything from the swap meets to fit the Volvo wheels, when I remembered years and years before when Dean Moon had made up a set of his spun aluminum wheel discs for my go-kart. To the phone, and sure enough the company still makes 'em. I got some 8-inch diameter units and they work perfect on the Volvo wheels. Someday I may even go for some old Halibrand type slotted mages, which would be in keeping with the looks of the car. Providing the swap meet price is right.

Ceridono had been building his SpeedRodder channeled Deuce roadster as the Nineties wore down (a series in Street Rodder magazine), and when it was finished Bill Smith at Speedway Motors asked Ron to bring it to Lincoln, Nebraska during the very next Rod & Custom magazine

Americruise. Ron thought that Pegge and I should come along in the Dawg. But I knew that Pegge would not be able to handle the heat, so I whipped up a Vintage Air A/C from parts laying about the garage. We did the trip in July and never once used the air.

THE COUP D'GRACE

No, that should be Roadster, shouldn't it? Anyway, in 1999, my wife Pegge and I decided to fly down to Australia and be the guests of Larry O'Toole. Larry publishes the Australian Street Rodder magazine and has camped out with us for years on his annual treks to the NSRA Nats. We always do the salt SpeedWeek, and he had been hammering for me to come do Lake Gairdner with him. That's the OZ salt flats.

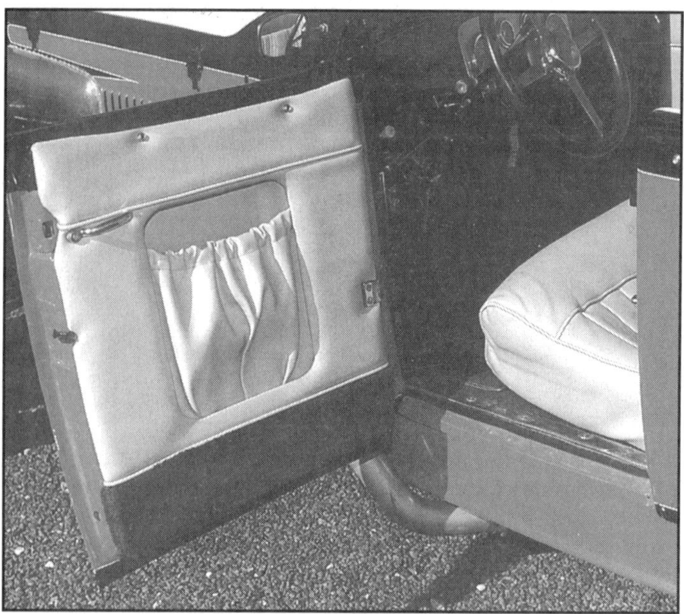

First thing you learn about a basic hot rod is that storage room is vital. Even in the door cavity, which is where ladies keep essentials and men carry survival supplies.

Right—Hood of the Dawg is most distinctive feature. Originally meant only as a pattern for a later aluminum unit, the hood attracted Bonneville legends to sign their names. Some other people of note were also asked to sign. Fading of some of the signatures occured and the signers are no longer with us. When Carl Brunson finally painted the body, this centerpiece was preserved.

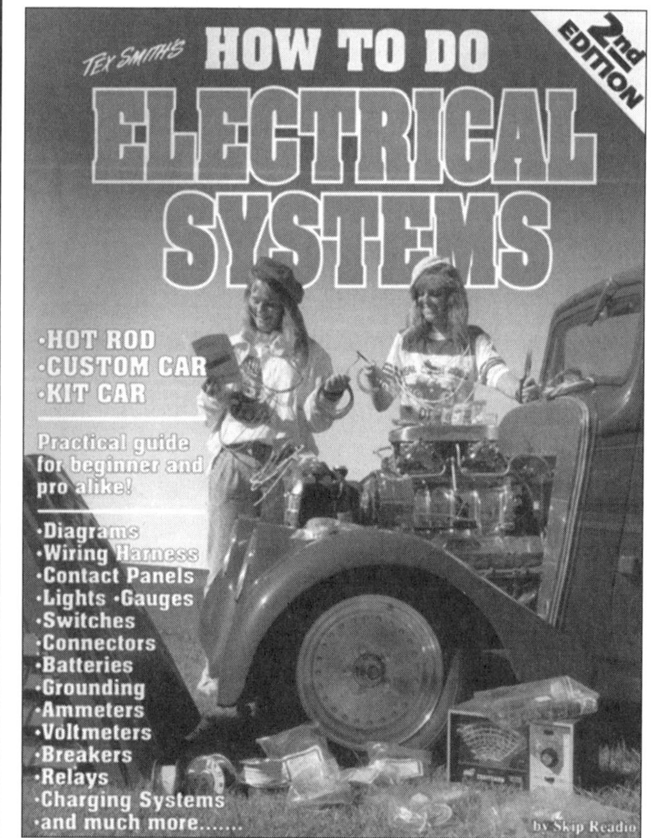

How to Do Electrical Systems

This book takes the mystery out of the complexity of hot rod and custom car electrical systems. Anyone can use this book to wire and troubleshoot practically any special built car with its easy to read diagrams and practical tips. This book includes wiring schematics for a myriad of accessories common to contemporary or custom rods as well as a troubleshooting section which make it an invaluable onboard companion for every builder. The guide to small electrical repairs or complete wiring systems, whether from a kit or completely from scratch.

Hot Rod Library, Inc
12 North Main St. C-3
Veyo, UT 84782
Toll Free: (800) 513-8133

Just after going on the road, the Dawg couldn't resist a fireplug in Tex's hometown.

Again, note the hubcaps in this early photo and Tex's beaming smile for another fun filled summer before Idaho snows set in.

At the car's second home, the Bonneville salt flats is where the Junkyard Dawg basic hot rod really struts. Note the Moon go-cart hubcaps and shiny finish.

This is one rod at home wherever it appears, and it is everywhere in America. This photo was taken at the annual Las Vegas rockabilly fest, which has dozens of funky dressed people and great bands.

So, Pegge and I drove down to Las Vegas and I trailered the roadster so Carl Brunson could spray on a new coat of primer. The car was looking a tad grungy. What I didn't know was that as we left for the airport, Pegge lagged behind and whispered to Carl "Paint it."

Well, there went the old image out the window. When we came home some six weeks later, Carl rolled a bright red car with black scallops out of his shop. Shock city. He had even done a massage of all the sheet metal. Which meant that in keeping with my new status as a painted car owner, I had to scrounge around for a reasonably priced tan nauga upholstery job. Ceridono figured I had moved on to the show car crowd for sure.

It is in this state of being that the Junkyard Dawg remains. It is driven constantly with very little maintenance or attention. Just get in and drive. On occasion, but not so much that the car might become spoiled, the Dawg is washed. After each and every session of driving on the salt flats, it sits over the lawn sprinkler for a couple of days to wash away any residual salt.

Dependable? Absolutely. Funky? Yep. Great to drive? About as good as they get, and it is comfortable. I sit down behind the windshield, with almost no wind turbulence. The only change I anticipate now is reducing brake pedal effort by adding power. Otherwise, see you down the blue line highway!

Powertrain. Engines/trans/rearends

By Jim Clark

Choosing the best combination for your project.

SELECTING A BASIC POWERTRAIN

Keeping with the theme of this book, wherein the guide is that Enough-Is-Enough and Too-Much is often way too much, the same criteria applies to a sufficient powertrain. Sufficient and significant are not the same thing. If the car has been carefully planned, part of the equation has been to decide how much horsepower is enough, how much of that horsepower can be put to the road, and how economy (initial and ongoing costs) will be affected. On the other hand, it seems to be the penchant for most hot rod enthusiasts to believe that when it comes to horsepower, enough is never enough!

During the first considerations of engine/transmission/rearend the builder of a basic rod or custom too often envisions a massive amount of power with lots of visual goodies such as chrome plating and superchargers. Kind of a dream time wish list. At the same time reality says that the used engine and transmission languishing in the garage corner must be utilized. Form (the rod) follows function (the cost). Even with such constraints, it is very possible to have a basic rod that will boil the hides on a whim and still give great reliability and decent gas mileage.

Which really is the neat thing about a basic hot rod. You don't need to mortgage your life to enjoy one.

This is the New Millennium, for hot rodding that means we do not have to use powertrains from the 1920s to have a Real Hot Rod. Not even grunt motors from the Fifties or Sixties. A good basic hot rod can have anything from a Model C Ford four-banger to a new V10 or a 400-horse riceburner. This is what immediately sets a basic rod apart from a Nostalgia ride or a Rat Rod, yet the same basic hot rod can use any kind of antique engine the owner wants. Which is why so many high profile rodders want such a car in their stable.

ENGINES: FOUR-BANGERS

American hot rodding was founded on the four-cylinder engine. Not because there were no options, but because the four-bangers were plentiful, simple to understand and modify, and inexpensive. Too, during the infancy of the American automotive industry, there was a huge amount of

The Studebaker V8 engine was one of the very first OHV designs of the early 1950s to find wide favor as an engine swap. It was small in dimensions and light in weight.

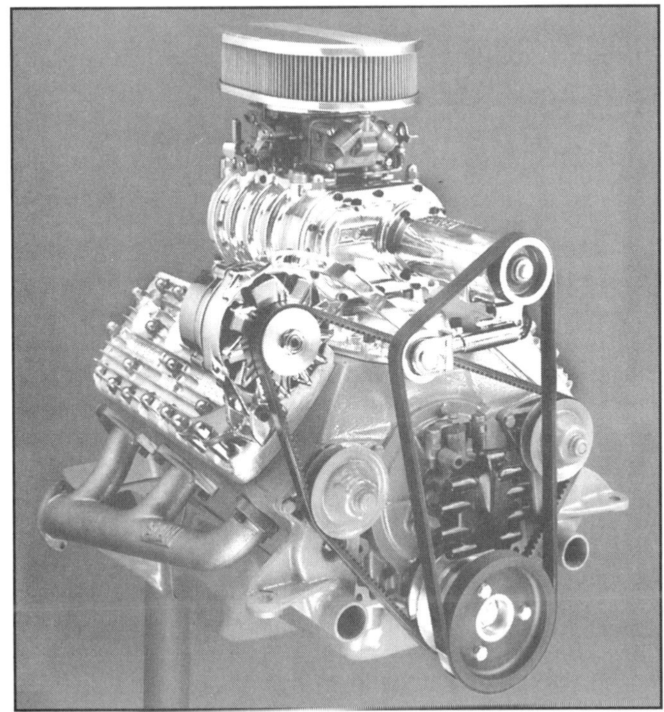

Four examples Above & Left—The Ford flathead V8 is the very essence of hot rodding, and it has achieved a popularity today that would rival the late Forties. It is especially popular when mated to a Ford C4 automatic or one of the modern 4-speed trannies.

The four-cylinder Ford engine has a new group of camp followers, since the Model A design can be made to live at highway speeds and the B/C design takes very well to modification.

cross-pollination among inventors, designers, and engineers. Consequently, interchange was common practice. At the same time, the fours appearing in the late teens were smaller in size and weight than the 800 cubic inch behemoths they succeeded.

There has been renewed interest in the Models A-B-C Ford four-cylinder engines in recent years, although a cadre of restorers and rodders have worked with the Dearborn product for years. In fact, the Ford four maintained supremacy at the dry lakes until the Ford flathead V8 came into being. A basic hot rod, especially the lakes modified style, is especially well suited to this engine.

At the same time, there is a very wide selection of more modern fours that are actually superior to the early Ford units. Examples would be the Pinto, the GM fours from the sixties, and even some great imports such as Fiat. Too, the lowly VW air cooled four can be made to produce prodigious power, while the small Asian front-wheel-drive fours are now producing upwards of 400 hp. German, English, French and Scandinavian four-cylinder engines are a good starting point, as well. In a time when gasoline prices escalate, the hot four-banger engine is looking more and more desirable to many rod builders.

SIXES

Although the American V8 engine reigns supreme in the fancy of rod builders worldwide, there is a great deal to recommend the six-cylinder, as either an inline or a V6 version. A few rodders worked some prodigious magic with the inline sixes during the late Forties and early nineteen fifties, the best known were Chevy and GMC truck types. These inlines were highly favored as high-torque workhorses in the American south, and they could often be modified to regularly outperform V8s. That continues through today.

What is not so well known about the inline design is that there were some excellent versions from other manufacturers, such as Studebaker, Hudson, Chrysler, Ford, etc. These were largely the flathead designs, and some were famous for stubborn reliability rather than for any performance potential. Still, there was a modicum of aftermarket bolt-on equipment made for a wide range of inline sixes; a fact not lost on nostalgia rod builders. The Ford flathead six, those of an earlier

Chrysler inline sixes are not nearly as well known as those are from GM, but the slant-six became famous as being indestructible. The flathead MoPars were all good, except for the Plymouth, which gained fame as a flat crank special!

Obviously, the small-block Chevrolet V8 became an overnight hot rodder choice in l955 and has remained so since. The price of an engine rebuild kit tells it all, with the little Chevy components about half the price of anything else.

Cadillac OHV engines of the Fifties and Sixties were always kind of upper crust in rodding circles of the day, in a basic rod they still invoke a kind of status denied the more mundane pavement cruncher.

The GM fours such as produced for Pontiac and the Chevy 2 make excellent banger motors for any basic rod. They take supercharging very well.

Above & Right—The Chevy (any GM) big block engine has plenty of grunt from cubic inches, but it is also heavier and larger in every dimension.

Above & Left—The Oldsmobile V8 of the Fifties is a good one for rodding, since it can easily be bored to over 400 cubic inches. It also has a penchant for running very cool behind early Ford and Chevy radiators.

Above & Top—The best known V8 from Chrysler Corporation is the Hemi, introduced in 1949, and used in Chrysler-DeSoto-Dodge cars for many years. These engines come in several different displacements, and the outer dimensions vary widely. The design has been updated several times through recent years.

Above—Chrysler small-block engines were offered in a wide range of sizes and had a lot of speed equipment available for them, though less than the little Chevys.

design with a separate intake manifold, can be made into good performers. With modern transmissions, overdrives, and better rearend gears, the sixes are great for basic hot rods.

There are a lot of non-American inline-six-cylinder engines that work great in rods and customs, the best known being the overhead cam Jaguar. But in Australia the inline six is the base engine for production cars of moderate size, with GM and Ford long term advocates. Since the 1960s, Chrysler has been known for an outstanding hemi-head inline six that was a design carryon of the slant six. Some of these Aussie inlines feature flow-through heads, and they are known for excellent horsepower and torque curves.

The V6 engine made its first big impression with street rodders during the first gas crunch of 1974. All of a sudden, modern fours such as the Chevy 2 and the Pontiac were everywhere in an attempt to beat the pump gas prices, but the V6 was the way to go. Granted, the loss of 2-cylinders can be a bitter pill for the tire smoking crowd, but this engine design has some plusses as well, such as reduced weight and engine length. There is a big supply of V6 engines in American junkyards, so the prices are favorable.

EIGHTS

American rodders tend to think of any eight-cylinder engine as being a V-configuration, but there were plenty of inline eights made up into the 1950s. Unfortunately, most of these are long, heavy, and not known to sip fuel. On occasion, a Buick straight-eight OHV or a Packard flathead eight will show up in a basic rod.

It is the V8 engine that predominates the

Above—The big Buick V8s introduced in the late sixties offered all of the brute torque of the other GM behemoths but filled up the engine bay on most anything they were installed in. The most successful of these were the ones built by Kenne-Bell.

Above Right & Right—The Nailhead Buick, identifiable by the vertical rocker covers, offered all of the torque provided by the other long-stroke V8s introduced at the time but fit in narrow engine compartments almost as well as the small-block Chevy. It's major drawback was the left side starter location that often interfered with early steering box types that mounted to the left frame rail.

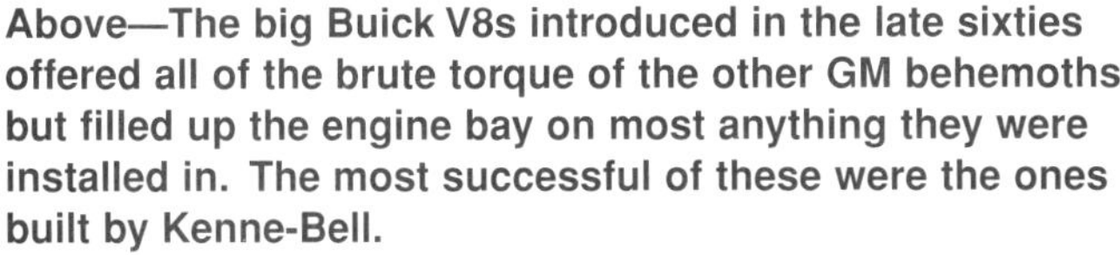

Below & Below Right—The GM series inline-six-cylinder engines are longer than most V8s, but they have been favorites of some rod and custom builders since the l930s. The GMC six is especially favored, and there is still some power equipment available at swap meets.

Above & Right—Small-block Fords were comparable to the small Chevy V8s but the front distributor and oil pump location made the deeper front sump in the pan interfere with many front suspension systems.

Bigger displacement Ford V8s were good engines but their size and weight were major drawbacks. These earlier versions had the distributor and oil pump at the rear.

When money is no object exotic engines like this Ferrari can be used to create a unique combination.

Newer 4-cylinders like this GM Quad 4 provide lightweight cars with dazzling performance and economy in a modern high-tech package.

In an attempt to save fuel during the many gas crunches rod builders turned to alternatives like the air-cooled Corvair and this Volkswagen to power lightweight rides.

Straight-8 Buicks offered plenty of power and loads of torque but their length made them too long for most applications. This example has a home-built dual turbocharging system fabricated from a V6 Grand Sport.

American hot rod scene. These range in size from the diminutive Ford V8-60 to little seen flathead V8s from Cadillac in the Forties, to gargantuan cubic inch monsters now common in drag racing. Of course, the Ford flathead V8 is most often associated with early hot rodding, but by nature the hobby/sport spawns some really interesting variations.

Far and away the basic rod combination that is seen most today is the small-block Chevy 350 with a 350 automatic transmission.

In nostalgia rodding, there is an emphasis on V8s of the Fifties, such as Cadillac, Oldsmobile, Pontiac, Chevrolet, Ford, Studebaker, Packard, Chrysler, DeSoto, Dodge, Plymouth, ad nauseam. These are all overhead valve/short stroke designs, but there is a considerable difference in weights. Too, there are the small-block engines introduced mostly in the early 1960s, as well as the aluminum V8s from GM. The selection of V8 engines is huge, which is why so many different models are showing up in basic rods.

T'OTHERS

Comes today, with some V10s in regular rod use, and even the old Lincoln Zephyr V12 flatheads appearing. Too, there were V16 Cads produced as well as similar engines of now-obscure fame.

All of these are fair game for the basic hot rod builder, because this is really what basic is all about. Pure hot rodding, and that means being creative in the engine compartment. Of course, much of this is also made possible because of the very wide range of good, strong transmissions and rearends produced since 1950.

TRANSMISSIONS

As any older and experienced hot rodder will confirm, the really weak link in early day rod building and racing was the transmission. They were prone to breaking; usually it wasn't a matter of IF but of WHEN. Some of the heavier production cars had better gearboxes, such as the Packard, but getting them adapted was a late-arriving grace that was upstaged by the high performance automatic.

When the automatics started to appear in numbers, companies such as B&M jumped on the bandwagon with performance rated GM Hydra-Matics and Ford Cruise-o-matics. The earliest versions were cast iron and heavy, but they could be made to live, a big plus since Detroit was still concentrating on the three-speed manual. Things began to change as the first American made four-speed manual boxes appeared, and the floor-shift crowd was delighted when hot rodders started to produce overdrive add-on's.

Things in both arenas have continued to improve dramatically, to the point where just about any modern automatic or standard transmission can be mated to virtually any kind of engine. For the basic rod, this means that total reliability can be had for a reasonable cost.

REARENDS

As with the engine and transmission, a contemporary basic hot rod or custom car can utilize a wide selection of final drive components. Although the Ford 9-inch rearend seems to be the most common, the Ford 8-inch is very good. So are the MoPar rears, as well as the GM designs. For today's rod builder, the most obvious starting point is the brake backing plate flange-to-flange measurement, which determines the distance between the rear tires and the body. Since most rearends made after 1955 are capable of handling lots of power, gear and axle strength are not nearly the problem as before.

And, as with the engine, a basic rod can use whatever rearend the builder might choose without the car loosing any of its curb appeal.

KITS: YOUR BASIC CATALOG RIDES

By Jim Clark

BASIC KITS

As pointed out several times, a basic hot rod can be no buck, some buck, or lotsa bucks; it all depends on the financial inclination of the owner.

While there have been starts and stops in the

Curt Hamilton's early T roadster pickup kit.

basic kit car approach to car building, most of these attempts have been directed toward the dune buggy and sports car crowd. In hot rodding, the kit car concept goes back to the early 1960s, when Curt Hamilton and Bud Lang got the fiberglass Model T body in strong production.

Initially, those 'glass bodies were directed toward drag racing applications, but street rod builders grabbed the units for their very own, spurred somewhat with the great success of the TV show 77 Sunset Strip. Norm Grabowski had built a street version of the venerable dry lakes modified roadster, which was used on the TV show, and the idea spread across the nation instantly. The reason was simple: Here was a car that was very simple,

inexpensive to build, and was unmistakably a hot rod. It was about as basic as a rod could be.

Before long, mail-order frames and building components were available, while drag racing front tubing-axles and suspension components were easily adapted to what was rapidly coming to be known as "Fad Cars". The hot rod magazines were full of how-to articles on this type car, and photo features amassed. Car shows came to be dominated by these fiberglass creations. What was not so apparent to the outside spectator, however, was how much fun the Fad Cars were.

These Model T based bodies were used by some of the very early turn-key street rod builders, at one time the Dragmaster Company (of drag racing fame) featured a fiberglass bodied, round tubing framed, small block Chevy driveaway rod for just $5000. It was complete in every way, and a

Mickey Lauria's Total Performance T-bucket kits.

large number of them were produced. Eventually, Mickey Lauria from Connecticut started Total Performance to produce such T's in any form of completion the buyer wanted. These cars continue through today and have come to symbolize the best of what is generically a Fad T.

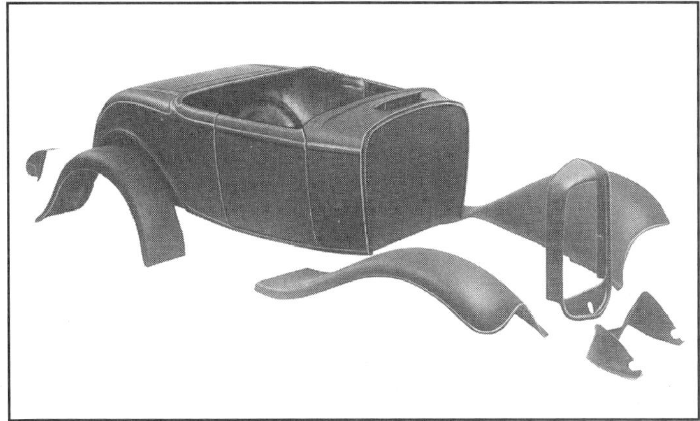

Early Speedway 1932 Ford roadster kit.

Reproduction steel Deuce roadster body from Rod Bods in Carson City, Nevada.

Modern all-steel 1933-34 Ford Cabriolet body from Steve's Restoration in Oregon.

Dee Wescott preping one of his Fiberglass coupe bodys.

In the l950s, Dee Wescott of Oregon began to make Model A parts from fiberglass, perfecting the process into one of the premier manufacturers of larger rod bodies. Today, these Wescott body styles reach into the l940s designs.

Still, it was some years before the fledgling street rod industry began to investigate the larger Ford car bodies, the manufacturers learning as they went on how to package a real kit rod. There have been fits of special kit cars available through the last three decades, but for the most part total production numbers were limited. Today, such kits are available for a surprisingly wide array of hot rod and custom car styles, thanks in large part to the evolution and distribution of l932 and later Ford/Chevy chassis. But as the body and chassis kits become ever more sophisticated, so does the ultimate vehicle cost.

The Model A Ford bodies were followed in short order by l932 and l933-34 Ford bodies. Bill Smith, the legendary owner of Speedway Motors in Lincoln, Nebraska, seized on this parts supply to create his own version of a later Ford kit car. The Speedway 1932 Ford lowboy roadster has been around for years, but has only recently been getting the serious attention from home builders that it should receive.

There are a number of low and high dollar kit cars now available to fit most any bank account, in styles ranging from the type of T that Hamilton and Lang invented to the almost exotic modern Lakes Modifieds as produced by Real Hot Rods and Daryl Zip.

With good bodies widely available and enough mail-order production parts available to create a brand new "old" car, the rod building shops appeared. Some argue that every hot rod these professional builders assemble is still nothing more than an upscale kit car.

But it must be pointed out that a typical kit hot rod, at any price range, is not at all the kind of vehicle called a rat rod, or a scrapper. The kit car is just as basic a hot rod, however, and it offers a great starting point for anyone new to the hobby.

Total Performance

Total Performance, Inc was founded in 1971 by Mickey Lauria. Today, Total Performance, Inc is one of the largest street rod manufacturers in the hot rod industry. They are recognized as the quintessential producer of the Model T hot rod, for both kits and complete cars.

Shown here is a sampling of what they have to offer. Complete information about their full line of products is available on their web site tperformance.com.

Wescott's Auto

Wescott's Auto Restyling was founded in 1954 by Dee Wescott. Early experience with the repair of Corvettes led to the production of fiberglass replacement parts. In 1969 Wescott produced a fiberglass 1931 Ford coupe body in response to a challenge claiming that opening doors were not possible on 'glass cars. In '71 they produced a roadster body, leading to the full line of early Ford bodies and accessories they now offer. Some of those are shown here.

For a catalog displaying the full line plus a large inventory of 1926-48 Ford replacement parts go to their web site wescottsauto.com.

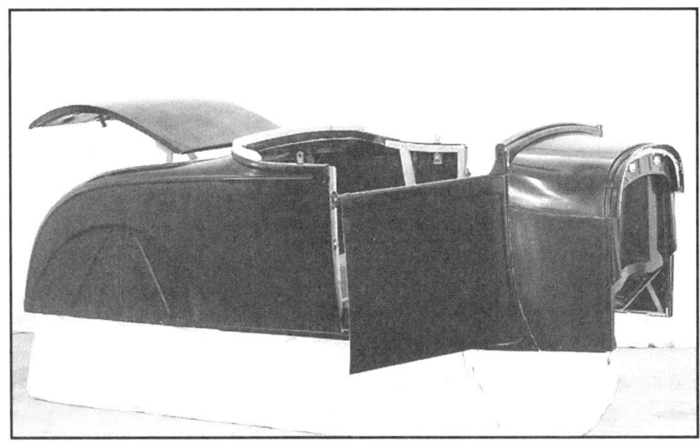

Speedway Motors

Speedway Motors, Inc was founded in 1952 by Bill Smith. Today they are the largest manufacturer, distributor and retail center for the street and hot rod industry. They began producing fiberglass bodies for race cars and the street in 1955. They feature a number of kits including their Lo-Boy '32.

Shown here is a sampling of what they have to offer. Complete information about their full line of products is available on their web site speedwaymotors.com.

New Age Motorsports

New Age Motorsports is a relative newcomer to the street rod industry. They are the manufacturer of fiberglass bodies, chassis and complete turnkey cars. These include a '32 Ford Roadster, three-window coupe, five-window coupe (American Graffiti style) and '34 three-window coupe. They make chassis for all models. Their 'glass bodies are equipped with a full-steel tubing interior skeleton. A feature that adds a lot of rigidity to them while offering an enhanced level of passenger safety.

Shown here is a sampling of what they have to offer. Complete information about their full line of products is available on their web site newage-motorsports.com.

ADAPTS TO
VIRTUALLY
ANY CHASSIS!

ELIMINATES
LEAF SPRINGS

THE ORIGINAL AIR RIDE SUSPENSION!

SPECIFIC VEHICLE AND CHASSIS APPLICATIONS
NUMEROUS APPLICATIONS
LOWERS RIDE HEIGHT
IMPROVES HANDLING

PARALLEL
WITH SHOCKWAVES

THE CHOICE OF
PROFESSIONAL
BUILDERS!

2-WAY AND 4-WAY CONTROL
MODULAR DESIGN
DIGITAL AND ANALOG GAUGES
REMOTE MOUNTING
FASTER RISE TIME

FOR THE REAR

SAME GREAT FEATURES AS OUR
ORIGINAL SHOCKWAVE!
CALL US FOR
SPECIFICATIONS AND DIMENSIONS
FOR YOUR NEXT CHASSIS

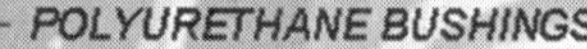

SHOCKWAVE™
by Air Ride Technologies

POLYURETHANE BUSHINGS

ANODIZED BILLET ALUMINUM
CONSTRUCTION

PROVEN-PATENTED
SEALING TECHNOLOGY

FIRESTONE BELLOWS

STAINLESS FASTNERS

QA1 BILLET
ALUMINUM SHOCKS

12 POSITION
ADJUSTABLE VALVING

CALL FOR YOUR FREE CATALOG
TECH AND SALES LINE

812.482.2932

www.ridetech.com

THEN YOU DRIVE 'EM!

I first met Don Dillard somewhere west of Laramie. When I don't remember. Where I don't remember. Probably Bonneville. Or the Pleasanton rod run, or Las Vegas, or somewhere on the east coast. Or down in Australia.

Dillard lives in California, but hundreds and hundreds of hot rodders wouldn't know that because he pops up everywhere, kind of like Bob Klessig of Wisconsin. And he is always in his primered

THE CALIFORNIA FLASH or, There's Dillard...Again!

Model A coupe. But let Don tell the story:

Whenever I hear someone ask for my story, not that it happens all that frequently, I think of Steve Martin in the movie "The Jerk". "My story?, I was born a poor black child…"

I've been a gearhead all my life, even as a kid. My first car in the early '70s was a '36 Ford trunk tudor. Actually calling it a car is kind. A more accurate description would be an ambitious

project. I was in way over my head with that one and never got it close to running under its own power. I added to the parts pile for a couple years and then traded it for a '57 Nomad which was also a bit of a project but one that was within my means and skills to get running in a few weeks. Eventually that gave way to a long string of mid '60s to early '70s MoPars and some occasional drag racing. In late '96 I decided I was tired of all

the anal retentive MoPar resto freaks and I didn't really want to go drag racing every weekend so I sold every MoPar car and part that I owned. Then I went shopping for something that I could have fun with every day.

This '30 Model A coupe was in the local Auto Trader for a reasonable price. The owner had pieced together a rolling chassis with a TCI frame and a bunch of swap meet parts and spare parts from other projects. He had pulled the complete body off a stocker and already had unloaded the stock chassis at the Pomona swap meet. It came with a junkyard '65 327ci Chevy engine and a brand new TH400 transmission. The body had a fresh coat of red oxide on it. With the '55 Chrysler K-H wires and big 'n little radial it almost looked like you could hop in and take it for a spin but there was a lot of work to be done first.

I figured it would take me about 6-months of spare time to get it drivable and true to the usual formula it took closer to a year. A big part of that time was spent rebuilding the engine. I could have purchased 2 or 3 crate engines for the same money but I wanted the engine to retain some vintage flavor. It was wounded pretty badly so, it required quite a bit of machine work to save. It's been reliable as an anvil ever since I put it in the car and it has even survived the recent addition of a Comp Cams 280 Magnum cam and a set of Dart Sportsman 2 heads. I learned how to do a lot of things on this car. Things that I didn't have to do to the later model cars that I'd worked on before

like complete wiring, plumbing, steering, brakes, etc.

Since the body was a pretty nice stocker and it had the Chrysler K-H wires, my original plan was to make it a resto rod. Probably green with black fenders and yellow wheels. I planned to drive it primer for a few months to work the bugs out and then I was going to do the whole paint, polish and upholstery routine. As soon as I realized how much fun I was having driving it the plan changed quickly. I still eventually wanted to do the resto rod thing but the timeframe was going to have to be pushed way out.

Then in '98 when Carps and I were coming back from Pleasanton he took a profile picture of the car. When he got back to Australia he photo-shopped the picture to the way the car looks now and e-mailed it to me. I was sold. The plan immediately changed to make the car look like the pho-toshopped version. The summer of '99 my brother and I chopped it (see chop story) and right before the 2000 LA Roadster show I put the red steelies and WWW tires on it. The look was complete.

It's constantly getting little upgrades and repairs but the plan is to never have it off of the road for more than a few days. There have been a few incidents that have interrupted the fun but it always goes back together better than before. This is hands-down the most fun car I've ever owned. It has been all over the southwestern states and even to Louisville a couple of times. With it I've met some of the coolest people on the planet.

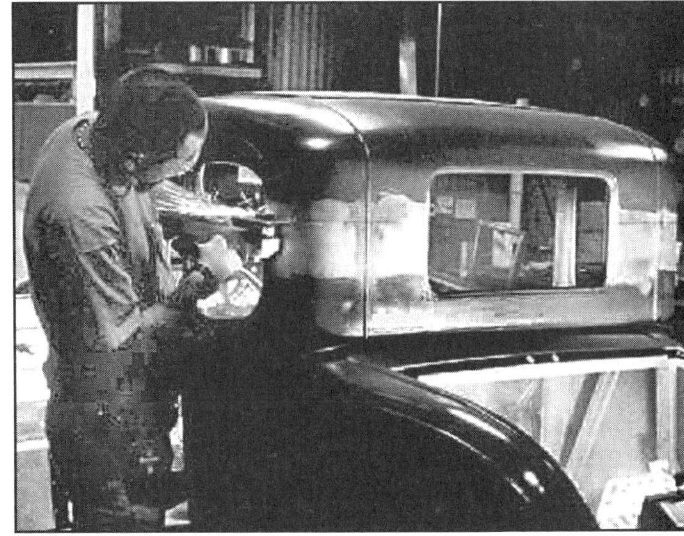

Chopping the Top of a 1930 Ford Coupe

During a family barbecue over the 4th of July weekend in 1999 my youngest brother, Sam (His name is actually Derron, but that's a whole different story), and I conspired to chop my Model A coupe. I asked him how long he thought it would take.

His reply was about 4-hours to cut it and about 4-hours to put it back together.

OK, double that, because everything takes twice as long as you think it's going to when working on a car, and you got 16-hours. Cool, what are you doing next weekend? Let's do it!

The plan was for me to get a spare windshield cut 3-inches during the week. That way we didn't have to mess around with trying to find a glass shop open on Saturday. I would drive the coupe from my house to the shop where he works (185-miles) on Friday, we'd chop it, and then I'd drive it home Sunday evening.

I took several pictures of the process and share them here with you. I must apologize that some of them are a little fuzzy. I was using 800 film indoors, often at night, without a flash. I should have used a tripod to hold the camera steady with the slow shutter speed. Oh well, maybe next time I'll do it right.

Thursday night I used a DA sander to remove the paint from the area that would be cut and welded.

I left my house about 1:00pm Friday and drove up to the thriving metropolis of Lindsay, CA (pop. 8924). Got here about 4:00pm. The drive was without incident in spite of the temp in the high 90s. With all the window glass removed except the windshield (which was cranked all the way open) it was quite breezy. I kept the speed to around 65-70-mph (most of the time anyway) and

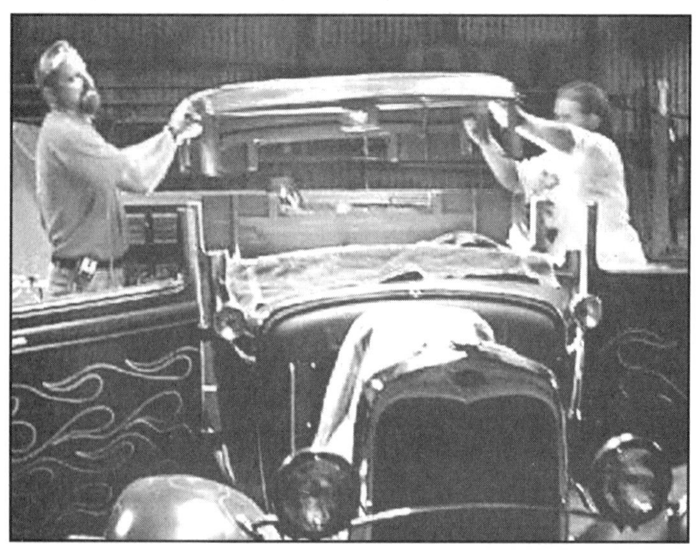

was rewarded with 16-mpg. After dropping my luggage off at mom & dad's place I went over to the shop where my brother works. They were done with the day's work, at about 5:00pm but it still took about an hour to get everything moved around so we could get the coupe into the shop and have enough space around it to work. Lil' bro's boss is one very cool dude in that he gave us free reign of his place of business to do the chop. Mucho gracias to Doug Deleo.

We got started at about 6:30pm. The first order of business was getting the old windshield out and cutting the frame to fit the new cut windshield. This is where the first problem reared its ugly head. The spare windshield that I had on hand is 1/2-inch narrower than the one that was in there so; my first task Saturday morning was to find a local glass shop that could cut the windshield that was in the car. So, we proceeded on

Friday using the cut windshield frame. We also took the trunk lid off to give a little more access to top rear of the roof. After bracing the inside of the car with what looks like a crudely constructed jungle jim we started marking and cutting. Most of the cuts were made with a speedecut, a 6-inch carbide cutting wheel that's about 1/16-inch thick and mounts on a 6-inch grinder. Finish cuts were made with a pneumatic sawsall where necessary. Sam and his buddy Kevin lifted the top off and set it on the floor. We were all surprised to see how rigid the top stayed. After -inches was cut off; Sam & Kevin set the top back on to check where addition grinding was needed to get it to fit. It was very close. There were only 3 spots that needed a little grinding. We did a little more grinding, the top went back on (for the final time) and we tacked it all around. Then we spent about a half-hour standing around commenting on how bitchin it looked with the 3-inch cut. At about 10:30 pm we called it a night and cleaned up enough to lock up the doors. It was a good day.

Saturday: I got the original windshield cut 3-inches at a local glass shop and got some rubber to set the glass in the frame. After running a few errands with my dad we got over to the shop at about noon to get started. It took about 1-hour to get the work area cleared out before we could begin work. The first task was to get the windshield put into the frame, and check the frame for fit on the car before we started welding everything up. This was the main area where we had some problems. The rubber was a little too thick and in the process of trying to squeeze and tap the frame onto the glass, I tapped a little too hard and/or a few too many times and broke the glass. So, we went to plan B. We used the other cut windshield that was 1/2-inch too narrow with the rubber that was too thick. We got the frame installed around the glass using some furniture clamps to apply pressure this time instead of a hammer. I'll take this windshield out and take the bare frame to the glass shop and have them cut me a new windshield after I get home. I'll also have them cut down the other 5 windows at the same time.

Messing with the windshield took up quite a bit of time. Once that was done and it was stashed safely away in the office. We got busy welding and grinding on the top. That's about all we did the rest of the day, welding and grinding and drinking lots of ice water and sodas. It was in the high 90's–low 100's all weekend. When we called it a day around 9:00pm, we had worked on it about 7 more hours and most of the grinding and welding was done. This included cutting the doors and welding and grinding on them. There was still a little work to do on the quarter-windows to make the surface the glass rests against flat and the windshield posts needed a little work to make them fit perfectly. It was looking real good.

Sunday: We went to church, then did a little shopping and had lunch (love them In-N-Out double-doubles) before getting to the shop at about 2:00pm. A little more fitting and grinding around the windows was done and we got the window frames cut, welded, ground and polished. Before putting the seat back in and the trunk lid back on, I threw a milk crate in it to sit on and drove over to the self-service car wash to vacuum out the stuff.

We got the seat and lid re-installed, all the stuff put back into the shop and we were sitting at mom's dinner table by 6:30pm for a home cooked meal.

I wimped out and didn't drive home Sunday night though. It just seemed like a much better idea to go for an evening swim and get a good night's sleep before making the 3-hour trip. So, I drove back home Monday morning.

All together we had about 16-hours of steady work to get the job done. Pretty good considering neither of us had ever chopped a top before. We've both cut several cars up for one reason or another, but we never put those back together again; thanks to Doug Deleo for the use of the shop. Tools like the speedecut, the Drag Gun plasma cutter, the dynafile, and even having several grinders with different types of wheels on them saved us tons of time.

It was quite an adventure and the best part is now the car looks BAD!

Wheelbarrow Firewall for a '30 Coupe

When I bought my Model A coupe it already had a junk SBC and a new TH400 mounted in the frame. The stock body was bolted to the frame with a hole cut in the firewall to clear the SBC and the floorboards were missing. I checked into the commercially available firewalls for Model A street rods and promptly got a case of sticker shock. $200–$250 for a piece of sheetmetal with a couple of breaks and beads rolled into it seemed a bit steep to me. So, I went in search of a custom solution that would have a little more character than a store-bought piece and could also be done for a reasonable cost.

I recalled hearing somewhere about someone making a firewall from a wheelbarrow bucket. I checked my trusty, rusty and well-used wheelbarrow and it did indeed have the compound curves that were desired for the Model A firewall. I ventured to my local Home Depot to procure a shiny new wheelbarrow bucket. I tried in vain to get them to sell me just the bucket at a discount, but no dice. I had to buy the whole kit for $26-plus.

I started by making a plywood floor to fit around the transmission. I trimmed the wheelbarrow bucket down-to-size and welded a flange around the edge. With this bolted to the existing Model A firewall, I then formed the toeboards, a

piece to cover the large "V" cut in the plywood floor, and a transmission hump to cover the transmission bellhousing. With these welded together and primed it was ready to bolt into the car.

Tire Damage on the way to AZ in November 2001

As those who were there know, I didn't make it to Scottsdale for the Goodguys event 11/16 - 11/18. I left directly from work Thursday afternoon to head over there but had some car problems out in the middle of the desert. Right around sunset I was buzzing along in the left lane about 50 miles west of Blythe when I was startled by a big BOOM! There was smoke everywhere, the engine wasn't running and I was skidding all over the highway. I don't remember very much between the BOOM and getting the car safely off the road on the left shoulder but I do remem-

ber thinking the car was going to roll as it was sliding sideways. Thankfully it stayed upright. I got out and assessed the situation after I stopped shaking and my heart rate got back to normal.

The BOOM was the left rear tire doing a Firestone/Explorer impersonation. The entire tread came off the tire and took the fender with it. The quarter panel got tweaked pretty bad too and there is a small dent in the front fender where the tire hit it. The inner tube kept air in it for a while and it didn't appear that there was any additional damage. Since the rear tires are 235's and the spare is a 155, and the ground off the side of the road was very soft sand, and I have AAA, and my cell phone was working out there in the middle of nowhere, I decided to just call a tow truck.

By the time the tow truck got there I had decided to go back to Indio to get a tire and just drive the car home if it would make it. The tow truck took me to a Pep Boys and while they were putting on a tire I took the mangled fender, running board and fender bracket off. I stowed them away. The car drove home OK.

The Road to the Ego Rama

After the Bonneville/Pleasanton trip this year I decided to take my coupe to the drag strip a few times to see how it would do and to see what areas needed some attention in preparation for the Ego-Rama. I didn't know for sure at that time if I would get voted in but it doesn't hurt to be prepared.

The first outing at the track told me what I already knew. Traction was a big problem. I at least needed a posi or Trac-Loc in Ford terminolo-

gy. Lower gears than the 3.00's that I used for highway runs and some tires stickier than the 235/75-15 WWW's would help too. The tech guy at the track laughed at my old helmet with its SNELL 1980 sticker and he made a few suggestions as to what safety improvements I could make in the future.

I scored a rebuilt 9-inch 3.50 Trac-Loc third member from a guy who is always at the swap meet selling used race parts. He didn't have them with him at the swap meet though so, I had to make the trip down to Garden Grove to pick them up. That's not a really long trip from Irwindale but with LA traffic, that pretty much burned up a whole evening after work one day. My usual trick of using a wheel or brake drum as an axle-puller wouldn't work this time so, I spent another evening calling and running all over town looking for a slide hammer with the proper axle flange attachment. I finally got it in and all bolted back up and there was a terrible whine on deceleration. Something was definitely wrong with the gears. I called the guy that I got them from and he said he'd swap them for another third member and if that didn't work, he'd refund my money. It's nice to do business with people who will stand by their product. Al Clark is a stand up guy. The second

third member went in a bit quicker and everything worked fine. Traction was considerably improved but it was obvious that the WWW radials were not going to be up to the task of hooking up at the drag strip.

I decided to try a set of the BFG Comp TA Drag Radials. It looked like the 245/60-15s would fit the car. At 26.1-inches tall they would lower the gear ratio a bit more too. I took a set of '56 Ford pickup wheels to the place that widens them for me and told them to put the centers on 7-inch rims, reversed with zero back spacing. I picked them up a week later sandblasted and primered for $80. Because I was in a hurry to get to the powdercoaters, I neglected to check them closely. The powdercoater said he could get them done that day and to come back at 1:00pm to pick them up. I got back there in time to see them coming out of the oven. They looked great but as I stood there admiring them while they were cooling, I realized that they had about 1.5-inch offset. Now that they were already powdercoated it was too late to take them back to have the offset corrected. My fault for being in a hurry and not inspecting them when I picked them up at the wheel shop. I'll be more careful in the future. Fortunately, the wheels and tires fit on the car OK with the extra offset. Getting the tire closer to the fender lip actually worked better aesthetically with the short rear tires.

I made a driveshaft safety loop and installed it before the second trip to the track.

The next trip to the track showed that the traction problem was solved. The car hooked right up but now it bogged off the line. Most likely this was from fuel sloshing into the vent of the primary fuel bowl of the 3310 Holley. There were a few other areas that needed to be addressed too. The TH400 didn't have a shift kit so, it wanted to shift out of first at about 4500 rpms, the column shifter wouldn't allow me to shift manually and with the small-valve heads, the engine didn't really want to pull past 4500 rpms anyway.

I made a list of things I wanted to fix, upgrade or change before the Ego-Rama but I didn't want to tear into the car until after the Rattle Can Nationals/CHRR weekend. That made things a little tight time-wise giving me exactly 5-weeks to get this list of things done:

Fresh set of big-valve heads.
New cam and lifters.
All new engine gaskets.
Weld cracked front fender brackets.
Modify TH400 to allow it to hold 1st gear.
New NHRA approved shifter.
New steering column, necessary because the column shifter was not being used any longer (it was ugly as sin too).
New turn signal switch and ignition switch, the old ones went with the old column.
New dash panel, necessary to add a Tach and vacuum gauge.
Re-wiring under the dash for all the new stuff.

While I was tidying up the interior I decided to add some door panels and kick panels too.

As soon as I got home from the CHRR on October 5, I tore the car apart to start on the upgrades. Working space and storage space for the disassembled parts was pretty tight because I lost the free storage space for my Plymouth and now it was back in the shop too along with the Cadillac, the '32 and a 56 Ford pickup cab. I removed the front sheetmetal, radiator, engine, transmission, steering column and dash. I also put the engine on the stand and tore it down to the short-block that Sunday afternoon and evening.

Monday morning at work I got a phone call from my sister-in-law informing me that my sister, who had been in very poor health for quite some time, was not expected to live. I dropped everything and went to be with her and my family. She died that night. The rest of the week was spent with my family. It was tough for all of us but we're strong, close and we give each other a lot of support. I got back to the shop the next week but couldn't find the energy or motivation to get much done on the coupe. After the memorial service on October 19 I got back in the groove and got focused on getting the car back together. With only 3 weeks to go I was wishing I hadn't taken it apart.

Somewhere along the way I decided against using the Drag Radials for the Ego-Rama. They didn't have much tread depth even when new and as soft as they are I feared they might be totally worn out before getting to Arizona. They also changed the look of the car considerably. It still looked OK but not as good as with the WWW's. I got a set of WWW recaps at the Long Beach swap meet to replace the radials that were on it. They're sort of like cheater slicks. They fit the car better and look better than the radials ever did and they hook up pretty good too. My bud Frank Klein hooked me up with a machine shop that he does business with and I got a fresh set of Dart Sportsman II heads, I got a Comp Cams 280 magnum cam, a B&M Pro Ratchet shifter, SW Tach and Vacuum gauge, miscellaneous carb and ignition parts from Service Center, and the steering column, steering wheel, steering U-joint and turn signal switch from Limeworks.

I ran into another snag when re-assembling the engine. The center two holes in each head for the intake manifold bolts were drilled 15-degrees off from the other holes. To get the intake manifold to fit I had to re-drill the center holes at the new angle and then use longer bolts and 15-degree alignment washers. Jay Carnine generously made the washers for me in short order and Hoyt Martin

picked them up on his way through Visalia the next day.

Hoyt helped on a lot of the other projects too. He sorted out most of the under-dash wiring changes and welded-up the cracked front fender brackets. Tony Waggoner gave me the instructions on how to modify the TH400 to hold first gear without putting in a shift kit. Frank Sendra came by a couple of times to help with whatever I was working on that day. Rotten Rodney helped out a couple of weekends by doing most of the door panel & kick panel fabrication & installation and helping with all the last minute details and Frank Klein helped with tools, answering almost daily questions, diagnosing problems and helping with the final cam break in. Without the generous help of these friends I never would have been ready. Thanks guys, I really appreciate it.

That last 3-weeks is mostly a blur as far as what was done on what day. I was working on the car after work every night until about 10:00 or 11:00pm. Someone was there almost every day helping with something. It was all back together and ready to fire for the first time on the morning of November 1. I had a few problems during the cam break-in procedure and had to shut the engine off a couple times. The first was a severe oil leak at the front of the oil pan. Even though I got rid of the cheapo chrome timing cover I still had the cheapo chrome oil pan and the front was not sealing even with the thick one-piece Fel Pro blue gasket. The second problem was it ran out of gas. There were still some problems with the way I had the fuel gauge and switch wired. I got a couple wires crossed when swapping the dash and it was blowing the fuse as soon as it was turned on.

After breaking in the cam, I re-adjusted the valves but the engine still rattled like the rockers were out of adjustment and I couldn't get it to run with anything less than about 16 degrees BTDC initial timing. I tried everything I could think of trying to get rid of the rattling. I was seriously stressed out. The car wouldn't run right, the start of the Ego-Rama was just a few days away and I couldn't figure out why it was running so badly. Frank Klein came over on Wednesday to see if he could help. After adjusting the valves two more times and swapping-out the roller-tip rockers for the stockers he suggested that the cam might be flat. We checked that and sure enough, we found that #7 intake was barely opening. I wasn't happy about how much work I now had ahead of me but it was a relief to know what the problem was. Wednesday night we pulled the radiator off the car and tore the engine back down far enough to replace the cam. When I got the cam out I saw that #1 exhaust, #2 exhaust & #7 intake were all flat. Thursday after work I took the cam back to Service Center. They agreed to give me a new one with lifters, no charge. Again, it's good to do business with people who stand by their products. Unfortunately, they didn't have it in stock and I had to go back Friday afternoon to get it. Thursday evening I cleaned everything up and got it ready to slide the cam in and bolt it all back together. Friday afternoon when I put the 2nd new cam in one of the cam bolts broke with less than 20–lb-ft of torque. At this point I was almost ready to shoot myself. What ELSE could possible go wrong? Luckily (?) I got the broken bolt out pretty easily and quickly. Friday evening we got it all back together ready to break in the 2nd new

cam. This time I used molybdenum disulfide break-in lube (and lots of it) that has always worked for me in the past instead of the little packet of red stuff that comes with the cam. Frank Klein came over to help with the break-in procedure and everything went well. After break-in we adjusted the valves again and the engine ran great. Rod and I spent the rest of Saturday finishing up a bunch of the other projects.

The first road test was on the way to breakfast Sunday morning. It ran good with no leaks and it pulled hard in first gear all the way to 6000 rpm. At that rpm the PVC can't evacuate the pressure fast enough though and oil starts coming out of the breather on the front of the intake manifold. I'm going to have to re-engineer that breather. For now the solution at the drags will be to tie-wrap a shop rag around the breather to soak up purged oil.

All we had to do Monday before heading to Burbank to meet up with the other Ego-Rama participants, was give it a thorough washing, mostly to get all the motor oil off the primer, fix a couple of rattles and buy a few supplies. I was amazed that we got it all done in time. A few days earlier I was sure that I was going to have to wimp-out and call the R&C guys to tell them that I took my car apart and didn't have enough time to get it back together. Thanks again to all my friends who helped me make it to the event on time.

Even though I only was able to participate in 2-days of the Ego Rama, I met some really great people and have some new friends. Several of my existing friends REALLY stepped up to show how strong the friendships are by helping me when I needed it most, both in thrashing to get the car ready and helping me when I got hurt. I'll never forget it. Tuesday night we were getting ready to leave the Bar-B-Que and I had the car backed in at an angle, about 2-feet from the wall of Randy Clark's new body shop. I opened the door to the coupe to fire it up and let it warm up a bit before we headed to the hotel. I must have left the car in reverse when I parked it because when it started it lunged backward hitting the wall and throwing me onto the ground.

After a 911call came the cops, paramedics, emergency, x-rays, CAT scans and then at 4:00am in the rain I was discharged. Lucky for me, Rotten Rodney got me to his place and took care of me for a few days until I could get out of bed long enough to go to the bathroom. Friday he got me to my doc for a quick check and then handed me off to my mom and dad. They took me home and watched after me for about a week until I was able to get up and around and take care of myself. I've weaned myself off of the prescription pain meds because I don't like the side effects. Just Advil and a muscle relaxer before bed. I still have a headache but the hole in my head is healing OK. My lower back is still sore but it gets better every day. I figure I'll be about 75% recovered by Thanksgiving. It might take a month or so to get back to 100%. The car isn't too bad. The left fender got banged up (again on the way to AZ). We left the car at Randy's shop that night. Rod picked it up and took it to the shop where he works the following Monday. It wouldn't surprise me a bit to get it back repaired, that's the kind of friends these guys are. No matter if it's not, they've already done a lot for me.

In the process of making changes I installed a B&M Pro Ratchet shifter WITH the neutral safety switch. We went through great lengths to ensure that the switch was installed, adjusted and working properly. That's what's so baffling to me. How did this happen? Oh well, I'll never trust a neutral safety switch again. I'll run them, but I won't bet my life or health on them.

Even though I wasn't able to complete the Ego-Rama this year all the effort was not in vain. I finally got off the dime and made some of the upgrades that I've wanted to do for a while and the car is that much closer to being ready for the 2004 Ego-Rama. That's right, like the governor said, "I'll be back."

Inbetween major projects like a '55 Chevy Bel-Air and a '48 Ford woody, Clare Patterson wanted something to drive. Like to rod runs and picnics and stuff. A low buck, dependo-rod for any weather condition, said weather conditions being part of the Kent, Washington lifestyle. When this Olds 88 coupe came possible from a retired lady in Kennewick, with only 24,683 miles, he jumped at the chance. After all, the 88s were considered the first of the GM factory race cars, and this one was hardly broken in. Some $7000 later, and what can only be described as minimal changes, Clare had a cool custom croozer.

This is a pure example of a Mild Custom, but because the cars were so hot in stock trim, they are also early Fifties era muscle cars. And because a car such as this fixes up with so little extra work need, it is definitely a basic hot rod.

BASIC BLUE HEAVEN

By James Handy

Other than replacing the stock lifters with 1953 Cad items for better oiling, the engine/transmission/chassis are nearly stock 1950 Oldsmobile.

Inside all is original light grey broadcloth, so quiet it is hard to be overpowered by the mellow glasspacks.

Left—The sweetheart cruiser is virtually stock, the custom 15-inch wheels seem to be the most obvious outward sign of a special vehicle. Clare painted the original crest blue color himself, in lacquer. Larry Waller added mild pinstriping.

Right—The car was lowered 3-I/2-inches front and 3-inches rear by cutting and recoiling the springs. Add the reduction in tire diameters and total car drop over stock is 5-inches.

Above Left—Clare Patterson built a legend in Northwest rodding by creating his own period perfect gas station, where else to wash a mildly dechromed Olds 88.

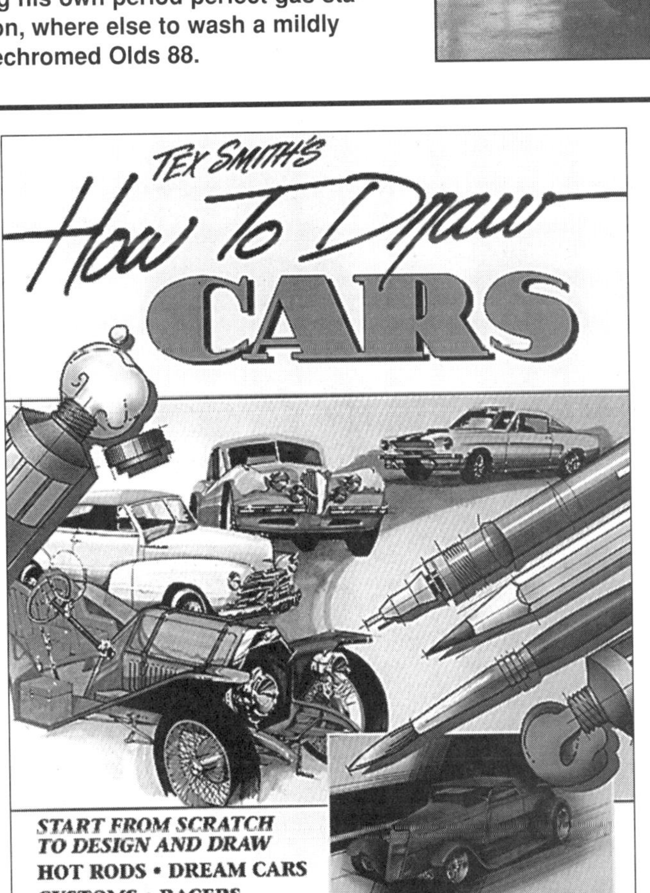

How to Draw Cars

At one time everyone has attempted to put on paper a rendering of their dream car. Aside from those with natural talent, most of us need help. This book contains over 200 pages on everything anyone needs to know to go from simple doodles to a professional drawing. It contains practical, illustrated instruction on everything from tracing, drawing, and painting cars to designing customs, rods, and dream cars of your own. In addition, there is a section on computer art, as well as a bibliography chapter which hi-lights some of the more prominent automotive artists of the day.

**Hot Rod Library, Inc
12 North Main St. C-3
Veyo, UT 84782
Toll Free: (800) 513-8133**

By Dan Hostetter

The Extraordinary Adventure of Mr. Perkins.

Eric Perkins slid behind the wheel of his black, channeled 1932 three-window coupe one bright morning, after kissing his wife and two daughters goodbye. The engine came to life, the shift lever found Drive, and our hero headed off on what was to become a unique and totally unexpected adventure. Somehow this happens often in basic hot rodding.

The plan was to head south from his home in Montesano, Washington to a large California rod run, but to leave a week early and pick up another lesser-known run on the way. This "other" rod run happened to be the Bonneville Cruise-In, a super laid-back affair that is not always held, but when it is the outing includes the Bonneville salt flats Speedweek in August.

This was to be Perkins' first time at the salt races, as he puts it, "I'm not a racer, rather more of a car fancier." However, he had read about the salt for years and vowed to see it someday. Eric arrived a day early in the host town of Wendover, Utah/Nevada and began preparing his coupe for

This 1932 Ford three-window looks low because it really is! Eric Perkins found an overlooked Northern California Fifties survivor and gave it the full restoration. The body is channeled over the frame and the top chopped 4-inches, Grille shell is stock height, just dropped between the frame horns. Note the flipper hubcaps on this side and Eric's totally period attire.

Simple sheet stock mounts period perfect Stewart Warner dials to the stock closed car dashboard, the Banjo steering wheel is original '36 Ford while the steering column drop was an accessory from way back.

Inside this time machine is basic hot rodding as it is best practiced, with parts and pieces coming from whatever source will get the job done.

the drive on the dreaded salt. He had heard stories. Driving on the salt is always required, because the display area for the Cruise-In is next to the race car pit area, some two or so miles from the paved road end. Eric crept onto the salt at a blazing 5-7 mph!

The jet-black Deuce coupe attracted considerable attention from spectator and racer alike, with its obvious theme of the mid-50s. Complete with wide whitewalls on red wheels featuring Ford hubcaps and beauty rings on one side…while sporting full cover spinner on the other. The same car but different from either side. Powertrain is street rod standard – 327 small-block Chevy with turbo 350 auto trans ahead of a '57 Chevy rearend. The only "real modern equipment is a SAAB rack and pinion steering mounted on an ancient Dago'd axle. Well, I suppose one should also include the 1968 Corvette seats upholstered in Lincoln Continental maroon. The dash has a business look, with seven

early Stewart Warner gauges fronting a 1936 Ford banjo steering wheel.

Pretty much standard stuff, perhaps, but what attracts the onlookers is the body proportions. The body has been channeled width of the frame, and the top chopped 4 inches. But it retains the fenders! The '32 grille shell remains unchopped, just lowered between the frame horns to continue the proportions. For any purists out there, this car was originally built in northern California in the 1950s, so it is truly authentic of the period.

Eric has loved Deuce three-windows since he was 10-years old and getting into his brother's HOT ROD magazines. Two cover cars that caught his attention were the Bill Breece passionate Purple coupe and Lloyd Bakan's DeSoto Hemi powered three-window.

But, Eric's first car was a VW. Which friend John Huggens showed him how to chop. He loved it and from then on Eric would hang out in customizing body shops studying the techniques of metal work. His guru was Von Hunter, a Portland, Oregon metal wizard. So, for the many following years, Perkins has owned over 35 rods and customs and has chopped most of them. Yet he makes a profession of servicing IBM computers.

Eventually Eric found the faded yellow '32 you see here. So, fast forward. Though the salt looked menacing on that first day, it soon lost the threat. He had a few days to kill before the California rod run, so he did what real hot rodders do so well…he helped a new found acquaintance with a race car. Bud Jones and his fuel flathead lakester.

Things went fine and on Thursday morning during record runs, he watched and listened as Al Teague thundered his streamliner through the lights at an incredible speed of 382 mph—within 18 miles of the magical 400 mark. That same day, Bud Jones turned over the driving chores of his lakester to Perkins. The rules state that a driver's first run must be kept below 125 mph, so Bud told Eric to shift at 5500 rpm and then "stand on it. The motor will lug down and pull you through at a slow speed". Eric obeyed, but when he cleared the 3-mile clocks, he had traveled in excess of 162 mph. The race guys weren't pleased, but they understood what had happened and granted a "C" license, good in the 125-175 mph range.

Since Eric now had a C license, he could go for his B certificate. Jones strapped the jazzed Mr. Perkins into the lakester. Bob Higbee the legendary starter waved him off, and Eric made a 182 mph down the straight black line. Again, within 18 mph of a legendary speed mark, that of 200 mph.

Last we saw of Eric he and Bud had their feet propped on the race car trailer having a cool one and discussing the next year. The California rod run? Oh, it was forgotten. Once you've had salt, it is hard to go back to sugar!

The proportions are square on with the Perkins coupe, but it takes on new meaning when a stock height car is alongside. Front this side, check the wheels.

I define a hot rod as a modified vehicle, race car, experimental vehicle, etc. This coupe of mine is a basic hot rod, and it is used like most people treat a "regular" car. I drive it every day, in all kinds of weather. It is a great vehicle in terms of dependability, it gets good gas mileage, and it brings back the old days of rodding with the styling.

As a builder of street rods for a living (Rod Techniques, Deer Park, NY) I felt that people needed to see, or remember depending on the age group, a traditional rod. We all seem to get caught up in "keeping up with the Jones" when building a car. I see people spending lots of money on their rods, adding details and parts that aren't necessary or don't fit the style of the car. The object of building a nice car is to follow a theme that works.

This coupe was built as an example of an early hot rod, and other than the 12-volt electrical system, it's a '40s style car. It gets a lot of attention.

Friend Andy Zucaro and his dog made the ultimate sacrifice and donated this 1931 Model A coupe body to the project. It had been the dog's house! Now it is channeled over the Z'd frame 5-inches in front and 4-inches in back, the top is chopped 4-3/4-inches. Brakes are '4l Ford, wheels are l6-inchers from same car, dropped axle has split wishbone. Definitely a driver, this coupe logs over l0,000 miles per year.

DOGHOUSE DRIVER

By Sean Vesely

Above—Red and white interior to match the body paint was stitched by Ed Lada. Stewart-Warner gauges are in a flat panel ahead of the Ford banjo steering wheel.

Above Left—Modifications to the Ford 8BA flathead engine are limited to a Mallory distributor (added after these photos) and a l2-volt generator. The radiator and grille shell are '32 Ford.

Left—1939 Ford transmission hooks to the '4l Ford rearend via a shortened torque tube, tube shocks and Model A spring finish off the final drive. Taillights are real hot rod standard l939 Ford teardrops.

Dale Seaholm, standing, and his dad Terry are well known rodders in the western U.S., mostly because they are on the road as much as possible. That lean-back windshield has chopped swap meet posts to mount a donated glass frame.

You can't tell by looking at it now, but in the late Fifties/early Sixties this particular Model A spent most of its moving time on the drag strip. Powered by a blown Olds it was a regular throughout the northwest U.S. When it was retired from the quarter-mile, all the running gear was stripped, along with anything else of value, and then it was abandoned to the elements. Until 1976, when basic rodder supremo Terry Seaholm found the hashed up mess.

But you gotta understand that Seaholm is not your run-of-the-mill hot rodder. He has been over and under, in and around practically every form of automotive performance, at most every price level, and he relishes the hunt for usable old car parts. In short, a swap meet junkie.

Other than the body, there was very little to begin the resurrection. Years of abuse and many crude modifications left the frame unusable. A new chassis of 2x3-inch rectangular tubing was made; the side rails following the '29 bodylines. A dropped and drilled '33 Ford axle with '28 Ford spindles and brakes was added, the lot mounted out front suicide-style. Deviating from the norm, a Saab rack-and-pinion steering gear was mounted solid to the beam axle; connected to the steering downshaft via a Don Hardy Race Cars flex shaft. Terry reports it all works great.

For power, Terry chose a 153 cubic inch Chevy II four-banger, originally modified to run a midget racer. It is loaded with a bevy of almost forgotten speed parts, including an Ansen 8-port aluminum head, built in l962 by Lou Senter. More Ansen goodies are included, such as the valve cover and side plate. The block is bored .060 and fitted with small-block Chevy pistons having 9:l compression. Connecting rods are stock, as is the crankshaft. A cam designed by the late Tex Roberts and ground by Delta Cams in Tacoma, Washington controls the valves.

Originally the special head was designed to operate at flat-out rpm, so the ports and valves don't lend themselves to low speeds. Terry went through several carburetor and intake manifold combinations before settling on a pair of variable venture SU sidedraft carbs. Now the engine idles quite nicely. This being a crossflow head, Seaholm made up his own header.

Five years of scrounging parts and building have been followed by nearly two decades of hard diving. Just your everyday resurrected roadster.

Above—Paint scheme is red scollops over a shiny black base highlighted by white pinstriping. Handmade grille insert is painted red matching the scollops. Suspension is painted black, except for the friction shocks.

Above & Right—In addition to being plenty freeway friendly, the Chevy II four-cylinder is thrifty at the corner gas station. Transmission is a Muncie wide-ratio 4-speed.

Right—The four-spoke champ-car style steering wheel looks like a Bell Auto item, but is really from an Essex and fronts an aftermarket type dash cluster with curved glass Stewart Warner gauges. Upholstery is red tuck 'n' roll.

Below—There are louvers everywhere, 176 all the way down the Terry-built belly-pan and up the rear deck panel. Just peeping out underneath is a Halibrand quick-change in a Ford V8 rearend with '40 Ford brakes. The taillights are '41 Ford items, frenched in best Fifties style.

Below—Drilled dropped beam-axle mounts Ford drum brakes, early Kelsey Hayes wire wheels, Dunlop motorcycle tires in front. Friction shocks mount ahead of the King Bee headlamps and the 1931 Chrysler grille shell. Terry made up the grille insert from 3/16-inch steel rod. Mike Smith formed the 3-piece hood. After Terry sprayed the black lacquer paint, famed Northwest painter Dick Page laid-out the scallops and Junior Nelson pulled the stripes.

If you've had a lifetime around hot rods and race cars, you gravitate towards those that brung you to the golden age. In the case of Curly Wells, Model T and A Fords were the introduction to both street and track performance.

CURLEY'S CARS

By Oslo Wilhunkie

There are a lot of guys who will tell you how they "usta" build hot rods way back when. Curly Wells was one of those guys that "usta" build them, and he still built them that way when I did this story a few years back. I knew Curly well, and I can vouch that these two carry-overs from hot rodding's earlier days could run with the best of modern rods.

Curly's hot rodding interest got its start with a Rajo equipped Ford 4-banger, while he was attending high school. By 1939 he had begun racing in the then newly formed BCRRA (Bay Cities Roadster Racing Association), competing in events in the Northern California Bay Area. He drove for other owners, as well as chauffeuring his own cars during the 1939-41 seasons.

This promising racing career was cut short by

WW II. After serving in the Army Air Force, Curly resumed racing in 1946, but by then roadster racing was beginning to wane, so he moved over to driving midgets and sprints cars while earning a living as an automotive machinist.

Though his circle track career was long ago, Curly managed to keep history alive into the 1990s with another roadster. This blast from the past was full of parts and pieces that would have made it competitive on the pre-war racing circuit. The hot setup back then was a 4-port Riley head, and judging by the way this latest car still runs it's easy to see why the Riley was so potent.

Inside the Ford B block, one of Curly's own counterbalanced cranks spins inside owner-built steel main caps. A homemade manifold holds twin Dellorto carburetors (the one concession to modern

Right—Wells sits low in the saddle of his '27T. After he warmed it up likely passengers had to want a ride pretty badly to crawl over that aluminized exhaust pipe. The bark of a 4-port Riley through a long stack is remarkable.

Left—Different T body, different time, same engine. Back in the days of roadster racing Curly was known as being a hard charger, here he collects a trophy from race queen at a pre-WW II event at San Jose, California.

Below—Bottom of the T roadster body was trimmed to conform to the Chevy frame rails. Friction shocks and '39 Ford taillights are found at the rear, as is a Halibrand quick-change center section under a Model A crossmember.

No repops here, bub. The Bell champ car steering wheel and Auburn dash are gennie oldies. Floor is down inside the frame rails to get folks out of the wind, but then they must share riding space with the transmission and torque tube. Windshield wiper is an "armstrong" version.

The legendary Riley 4-port head is awesome after nearly a century of use. One of these conversions on a Model B Ford block makes for impressive performance from a mere 200.5 cubic inches. Header exits right and continues down right side in front of passenger door.

Left—Windshield consists of the lower parts of Model T posts grafted to Model A upper posts and glass frame. Rudge knock-off wire wheels are not an everyday item; the exhaust pipe rear support was made from a Ford fender bracket.

day mechanicals). The cam is one of the legendary Ed Winfield units. Transmission is a Model B with Lincoln zephyr 25-tooth gears, while the early Ford rearend utilizes a Halibrand quick-change housing with 3.48 street gears and 4.11 gears for the drags. Curly was a regular at nostalgia drags, where he posted an impressive 14.98et at 93mph.

As was common in the heyday of roadster racing, the Ford body sits on a '28 Chevy frame modified with Ford cross-springs front and rear. Passengers sit on homemade seats, separated by the transmission and torque tube. Steering gearbox is '27 Whippet topped with an original Bell steering wheel. The raked windshield and the single exhaust pipe down the body side are, well, the way they "usta" do it.

Twin Dellorto carbs are a departure from original, but they make tuning much better. An AMC alternator is used, along with an accessory Model T water pump. The Whippet steering gear was often used for a through-cowl route to the pitman arm.

Because the Chevy frame has a high and wide kickup at the rear, much was trimmed from deck area of the T body. After these photos were taken the body was cherried and painted bright yellow with red scallops. A DeSoto grille replaced the A unit, and a hood was fabricated.

You see one of these radiator badges and you know full well that someone knows how hot rods "usta" be built.

Above—Zootie pickup features a wood dash panel with a gaggle of vintage Stewart Warner instruments in a metal insert, next to the key lock is a push button starter switch, a dead giveaway to old timey.

Right—For chores around the homestead, Curly relied on a very nice '29 Model A roadster pickup. With sheetmetal as straight as they come, body and wheels are red, fenders are black.

The other mount that Curly kept tabs on is a '29 roadster pickup that he came across in 1959. This A-bone is also B engine powered, with a two-port Riley head, the same head he used in 1938. Cam is again by Winfield, but the lubrication is a unique adaptation of a Dodge oil pump driven off the timing gears. Like the roadster, the pickup used a B trans with Zepher gears; rearend is a Ford type Columbia 2-speed.

Steering for the truck is a '25 Franklin gear topped with a '35 Chevrolet accessory wheel. The pickup runs just great; Curly cranked the quarter-mile in low 16 seconds with a top end of 83-plus mph. Yessir, Curly Wells was one modern time hot rodder who knew what basic hot rodding is all about, and he personally knew how it "usta" be.

Above—This Model B 4-banger powering the pickup features a Riley 2-port head, Winfield cam and a unique Dodge oil pump adaptation that is driven off the timing gears.

Above—This Model A rides on Kelsey-Hayes wire wheels and 16-inch rubber. Nerf bars are owner-built at both ends; the trailer hitch was used by Curly to haul one of several original Mullins trailers.

Right—Top and side curtains offer passenger protection when things get ugly outside. At least a little bit. Top rear panel has a Gypsy curtain that can be rolled and snapped to the top bow for added ventilation.

THE Online Place
for Pre '76 Cars, Parts, and Vendors !

Sell Your Car.....
Sell Your Parts....
Find A Car.....
You'll Find it All Here....

www.HotRodHotLine.com